Hot & Spicy Mexican

Also by Dave DeWitt, Mary Jane Wilan, and Melissa T. Stock

Hot & Spicy & Meatless

Hot & Spicy Chili

Hot & Spicy Latin Dishes

Hot & Spicy Southeast Asian Dishes

Hot & Spicy Caribbean

Hot & Spicy Mexican

Dave DeWitt
Mary Jane Wilan
Melissa T. Stock

Illustrations by Lois Bergthold

PRIMA PUBLISHING and colophon are trademarks of Prima Communications, Inc.

Portions of this book first appeared in *Chile Pepper* magazine. Used by permission.

Library of Congress Cataloging-in-Publication Data

DeWitt, Dave.
    Hot & spicy Mexican : the best fiery food from south of the border / by Dave DeWitt, Mary Jane Wilan, and Melissa T. Stock.
        p.   cm.
    Includes bibliographical references and index.
    ISBN 1-55958-654-0
    1. Cookery, Mexican.   2. Cookery (Hot peppers).   I. Wilan, Mary Jane.   II. Stock, Melissa T.   III. Title.
TX716.M4D49   1996
641.5972—dc20   96-3921
                                                                                   CIP

96 97 98 99 00 AA 10 9 8 7 6 5 4 3 2
Printed in the United States of America

How to Order:
Single copies may be ordered from Prima Publishing, P.O. Box 1260BK, Rocklin, CA 95677; telephone (916) 632-4400. Quantity discounts are also available. On your letterhead, include information concerning the intended use of the books and the number of books you wish to purchase.

This book is for José Marmolejo, who vastly increased our knowledge of Mexico's culinary delights. We particularly remember the Oaxaca experience, the Mexico City subway, and the mescal tasting in Austin!

Acknowledgments

Special gratitude to Chuck Evans for the use of his extensive Mexican food library, and to Jeanette DeAnda, for her excellent translation assistance.

We'd also like to thank the following people for their help on this project: Lula Bertrán, Cindy Castillo, Jesus Martín Cortez, Josefina Duran, Marta Figel, Lorenzo Fritz, Kathy Gallantine, Nancy and Jeff Gerlach, John Gray, Antonio Heras-Duran, Patrick Holian, Jay Lewis, Leo Nuñez, Jim Peyton, Mark Preston, María Marcela Ramonet, María Lila Robles-Uscher, Robert Spiegel, Susana Trilling, and Robb Walsh.

Contents

Introduction

It has often been written that the only national cuisine of Mexico is the cuisine of chile, and the fact that this is the only book in the *Hot & Spicy* series that is devoted to a single country is evidence for the accuracy of that statement. Simply said, here we have attempted to define the way chile peppers are used in Mexican cuisine. First and foremost, in Mexico more than in any other national cuisine in the world, chiles are utilized as a food as much as a spice. In massive quantities they are puréed into sauces, stuffed whole, and used as rajas, or strips. Our collection of Mexican recipes celebrates their appearance as a primary vegetable in the cuisine.

Important breakthroughs in this book include:

- A wide selection of recipes in which chiles are the principal ingredient, including chiles rellenos, salsas, and pickled chiles
- The most complete glossary of Mexican chile terminology ever published, along with a detailed glossary of other Mexican food terms and techniques
- Regional hot and spicy recipes covering most of the states of Mexico

Readers and cooks should remember that this is a book focusing on chile-oriented Mexican dishes, and is not intended to be a complete coverage of Mexican cuisine, which is impossible in a single volume.

We have spent considerable time in Mexico, from watching the Sonoran *chiltepín* harvest in La Aurora, to collecting *chilhuacle* chiles at the stand of Eliseo Ramirez in the *mercado* in Oaxaca, to studying Spanish in Cuernavaca, to visiting other Mexican chile capitals such as Monterrey, Puerto Vallarta, and Quintana Roo. Hopefully, our love and appreciation of Mexico come across in this volume.

Fortunately, chiles and other Mexican ingredients are increasingly easy to find in the United States and Canada. Not only are they appearing in Latin markets and supermarkets, they are available from numerous mail-order sources (see Mail-Order Sources, page 279).

We continue to use the same Heat Scale that we devised for *Chile Pepper* magazine and the other books in the *Hot & Spicy* series: Mild, Medium, Hot, and Extremely Hot. Each rating takes into consideration the types of chile in the dish, the number of chiles used in the recipe, and the degree of dilution. The relative heat of each recipe can be easily adjusted.

We hope you enjoy our hot and spicy trek south of the border. For more coverage of Mexican and other hot and spicy cuisines, subscribe to *Chile Pepper* magazine, P.O. Box 80780, Albuquerque, NM 87198, (800)359-1483.

The Soul
of the Mexicans

Chile is so ingrained in the culture of Mexico that chile expert Arturo Lomelí wrote: "Chile, they say, is the king, the soul of the Mexicans—a nutrient, a medicine, a drug, a comfort. For many Mexicans, if it were not for the existence of chile, their national identity would begin to disappear."

Early Origins

In southern Mexico and the Yucatán peninsula, chile peppers have been part of the human diet since about 7500 B.C. and thus their usage predates the two great Central American civilizations, the Mayan and the Aztec. From their original usage as a spice collected in the wild, chiles gained importance after their domestication and they were a significant food when the Olmec culture was developing, around 1000 B.C.

About 500 B.C., the Monte Albán culture, in the valley of Oaxaca, began exporting a new type of pottery vessel to nearby regions. These vessels resembled the hand-held *molcajete* mortars of today and were called *suchilquitongo* bowls. Because the *molcajetes* are used to crush chile pods and make salsas today, the *suchilquitongo* bowls are probably the first evidence we have for the creation of crushed chile and chile powders. Scientists speculate that chile powder was developed soon after the *suchilquitongo* bowls were invented, and both the tool and the product were then exported.

A carved glyph found in the ceremonial center of Monte Albán is further evidence of the early importance of chile peppers. It features a chile plant with three pendant pods on one end and the head of a man on the other. Some experts believe that the glyph is one of a number of "tablets of conquest" that marked the sites conquered by the Monte Albán culture.

The Spicy Legacy of the Mayas

When the Europeans arrived in the Western Hemisphere, people of Mayan ancestry lived in southern Mexico, the Yucatán peninsula, Belize, Guatemala, and parts of Honduras and El Salvador. The Mayan civilization had long passed its height by that time, so there are no European observations about this classic culture. All that exist today are writings about their descendants; Mayan hieroglyphics, which are slowly being transliterated; and ethnological observations of the present Mayan Indians, whose food habits have changed little in twenty centuries.

By the time the Mayas reached the peak of their civilization in southern Mexico and the Yucatán peninsula, around A.D. 500, they had a highly developed system of agriculture. Maize was their most important crop, followed closely by beans, squash, chiles, and cacao. Perhaps as many as thirty different varieties of chile were cultivated, and they were sometimes planted in plots by themselves but more often in fields already containing tomatoes and sweet potatoes. Three species of chile were grown by the Mayas and their descendants in Central America: *Capsicum annuum*, *Capsicum chinense*, and *Capsicum frutescens*—and they were all imports from other regions. The *annuum* probably originated in Mexico, while the *frutescens* came from Panama, and the *chinense* from the Amazon Basin via the Caribbean. The Mayas also cultivated cotton, papayas, vanilla beans, cacao, manioc, and agave.

The importance of chiles is immediately seen in the most basic Mayan foods. According to food historian Sophie Coe, in her book *America's First Cuisines*, "The beans . . . could be cooked in plain water or water in which toasted or untoasted chiles had been steeped. Such a chile 'stock' might be called the basis of the cuisine, so frequently does it turn up. It is in everything from the tortilla accompaniment of the very poorest peasant to the liquid for cooking the turkey for the greatest celebrations. There is even a reference to it in the *Popul Vuh,* the Mayan sacred text, where the grandmother grinds chiles and mixes them with broth, and the broth acts as a mirror in which the rat on the rafters is reflected for the hero twins to see."

Coe speculates that the first sauces were used for tortilla dipping. "The simplest sauce was ground dried chiles and water," she writes. "From this humble ancestor comes the line which terminates with trendy salsas beloved of a certain school of today's chefs." The ground or crushed chiles—sometimes in a thick sauce—were used to preserve and prolong the life of a piece of meat, fish, or other game. Since there was no refrigeration, fresh meat spoiled quickly, and by trial and error the earliest cooks realized that chiles were an antioxidant, preserving the meats to some degree.

"But even the original inventors of tortilla-dipping sauces varied them when they could," Coe added. "The ground toasted seeds of large and small squashes, always carefully differentiated by the Maya, could be added to the basic chile water, or you could mix epazote with the water and then add ground, toasted squash seeds to the flavored liquid." As more and more ingredients were added, a unique family of sauces was developed that led to the *pipiánes* and *moles* of today.

For breakfast the Mayas ate a gruel of ground maize spiced with chile peppers, which is usually called *atole* but is sometimes known as *pozóle*. A modern equivalent would be cornmeal or masa mixed with water and ground red chiles to the consistency of a milkshake. A favorite drink was chocolate mixed with water, honey, and chile powder.

For the main, or evening meal, stews of vegetables and meats heavily spiced with chiles were served. One of these was *chacmole*, which combined venison with chile, achiote, allspice, and tomato—it was an offering to the gods as well as a nourishing entrée. Various reports describe sauces made with chiles and black beans being wrapped in corn tortillas and covered with chile sauce, which may be the earliest references to enchiladas. As Sophie Coe noted, "The accepted wisdom was that tortillas and beans were boring; it took chile to make the saliva flow."

The Mayas seem to have invented tamales, too. Coe cites the Spanish chronicler Gonzalo Fernández de Oviedo who reported in 1526: "They brought certain well made baskets, one with the *pasticci* (filled pies) of maize dough stuffed with chopped meat. . . .They ate it all, and praised that dish *pasticci,* which tasted as if it were spiced. It was reddish inside, with a good quantity of that pepper of the Indies which is called *asci* (the Antillean word for chile, modernized to *ají*)." Mayan tamales were quite sophisticated, with many different fillings, including toasted squash seeds, deer hearts, quail, egg yolks, dove breasts, squash blossoms, and black beans. The Mayas kept domesticated turkeys, ducks, bees, and dogs, and their main game animals were deer, birds, iguana, and wild boar. Armadillos and manatees were considered delicacies. As with the Incas, meat dishes were reserved for Mayan royalty.

Chiles are highly visible today in areas with a Mayan heritage. In the Yucatán peninsula, descendants of the Mayas still grow *habaneros,* tomatoes, and onions in boxes or hollowed-out tree trunks that are raised up on four posts for protection against pigs and hens. These container gardens are usually in the yard of the house, near the kitchen.

Aztec Chiles

In 1529, Bernardino de Sahagún, a Spanish Franciscan friar living in Nueva España (Mexico), noted that the Aztecs ate hot red or yellow chile peppers in their hot chocolate and in nearly every dish they prepared! Fascinated by the Aztecs' constant use of a previously unknown spice, Sahagún documented this fiery cuisine in his classic study, *Historia General de las Cosas de la Nueva España,* now known as the *Florentine Codex.* His work indicates that of all the pre-Columbian New World civilizations, it was the Aztecs who loved chile peppers the most.

The market places of ancient Mexico overflowed with chile peppers of all sizes and shapes, and Sahagún wrote that they included "hot green chiles, smoked chiles, water chiles, tree chiles, beetle chiles, and sharp-pointed red chiles." In addition to some twenty varieties of *chillis,* as the pungent pods were called in the Náhuatl language, vendors sold strings of red chiles (modern *ristras*), precooked chiles, and "fish chiles," which were the earliest known forms of *ceviche,* a method of preserving fish without cooking. This technique places the fish in a marinade of an acidic fruit juice and chile peppers—see Chapter 7 for recipes.

Other seafood dishes were common as well in ancient Mexico. "They would eat another kind of stew, with frogs and green chile," Sahagún recorded, "and a stew of those fish called *axolotl* with yellow chile. They also used to eat a lobster stew which is very delicious." Apparently the Aztecs utilized every possible source of protein. The friar noted such exotic variations as maguey worms with a sauce of small chiles, newt with yellow chiles, and tadpoles with *chiltecpitl.*

Father Sahagún, one of the first behavioral scientists, also noted that chiles were revered as much as sex by the ancient Aztecs. While fasting to appease their rather bloodthirsty gods, the priests required two abstentions by the faithful: sexual relations and chile peppers.

Chocolate and chiles were commonly combined in a drink called *chicahuatl,* which was usually reserved for the priests and the wealthy. The Aztec versions of tamales often used banana leaves as a wrapper to steam combinations of masa dough, chicken, and the chiles of choice. Sahagún wrote that there were two types of sauces called "chilemollis": one with red chile and tomatoes, and the other with yellow chile and tomatoes. These *chilemollis* eventually became the savory *mole* sauces for which Mexican cuisine is justly famous.

Aztec cookery was the basis for the Mexican food of today, and, in fact, many Aztec dishes have lasted through the centuries virtually unchanged. Since oil and fat were not generally used in cooking, the foods were usually roasted, boiled, or cooked in sauces. Like the Mayas, the Aztecs usually began the day with a cup of *atole* spiced with chile peppers.

The main meal was served at midday and usually consisted of tortillas with beans and a salsa made with chiles and tomatoes. The salsas were usually made by grinding the ingredients between two hand-held stones, the *molcajetes*. Even today, the same technique is used in Indian villages throughout Mexico and Central America. A remarkable variety of tamales was also served for the mid-day meal. They were stuffed with fruits such as plums, pineapple, or guava; with game meat such as deer or turkey; or with seafood such as snails or frogs. Whole chile pods were included with the stuffing, and after steaming the tamales were often served with a cooked chile sauce.

It was this highly sophisticated chile cuisine that the Spanish encountered during their conquest of Mexico. Christopher Columbus "discovered" chile peppers in the West Indies on his first voyage to the New World. In his journal for 1493, he wrote, "Also there is much *ají*, which is their pepper, and the people won't eat without it, for they find it very wholesome. One could load fifty caravels a year with it in Hispaniola."

Dr. Diego Chanca, the fleet physician for Columbus on his second voyage, wrote in his journal that the Indians seasoned manioc and sweet potatoes with *ají*, and that it was one of their principal foods. Of course, both Columbus and his doctor believed that they had reached the Spice Islands, the East Indies. Not only did Columbus misname the Indians, he also mistook chiles for black pepper, thus giving them the inaccurate name "pepper." But he did one thing right—he transported chile seeds back to Europe after his first voyage, which began the chile conquest of the rest of the world.

Explorers who followed Columbus to the New World soon learned that chiles were an integral part of the Indians' culinary, medical, and religious lives. In 1526, just 34 years after Columbus's first excursion, Captain Gonzalo Fernández de Oviedo noted that on the Spanish Main, "Indians everywhere grow it in gardens and farms with much diligence and attention because they eat it continuously with almost all their food."

Bernabe Cobo, a naturalist and historian who traveled throughout Central and South America in the early seventeenth century, estimated that there were at least forty different varieties. He wrote that there were "some as large as limes or large plums; others, as small as pine nuts or even grains of wheat, and between the two extremes are many different sizes. No less variety is found in color . . . and the same difference is found in form and shape."

The Aztec market in the capital, Tenochtitlán, contained a large number of chiles, and most of those had been collected as tribute, a form of taxation used by the Toltecs and Aztecs and later adopted by the Spanish. The payers of the tribute were the *macehuales,* the serfs or commoners; the collectors were Aztec officials or, later on, officials who worked for the Spanish. The tribute consisted of locally produced goods or crops that were commonly grown, and the tribute of each village was recorded in codices of drawn or painted pictographs.

According to many sources, chiles were one of the most common tribute items. The chiles were offered to the government in several different forms: as fresh or dried pods, as seed, in two 100-pound bundles, in willow baskets, and in Spanish bushels. After transport to the capital, the chiles were stored in warehouses and closely guarded, and then sold. Chile peppers were considered to be the most valuable of the tributes.

One of the most famous tribute codices is the *Matricula de Tributos,* which is part of the *Mendocino Codex.* This codex was compiled for the first viceroy of New Spain, Antonio de Mendoza, who ordered it painted in order to inform the Emperor Charles V of the wealth of what is now Mexico. Glyphs on the codex indicate the tribute paid to the Aztecs by conquered towns just before the Spanish conquest; the towns on one tribute list (in what is now San Luis Potosí) gave 1,600 loads of dry chiles to the imperial throne each year!

The *Mendocino Codex* also reveals an early use of chile peppers as a form of punishment. One pictograph shows a father punishing his young son by forcing him to inhale smoke from roasting chiles. The same drawing shows a mother threatening her daughter with the same punishment. Today, the Popolocán Indians who live near Oaxaca punish their children in a similar manner.

Wherever they traveled in the New World, Spanish explorers, particularly nonsoldiers, collected and transported chile seeds and thus further spread the different varieties. And not only did they adopt the chile as their own; the Spanish also imported foods that they combined with chiles and other native ingredients to create even more complex chile cuisines.

Creating a Cuisine

The arrival of the Spanish in Mexico had a profound effect on the cuisine of the country, as the ingredients the explorers brought with them soon transformed the eating habits of the Indians. However, the Aztecs and their descendants did not give up their beloved staples such as chiles, corn, and chocolate; they combined them with the new imports and thus created the basis for the Mexican cuisines of today.

Throughout the centuries, an astonishing variety in Mexican cooking developed as a result of geography. From the Yucatán peninsula, Mexico stretches more than 2,000 miles to the deserts of the north, and so the length and size of Mexico, combined with the fact that mountain ranges separate the various regions, led to the development of isolated regional cuisines. This geographical variety is the reason that the cooking of tropical Yucatán differs significantly from that of the deserts of Chihuahua and Sonora.

One common factor, though, in Mexican cookery is the prevalence of chile peppers. Unlike South America, where chiles are still mostly consumed by the Indian population, in Mexico everyone fell in love with the pungent pods. Chile peppers are Mexico's most important vegetable crop; they are grown all over the country, from the Pacific and Gulf coasts to mountainous regions with an elevation above 8,000 feet. Approximately 200,000 acres of cultivated land produce between 500,000 and 650,000 tons of fresh pods and 30,000 tons of dry pods, making Mexico number six among the chile-producing countries of the world. Although more than thirty different varieties are grown or collected in Mexico, the *anchos/poblanos*, *serranos*, *mirasols*, and *jalapeños* account for 75 percent of the crop. In 1988, Mexico exported 2,529 metric tons of fresh or dried chiles worth $4.6 million into the United States.

In 1985, each Mexican consumed about 14 pounds of green chile and nearly 2 pounds of dried chile. In fact, the Mexicans eat more chile per capita than onions or tomatoes. The favorite chiles are about evenly divided between those harvested fresh and those utilized in the dry form.

The *serranos* and *jalapeños* are grown for processing and the fresh market, where they are the chiles of choice for salsas. Over 90 percent of the *serrano* crop is used fresh in homemade salsas.

About 60 percent of the *jalapeño* crop is processed, either by canning or pickling or as commercial salsas. Of the remainder, 20 percent is used fresh and 20 percent is used in the production of *chipotles*, the smoked and dried form of the *jalapeño*.

How Many Moles?

Perhaps the most famous Mexican chile dishes are the *moles*. The word *mole*, from the Náhuatl *molli*, means "mixture," as in *guacamole*, a mixture of vegetables (*guaca*). Some sources say that the word is taken from the Spanish verb *moler*, meaning to grind. Whatever its precise origin, the word used by itself embraces a vast number of sauces utilizing every imaginable combination of meats, vegetables, spices, and flavorings—sometimes up to three dozen different ingredients. Not only are there many ingredients, there are dozens of variations on *mole*—red *moles*, green *moles*, brown *moles*, fiery *moles*, and even mild *moles*.

The earliest *moles* were simple compared with what was to come after the Spanish invasion. Ana M. de Benítez, who reconstructed pre-Columbian dishes based on Sahagún's descriptions, used four different chiles (*ancho, mulato, pasilla,* and *chipotle*), plus tomatoes, garlic, pumpkins, tomatillos, and chayote, as the basis of her *moles*. The addition of Eastern Hemisphere ingredients such as almonds, raisins, garlic, cinnamon, and cloves would eventually transform the basic *mole* of the Aztecs into a true delicacy.

Mole poblano, originally called *mole de olores* ("fragrant mole"), is the sauce traditionally served on special occasions (such as Christmas) that combines chiles and chocolate, a popular and revered food of the Aztecs. Moctezuma's court consumed fifty jugs of chile-laced hot chocolate a day, and warriors drank it to soothe their nerves before going into battle. However, the story of how chocolate was combined with chile sauces does not involve warriors, but rather nuns.

Legend holds that *mole poblano* was invented in the sixteenth century by the nuns of the convent of Santa Rosa in the city of Puebla. It seems that the archbishop was coming to visit, and the nuns were worried because they had no food elegant enough to serve someone of his eminence. So, they prayed for guidance and one of the nuns had a vision. She directed that everyone in the convent should begin chopping and grinding everything edible they could find in the kitchen. Into a pot went chiles, tomatoes, nuts, sugar, tortillas, bananas, raisins, garlic, avocados, and dozens of herbs and spices. The final ingredient was the magic one: chocolate. The chocolate, they reasoned, would smooth the flavor of the sauce by slightly cutting its heat. Then the nuns slaughtered their only turkey and served it with the *mole* sauce to the archbishop, who declared it the finest dish he had ever tasted.

This is a great legend, but a more likely scenario holds that the basic *mole* of the Aztecs was gradually transformed by a collision of cuisines. Regarding the use of chocolate, since that delicacy was reserved for Aztec royalty, the military nobility, and religious officials, perhaps Aztec serving girls at the convent gave a royal recipe to the nuns so they could honor their royalty, the archbishop. At any rate, the recipe for *mole poblano* was rescued from oblivion and became a holiday favorite. De Benítez noted: "In the book on Puebla cooking, published in Puebla in 1877, we find recipes for making forty-four kinds of *mole*; there are also sixteen kinds of *manchamanteles* (tablecloth stainers) which are dishes with different kinds of chiles."

In Mexico today, cooks who specialize in *moles* are termed *moleros*, and they even have their own competition, the National *Mole* Fair held every year in October at the town of San Pedro Atocpan, just south of Mexico City. At the

fair, thousands of people sample hundreds of different *moles* created by restau-
ranteurs and *mole* wholesalers. This fair is the Mexican equivalent of chili con
carne cookoffs in the United States; the *moleros* take great pride in their fiery
creations and consider each *mole* a work of art in the same way that chili cookoff
chefs regard their chili con carne. Often the preparation of a family *mole* recipe
takes as long as 3 days. Their recipes are family secrets not to be revealed to
others under any circumstances; indeed, they are passed down from generation
to generation.

"If one of my children wants to carry on my business as a *molero* and is
serious about it," *molero* Villa Suarez told reporter William Stockton, "I will
tell them all the secrets when the time comes." But he went on to indicate that
if his children were not interested in becoming *moleros*, his secrets would die
with him.

In 1963, a group of *moleros* formed a *mole* cooperative of sixty partners
who banded together for the good of their craft. They shared equipment such
as pulverizers and mills, and eventually organized a fair exclusively dedicated to
mole: the *Feria Nacional del Mole*, the National *Mole* Fair, held in conjunction
with the fairs of the local pueblos.

By 1982, the fair had grown so large that the committee moved the location and the date to accommodate all the visitors. The *mole* fair became a
national event and was eventually placed on the Secretary of Tourism's calen-
dar of fairs and fiestas. Each year bigger and better events were presented. As a
result, restaurants began featuring more *mole* specials and tourists had more
opportunities to experience the various *moles*. The National *Mole* Fair has certainly become one of the premier chile pepper events in the world.

The color of a particular *mole* depends mostly on the varieties of chile utilized. A green *mole* consists mostly of *poblano* chiles, while a red *mole* could con-
tain three or four different varieties of dried red chile, such as *chiles de árbol* or
cascabeles. The brown and black *moles* owe their color to *pasillas* and *anchos*,
both of which are sometimes called "chile negro" because of their dark hues
when dried. The dark color of *mole negro* can also be the result of roasting the
chiles until they are almost black, as is the custom in Oaxaca.

Other than chiles, there are literally dozens of other ingredients added to
the various *moles*, including almonds, anise, bananas, chocolate, cinnamon,
cilantro, cloves, coconut, garlic, onions, peanuts, peppercorns, piñons, pumpkin
seeds, raisins, sesame seeds, toasted bread, tomatillos, tomatoes, tortillas, and walnuts. Undoubtedly, some *moleros* add coriander, cumin, epazote, oregano, thyme,
and other spices to their *moles*.

But Puebla is not the only state in Mexico with a reputation for *moles*. Oaxaca, in the south, lays claim to seven unique *moles*—and dozens and dozens of variations. Susana Trilling, who owns the Seasons of My Heart cooking school located outside of Oaxaca city at Rancho Aurora, was our guide to the *moles* of Oaxaca. During a trip to her school, Dave was given lessons on preparing the famous *mole negro Oaxaqueño,* while Susana described her experiences with the seven famous *moles*. She later wrote about the *moles* in a *Chile Pepper* magazine article entitled "My Search for the Seventh *Mole*."

Susana wondered about the number seven, because there are seven regions in the state of Oaxaca, and, of course, 7 days in the week. But then she read *Tradiciones Gastronemicas Oaxaqueñas,* in which the author, Ana María Guzmán de Vásquez Colmenares, noted: "There must be something magical in the number seven, for the number of Oaxacan *moles* coincides with the wonders of the world, the theological virtues, the wise men of Athens—and for their wisdom which elected the number seven to represent justice."

"There may be seven *moles*," say the locals, "but thousands and thousands of cooks have their own private versions of all of the *moles,* so how many does that make?" One magazine writer suggested: "Oaxaca should be the land of 200 *moles!*"

For the record, the seven *moles* are: *mole negro, mole coloradito, mole verde, mole amarillo, mole rojo, manchasmanteles* ("tablecloth stainer"), and *mole chichilo*. They are all descendants of *clemole,* believed to be the original mole of Oaxaca. It was quite simple, being composed of *ancho* and *pasilla* chiles, garlic, cloves, cinnamon, and coriander.

The Oaxacan *moles* are characterized by unusual chiles that are unique to the region. In a discussion with chile vendor Eliseo Ramirez, Dave learned that there are sixty kinds of chile grown only in the state of Oaxaca and nowhere else in Mexico. Of those sixty, he carried about ten. Some of these unusual chiles include *chiles de agua,* which grow erect and are pointed at the end. The *chiles chilhuacle,* which are short and fat, come in two varieties: black and red. The red variety is called "the saffron of the poor" because a small amount of ground *chilhuacle rojo* gives a similar coloring to foods. Other unique chiles are the red-orange *chiles onzas,* the yellow *costeño,* and the *pasilla Oaxaqueña* (sometimes called *pasilla Mexicana*), a smoked *pasilla* that adds a *chipotle*-like flavor to *moles*.

In the market, Dave also learned an easy way to make *moles*. Instead of tediously grinding all of the ingredients on a *metate,* the cooks would go to the Benito Juárez market, buy all their chiles, nuts, and seeds, and have them custom-ground in the special *molinos*, or mills, in another section of the market. The result is a dark paste that is later converted into a *mole* sauce.

Susana Trilling describes the more tedious process: "The chiles are toasted black, soaked and ground, and blended with fried tomatoes, tomatillos, and roasted garlic, and onions. Then come nuts and seeds—some toasted, some fried. Almonds, peanuts, pecans, chile seeds, and sesame seeds. There are almost always more sesame seeds than any other seed or nut. They have to be fried slowly and carefully, with lots of love and attention. Hence the affectionate Mexican *dicho* (saying): 'You are the sesame seed of my *mole*.'"

There are other special ingredients that characterize the different Oaxacan *moles*. Avocado leaves, difficult to find in the United States and Canada, are used in *mole negro*. Fresh green herbs such as epazote and parsley are the source of the green color of *mole verde*. Pineapple and banana are added to *manchasmanteles*, while string beans, chayote and *chiles costeños* are ingredients in *mole amarillo*.

Many different meats are added to *moles*, from chicken to beef to fish, but by far the most common meat served is turkey. In fact, turkey is so important in *mole negro* that Mexican writer Manuel Toussaint noted that the turkey in the *mole* was as important as the eagle in the Mexican flag, and another writer suggested that to refuse to eat *mole negro* was a crime of treason against the homeland!

Mexican Chile Basics

In our Glossary of Mexican Chiles (page 259), we define the enormous number of varieties we encountered in our research. But many of these chiles are unavailable except in local markets, so here we describe the chiles that are the most commonly used in Mexico and in the recipes in this book.

Ancho/poblano　The *ancho* is the dried form of the *poblano*. The fresh pods range in length from 3 to 6 inches and in width from 3 to 4 inches. The fresh pods are roasted and peeled before they are used. Then they are stuffed for chiles rellenos, cut into strips, or chopped for use in vegetables. The reddish-brown *anchos* are usually toasted on a griddle and rehydrated before use. The *anchos* have a flavor that is often described as raisiny and are sometimes ground into a powder. This variety is rather mild. Substitute: *pasilla*

Cascabel The spherical *cascabel* is about an inch and a half in diameter and is most often used in its dried form. When dry, the seeds rattle in the pod and account for the name, which roughly translates as "jingle bell." *Cascabeles* are used in sauces and to spice up many other dishes, such as soups and stews. *Cascabeles* have medium heat. Substitute: *guajillo*

Chipotle Literally, a *chipotle* is any smoked chile, but it generally refers to a smoked *jalapeño*. They are dark brown or red, about 2 inches long and an inch wide, and come in two forms: dried, or canned in an *adobo* sauce. The dried *chipotles* are rehydrated before use, and are sometimes ground into a powder. These chiles have medium heat. Subsitute: none

De árbol *De árbol* means "tree chile," an allusion to the appearance of the plant. The dried pods are about 3 inches long and three-eighths of an inch wide.

They are used in cooked sauces of all kinds and are sometimes ground into a powder. The pods have medium heat. Substitute: *mirasol*

Guajillo Similar in appearance to New Mexican varieties, the *guajillo* is mostly used in its dry form. It is 4 to 6 inches long and about an inch and a half wide. The pods are orange-red, medium-hot, and are mostly used in sauces. Substitute: dried red New Mexican chiles

Habanero Grown in the Yucatán Peninsula, these lantern-shaped, orange chiles are the hottest peppers in the world. The pods are about an inch and a half long and an inch wide and have a distinctive aroma that is fruity and apricot-like. They are used primarily in their fresh form in Mexico, but also appear dried in the United States and Canada. The fresh pods are used extensively in salsas and other Yucatecan dishes. There is no real substitute for the flavor of fresh *habaneros*; use the hottest fresh chiles you can find, such as cayenne or Thai. Substitute for dried *habaneros*: *piquín*

Jalapeño Perhaps the most common chile in Mexico, the familar *jalapeño* is 1 to 2 inches long and about three-quarters of an inch wide. Unless they are smoked to create *chipotles*, the *jalapeños* are used exclusively in their fresh form in a wide number of dishes. They have medium heat and are often found pickled in cans. Substitute: *serrano*

Mirasol *Mirasol* means "looking at the sun," an allusion to the erect pods, which measure up to 4 inches long and about three-quarters of an inch wide. The medium-hot pods are used dried in sauces and meat dishes, and are sometimes ground into powder. Substitute: *de árbol*

Pasilla The fresh form of the pasilla is called *chilaca*, and it is used in a similar manner to New Mexican varieties or *poblanos*. In the dried form, the pods are 5 to 6 inches long and about an inch and a half wide. They are used in sauces and are sometimes stuffed. The pods are mild and are sometimes ground into powder. As the name "little raisin" implies, the pods have a raisiny aroma and flavor. Substitute: *ancho*

Piquín   These small, erect pods are less than an inch long and a half-inch wide, and usually resemble miniature bullets. The *chiltepines* are spherical *piquínes* that measure about a quarter of an inch in diameter. The pods of both are used in salsas, are added to soups and stews, or are ground into powder. They are hot to extremely hot. Substitute: dried *habanero*

Serrano   The *serrano* is used fresh in both the red and green forms and measures 1 to 3 inches long and a half-inch wide. It is the chile of choice in Mexico for fresh salsas and has medium heat. The name means "mountain chile" or "highland chile." These are often found pickled in cans. Substitute: *jalapeño*

Roasting and Peeling Chiles

Poblano and New Mexican chiles are usually blistered and peeled before being used in recipes. Blistering or roasting the chile is the process of heating the fresh pods to the point that the tough, transparent skin is separated from the meat of the chile so it can be removed.

To roast and peel chiles, first cut a small slit in the chile close to the stem end so that the steam can escape and the pod won't explode. Our favorite roasting method, which involves relaxing with a Negra Modelo *cerveza*, is to place the pods on a charcoal grill about 5 to 6 inches from the coals. Blisters will soon indicate that the skin is separating, but be sure that the chiles are blistered all over or they will not peel properly. Although the chiles may burn slightly, take care that they do not blacken too much or they will be difficult to peel. They can also be roasted by holding them in tongs over a gas flame, or in a very hot iron skillet.

After they are blistered, immediately wrap the chiles in damp paper towels and place them in a plastic bag to steam for 10 to 15 minutes. The best way to avoid chile burns is to wear rubber gloves during the peeling process. Remove the skin, stem, and seeds of each pod and process them any way you like: whole, in strips or *rajas*, or chop them coarsely. Place the chopped chiles in plastic ice cube trays and freeze them solid. Pop the cubes out and place them in Ziploc freezer bags and you'll have easy access to whatever amount of chile is needed for a recipe. The chiles will keep in your freezer for at least a year. About two cubes equal one chile.

Toasting and Rehydrating Chiles

Many recipes call for toasting chiles, and that is accomplished on a *comal* or griddle, or in a dry skillet over high heat. Use tongs to toast just long enough that the aroma is released, but not enough to burn the pods. After toasting, the pods are usually rehydrated in hot water until they flesh out and soften in color.

Salsas y Condimentos con Chiles

Chile Sauces and Condiments

Mexico, which grows more varieties of chiles than any other country, also has the greatest number of different kinds of sauces, and they are so important to the cuisine that an entire book could be written on the subject. We are presenting a mere sampling of Mexican chile sauces and condiments in this chapter—additional sauces are found within other recipes in this book.

In Mexico, most of the grinding of sauces is done in a *molcajete,* a stone mortar. As in many modern Mexican homes, we have substituted a food processor or blender, although some traditional cooks may prefer the old-fashioned method. Cooked sauces are generally fried in lard; we have substituted vegetable oil in deference to being culinarily correct in this day and age.

Since many common Mexican sauces such as Pico de Gallo and Guacamole are repeated over and over again in cookbooks, we have decided to focus our attention on the sauces that are not so well known outside of Mexico. Our first sauce, *Salsa Casera* or Homemade Chiltepín Sauce (page 20), shows how truly powerful the tiny, spherical *chiltepines* can be. Only small portions of this should be served; half a teaspoon will make a bowl of soup very hot. Less pungent but very flavorful is *Salsa Chile de Árbol,* or Chile de Árbol Sauce (page 21), which features the very popular *de árbol* chile along with other Mexican spices such as allspice, cloves, and cumin.

Two chile condiments are next. *Chiltepines en Escabeche* (Pickled Chiltepines, page 22) are a great delicacy in northern Mexico, where they are popped into the mouth while eating virtually any snack or main course. They are so popular that at least one manufacturer, Bueno Foods, packs them commercially. Another chile treat is *Chipotles Adobados* or Chipotle Chiles in Adobo Sauce (page 23). These too are available commercially, but we prefer the sweet heat of the homemade chiles.

From the Yucatán peninsula come five intriguing sauces. *Salpicón* (Yucatecan Radish Relish, page 24) combines *habaneros,* radishes, and lime juice for a startling taste combination, while *Xnipec,* translated as Dog's Nose Salsa (page 25), depends on onions and *habaneros* for its flavor. The word *xnipec* refers to the phrase from the Mayan language that actually means "even makes a dog's nose hot," referring to the fact that a dog's nose is usually cold. *Salsa Xcatic* (Xcatic Chile Sauce, page 26), a cooked salsa that's great with seafood, depends on the *xcatic* chile, but yellow wax hots make a good substitute. *Chiltomate* (Roasted Habanero–Tomato Sauce, page 27) is probably the hottest of all these, while *Recado Rojo,* or Red Seasoning Paste (page 28), is usually mild and is used to color and flavor *pibiles,* stewed pork dishes.

Salsa Borracha, or Drunken Sauce (page 30), is a classic Mexican sauce that is made all over the country with a variety of chiles; ours features *pasillas* and *serranos*. Another famous sauce, originally from Puebla but now made all over the country, is *Salsa de Mole Poblano* (Classic Mole Poblano Sauce, page 31) with its seeds and spices. Other *moles*, including the Oaxacan sauces, are found in Chapters 5 and 6. A closely related group of sauces, called *pipiánes*, are the sauces based on pumpkin seeds, or *pepitas*. We've included two of the most commonly served *pipiánes*, *Pipián Rojo* (Red Pipián Sauce, page 32) and *Pipián Verde* (Green Pipián Sauce, page 33). Both are usually combined with chicken or turkey.

Many Mexican states are renowned for specific sauces that are served at nearly every meal. For example, in Nuevo León, two sauces stand out. *Salsa Colorada de Nuevo León* (Red Sauce from Nuevo León, page 34), is a quite hot table sauce from that state that combines *piquín* and *cascabel* chiles. *Salsa de Agricultor* (Farmer's Sauce, page 35) is another favorite of that state; it is made from four different chiles. In Tlaxcala, *Salsa de Chipotle* (Chipotle Chile Sauce, page 38) is the sauce of choice, while the residents of Mexico City enjoy *Salsa del Diablo* (Devil Sauce, page 36), made with three varieties of chiles. In Querétaro, *Salsa Negra* (Black Sauce, page 39) reigns supreme.

The state of Chihuahua is probably the home of the widest variety of sauces in Mexico, and we close out this chapter with a selection of four of them. *Salsa Sabrosa Estilo Chihuahua* (Tasty Chihuahua-Style Sauce, page 40) contains eggs, tomato juice, and chiles, and is great when served over any kind of cooked eggs. *Salsa Brava Tarahumara*, or Tarahumara Bold Sauce (page 41), so named because of the Tarahumara Indians, combines three varieties of chiles with numerous spices, while *Salsa Verde Poblana* (Green Poblano Chile Sauce, page 42) depends on fresh green *poblano* chiles for its flavor and mild heat. *Salsa de Chile y Queso* (Chile–Cheese Sauce, page 43) is the authentic version of what came to be known as "chile con queso" north of the border.

Salsa Casera

(Homemade Chiltepín Sauce)

This diabolically hot sauce is also called *pasta de chiltepín* (*chiltepín* paste). It is used in soups and stews and to fire up *machaca*, eggs, tacos, tostadas, and beans. This is the exact recipe prepared in the home of our friend, Josefina Duran, in Cumpas, Sonora.

2	cups *chiltepines* (or other small, hot chiles)	1	teaspoon coriander seed
8	to 10 cloves garlic	1	cup water
1	teaspoon salt	1	cup cider vinegar
1	teaspoon Mexican oregano		

Combine all ingredients in a blender and purée on high speed for 3 to 4 minutes. Refrigerate for 1 day to blend the flavors. It keeps indefinitely in the refrigerator.

Yield: 2 cups

Heat Scale: Extremely Hot

Note: This recipe requires advance preparation.

Salsa Chile de Árbol
(Chile de Árbol Sauce)

This is the sauce that commonly is bottled in liquor bottles and sold in the *mercados* and at roadside stands in central and northern Mexico. It is sprinkled over nearly any snack food, from tacos to tostadas.

30	*chiles de árbol*, seeds and stems removed	¼	teaspoon ground cumin
	Water	¼	teaspoon ground allspice
1	tablespoon sesame seeds	⅛	teaspoon ground cloves
1	tablespoon *pepitas* (pumpkin seeds)	3	cloves garlic
		1	cup cider vinegar
		¾	cup water

Soak the chiles in the water until softened, about a half-hour.

   Toast the sesame seeds and pumpkin seeds in a skillet until they pop and are brown. Combine the seeds with the drained chiles and the remaining ingredients and purée for about 3 minutes. Strain the mixture through a sieve and bottle. It will keep for months in the refrigerator.

Yield: 2 cups

Heat Scale: Hot

Salsa Home Page

On the World Wide Web of the Internet, there's a home page that celebrates salsas from both Mexico and elsewhere. The Salsa Home Page is located at:

http://www.panix.com/~clay/cookbook/salsa.html

Chiltepínes en Escabeche

(Pickled Chiltepínes)

In the states of Sonora and Sinaloa, fresh green and red *chiltepínes* are pre-served in vinegar and salt. They are used as a condiment and are popped into the mouth when eating any food—except, perhaps, *flan*. Since fresh *chiltepínes* are available in the United States only in Arizona and Texas, adventurous cooks and gardeners must grow their own. The tiny chiles are preserved in three layers in a 1-pint, sterilized jar.

2 cups fresh red and/or green *chiltepínes*	3 teaspoons salt
3 cloves garlic, peeled	3 tablespoons cider vinegar
	Water as needed

Fill the jar one-third full of *chiltepínes*. Add 1 clove garlic, 1 teaspoon salt, and 1 tablespoon cider vinegar. Repeat this process twice more and fill the jar to within ½ inch of the top with water.

Seal the jar and allow to sit for 15 to 30 days.

Yield: 1 pint

Heat Scale: Extremely Hot

Note: This recipe requires advance preparation.

Chipotles Adobados

(Chipotle Chiles in Adobo Sauce)

Here's another pickled chile recipe, this time from Tlaxcala. These sweet–hot pickled chiles can form the basis of a sauce all their own if they're further puréed, or they can be served as a condiment with enchiladas and other main dishes.

½   pound dried *chipotle* chiles, stems removed
    Water to rehydrate

1   quart vinegar

1   head garlic, peeled and crushed

½   cup *piloncillo*, or ½ cup packed brown sugar

1   cup roasted and peeled green chile, such as *poblano* or New Mexican

2   medium tomatoes, chopped

6   black peppercorns

3   bay leaves

1   teaspoon ground cumin
    Salt to taste

Soak the *chipotles* in water until they rehydrate (at least an hour), then drain.

In a saucepan, add ½ of the vinegar, ½ of the garlic, and all of the *piloncillo*. Cook this mixture for about 20 minutes, then add the *chipotles*.

In another pan, combine the green chile, tomato, remaining garlic, peppercorns, bay leaves, cumin, remaining vinegar, and salt to taste. Cook for about 30 minutes, covered, over medium heat. Add the *chipotle* chile mixture, stir well, and store in sterilized jars.

Yield: About 1½ quarts

Heat Scale: Hot

Salpicón

(Yucatecan Radish Relish)

Nancy and Jeff Gerlach wrote in *Chile Pepper* magazine about collecting this salsa in their favorite region in Mexico, the Yucatán peninsula: "The first time we were served this salsa of 'little pieces' we were surprised by the use of radishes, which added not only flavor, but an interesting texture to the salsa. For variety, add some diced tomatoes or avocados." Serve this salsa over seafood.

2   *habanero* chiles, stems and seeds removed, diced; or substitute 4 *jalapeño* or 4 *serrano* chiles

1   large red onion, diced

8   to 10 radishes, thickly sliced

3   tablespoons lime juice, fresh preferred

3   tablespoons fresh cilantro, chopped

Combine all of the ingredients, except the cilantro, in a bowl and allow to sit for an hour to blend the flavors. Toss with the cilantro and serve.

Yield: ½ cup

Heat Scale: Medium

Xnipec
(Dog's Nose Salsa)

This classic Yucatecan salsa is definitely wild. *Xnipec*, pronounced "SCHNEE-peck," is Mayan for "dog's nose." Serve it—carefully—with grilled poultry or fish.

	Juice of 4 limes	1	tomato, diced
1	onion, red or purple preferred, diced	2	tablespoons cilantro, minced
4	*habanero* chiles, seeds and stems removed, diced		

Soak the diced onion in the lime juice for at least 30 minutes. Add all of the other ingredients and mix, salt to taste, and add a little water if desired.

Yield: 1½ cups

Heat Scale: Extremely Hot

The Importance of Chile in Mexico

The chile pepper is the national condiment par excellence, and it is used only in the native dishes. In the majority of typical Mexican dishes served for the consumption of foreigners who are interested in trying them, only a "pinch" of chile is used. They can even be made without this piquant touch, although thereby sacrificing their rating as genuine, classical Mexican dishes.

—Amando Farga

Salsa Xcatic

(Xcatic Chile Sauce)

This sauce was collected for us by Marta and Alan Figel, owners of On the Verandah restaurant in Highlands, North Carolina, where they have a large hot sauce collection. Marta was on assignment for *Chile Pepper* magazine at the time, and she described the principal chile in this salsa designed for use on seafood: "The Yucatán peninsula is identified with its native fiery chile, the *habanero*, and the lesser known chile *xcatic* (pronounced sch-KA-tik). Similar to a chile *güero*, it is pale green to bright yellow, much hotter, and resembles the New Mexican chile in shape and size."

9   *xcatic* chiles, seeds and stems removed, finely chopped; or substitute yellow wax hot or *güero* chiles

1   medium white onion, finely chopped

¼   cup vegetable oil

½   teaspoon salt

2   tablespoons white vinegar
     Freshly ground black pepper to taste

Sauté the chiles and onion in the oil for 20 minutes at low heat. Place in a blender with the remaining ingredients and purée until smooth.

Yield: 1 cup

Heat Scale: Medium

Chiltomate

(Roasted Habanero–Tomato Sauce)

This simple, all-purpose sauce calls for roasting the vegetables, a process that is typical of Yucatán and imparts a distinctive flavor. Don't worry about removing all the skins from the *habaneros* and tomatoes—some charred bits will give the sauce extra flavor. This sauce is wonderful over tacos of all kinds, as well as enchiladas, chiles rellenos, and tamales.

2	*habanero* chiles, roasted, seeds and stems removed, chopped	¼	teaspoon Mexican oregano
4	medium tomatoes, roasted, peeled, and chopped	2	tablespoons vegetable oil
1	small onion, roasted, peeled, and chopped	¼	teaspoon salt

To roast the vegetables, preheat a dry skillet until very hot. Place the un-peeled vegetables on the skillet and roast for 10 to 15 minutes, turning frequently. If you have a stovetop grill, roast the vegetables over the flame until the skins are blackened, about 5 minutes. The vegetables can also be roasted under a broiler. After roasting, remove the skins.

Place the tomatoes, chopped vegetables, and oregano in a blender or food processor and purée until smooth.

Heat the oil in a skillet and sauté the sauce for about 5 minutes. Add the ¼-teaspoon salt (or more to taste).

Yield: 2 cups

Heat Scale: Hot

Recado Rojo

(Red Seasoning Paste)

Here is a classic Yucatán seasoning paste from Jeff and Nancy Gerlach, who commented in *Chile Pepper* magazine: "This is the most popular of all the different *recados* and is very typical of Yucátan. It is used to add both flavor and color to foods, and is most commonly used for *pibíles*, or stewed pork dishes. The red color comes from the annatto seeds, which also add a unique flavor to this tasty paste. Available commercially as achiote paste, *Recado Rojo* is far better when prepared at home." Some cooks add red chile powder to this recipe.

4 tablespoons ground annatto seeds (see note)	1 cinnamon stick, 1-inch long
1 tablespoon dry oregano, Mexican preferred	4 whole cloves
	2 whole allspice berries
10 whole black peppercorns	½ teaspoon cumin seeds
½ teaspoon salt	3 cloves garlic, chopped
	3 tablespoons distilled white vinegar

Place the annatto, oregano, peppercorns, salt, cinnamon, cloves, allspice, and cumin in a spice or coffee grinder and process to a fine powder. Add the remaining ingredients and grind to a thick paste, adding a little water if the mixture is too thick.

Allow to sit for an hour or overnight to blend the flavors.

Yield: ½ cup

Note: Annatto is available in Latin markets or through mail-order sources.

The Puzzle of Mexican Chiles

In Oaxaca I met a lot of unfamiliar chiles, both dried red and green, and one beautiful fresh chile in its ripe, red stage, like a pimiento. Of course I bought some of each kind and took them back to Mexico City, where I could cook with them and see if the flavor was sufficiently distinctive for me to decide if it had no substitute. All this points up the problem with chiles. One has to learn to recognize them first by their looks and only later by their names, as these vary from place to place.

—Elisabeth Lambert Ortiz

Salsa Borracha
(Drunken Sauce)

There are many variations on Drunken Sauce in Mexico. It is usually made
with *pulque*, fermented agave juice, which cannot be canned or bottled. This
version is from Nuevo León and we have substituted beer since *pulque* is not
obtainable outside of Mexico. Serve this salsa over seafood.

20	*pasilla* chiles	3	pickled *serrano* chiles, chopped
4	cloves garlic	1	onion, chopped
¼	cup olive oil		Salt to taste
1	bottle flat Mexican beer, such as Bohemia, or more as needed		

On a griddle, toast the *pasillas* until they are aromatic, turning them often
and taking care not to burn them. Remove the chiles, allow them to cool,
and remove the stems and seeds. In batches in a food processor or blender,
purée the *pasillas* with the garlic, olive oil, and flat beer.

Transfer the mixture to a bowl, add the *serranos* and onion, and mix
well. Add salt to taste.

Yield: About 3 cups

Heat Scale: Medium

Salsa de Mole Poblano

(Classic Mole Poblano Sauce)

This subtle blend of chocolate and chile is from Puebla, where it is known as the "national dish of Mexico" when it is served with turkey. This sauce adds life to any kind of poultry, from roasted game hens to a simple grilled chicken breast. It is also excellent as a sauce over chicken enchiladas.

4	dried *pasilla* chiles, seeds and stems removed	½	corn tortilla, torn into pieces
4	dried red *guajillo* or New Mexican chiles, seeds and stems removed	¼	cup raisins
		¼	teaspoon ground cloves
		¼	teaspoon ground cinnamon
1	medium onion, chopped	¼	teaspoon ground coriander
2	cloves garlic, chopped	3	tablespoons shortening or vegetable oil
2	medium tomatoes, peeled and seeds removed, chopped	1	cup chicken broth
2	tablespoons sesame seeds	1	ounce bitter chocolate (or more to taste)
½	cup almonds		

Combine the chiles, onion, garlic, tomatoes, 1 tablespoon of the sesame seeds, almonds, tortilla, raisins, cloves, cinnamon, and coriander. Purée small amounts of this mixture in a blender until smooth.

Melt the shortening in a skillet and sauté the purée for 10 minutes, stirring frequently. Add the chicken broth and chocolate and cook over very low heat for 45 minutes. The sauce should be very thick. Use the remaining sesame seeds as a garnish.

Yield: 2 cups

Heat Scale: Medium

Pipián Rojo
(Red Pipián Sauce)

The chiles, tomatoes, and squash seeds make this a very New World dish, as squash has been a Mexican staple for millennia. Typically, cooked chicken or turkey is added to this sauce from southern Mexico.

1½ cups ripe tomatoes, chopped
½ cup tomatillos, chopped
1¾ *pasilla* chile, seeds and stem removed
1¾ *guajillo* chile, seeds and stem removed; or substitute dried red New Mexican
¾ cup water
¼ cup lime juice
½ cup sesame seeds
1 tablespoon squash or pumpkin seeds (*pepitas*)

1 cinnamon stick, 1 inch long, broken up
2 teaspoons crushed hot New Mexican red chile
½ cup French bread, cubed and moistened with chicken broth
¼ teaspoon achiote (annatto seed)
2 cups chicken broth
1 tablespoon flour

Combine the tomatoes, tomatillos, and chiles in ¾ cup water and ¼ cup lime juice in a saucepan and cook over medium heat for 10 minutes.

Toast the sesame seeds, squash (or pumpkin) seeds, cinnamon stick, and crushed chile in a dry skillet over low heat for about 10 minutes.

In a food processor or blender, process the toasted ingredients, and then add the cooked tomato mixture, stirring into a smooth paste. Add the bread, achiote, 2 cups of chicken broth, and flour and process everything until smooth. Return the sauce to the stove and heat through.

Yield: About 4 cups

Heat Scale: Medium

Pipián Verde

(Green Pipián Sauce)

This green sauce from southern Mexico is Mayan and the dish originally was made with turkey or duck. After the Spanish introduced chickens, scallions, onions, and cilantro to Mexico, this recipe evolved. Cooked chicken is usually added to the sauce, which is then served with black beans, corn tortillas, and sliced mango.

2	dried *chipotle* chiles Boiling water	½	cup canned tomatillos, drained and chopped
1	tablespoon pumpkin seeds	2	cups chicken broth
½	cup fresh cilantro, chopped		
1	cup scallions, sliced, including the greens		

Cover the chiles with boiling water and allow them to sit for 15 minutes to soften.

Toast the pumpkin seeds in a hot skillet until they start to brown, taking care not to let them burn. Grind the seeds in a blender or spice mill.

Combine the chile, toasted seeds, cilantro, scallions, and tomatillos in a blender along with 2 cups of chicken broth and purée until smooth.

Yield: 3 cups

Heat Scale: Medium

Salsa Colorada de Nuevo León
(Red Sauce from Nuevo León)

This is a significantly hot table sauce that is served at room temperature to add piquancy to any dish, but especially to soups and stews. It can be used for dipping tostadas. Generally, it is refrigerated for a couple of days before serving, but it can be served immediately.

20	dried *piquín* chiles, whole	1	teaspoon dried Mexican oregano
10	dried *cascabel* chiles, seeds and stems removed; or substitute 5 New Mexican chiles	2	cups vinegar
8	cloves garlic	3	bay leaves
1	onion, chopped	1	sprig fresh thyme
1	teaspoon ground cumin	1	sprig fresh marjoram
			Salt to taste

In a food processor or blender, combine the chiles, garlic, onion, cumin, and oregano and process to make a paste.

In a saucepan, combine the vinegar and bay leaves, thyme, and marjoram and bring to a boil. Turn off the heat, remove the saucepan, and allow the herbs to steep for 5 minutes. Remove the herbs, then add the chile paste and blend the mixture until smooth. Place the mixture back over the flame and cook for 5 minutes over medium heat. Taste, adjust for salt, and cool to room temperature.

Yield: About 2½ cups

Heat Scale: Hot

Salsa de Agricultor

(Farmer's Sauce)

With four different chiles used, this sauce from Nuevo León proves that the farmers can take the heat. This table sauce is served at room temperature to spice up soups and stews or any barbecued meat.

10	*piquín* chiles, seeds and stems removed	½	teaspoon ground cumin
10	*cascabel* chiles, seeds and stems removed	1	tablespoon Mexican oregano
5	*chipotle* chiles, seeds and stems removed	5	cloves garlic
		¼	onion
6	*ancho* chiles, seeds and stems removed	1	tablespoon paprika
	Boiling water	2	cups vinegar
½	teaspoon freshly ground black pepper	½	cup vegetable oil
			Salt to taste

Place the chiles in a bowl and cover with hot water. Soak them until they soften, at least 60 minutes. In a food processor or blender, combine the drained chiles, pepper, cumin, oregano, garlic, onion, and paprika and process, adding the vinegar a little at a time. Continue until the mixture forms a smooth sauce.

Remove the sauce from the blender and strain. Heat the oil in a saucepan and add the strained sauce. Sauté, stirring constantly, until the sauce thickens slightly. Add salt to taste.

Yield: About 3 cups

Heat Scale: Hot

Salsa de Diablo

(Devil Sauce)

A favorite in Mexico City, this spice-influenced salsa is interesting because it is one of the few Mexican sauces made with wine. The brave can use this sauce as a salad dressing, but its primary use is over grilled steaks—*carne asada*—or roasted meats, such as lamb.

15	*guajillo* chiles, seeds and stems removed
5	*chipotle* chiles, seeds and stems removed
1	tablespoon *piquín* chiles, seeds and stems removed
2	cups vinegar
4	cloves, crushed
1	cinnamon stick, crushed
½	teaspoon freshly ground black pepper

1	teaspoon Mexican oregano
½	teaspoon ground ginger
½	teaspoon mustard powder
	Salt to taste
½	cup cider vinegar
¼	cup vegetable oil
½	cup red wine

On a griddle, toast the chiles until they are aromatic but not blackened. Transfer them to a bowl and pour the vinegar over them to rehydrate. Let them sit for at least 4 hours, preferably overnight.

Place the chiles in a food processor or blender with any additional vinegar they were soaked in. Add the cloves, cinnamon, black pepper, Mexican oregano, ginger, and mustard and purée until smooth. Add salt to taste. Strain the mixture and add the cider vinegar, oil, and wine, stirring well so that it is evenly mixed.

Yield: About 3½ cups

Heat Scale: Hot

Note: Serve with meat.

Lusting for Mexican Food

Mexican food is an aphrodisiac which excites the passion for living. The cuisine is like a historical novel which has a gorgeously wanton redhead on its dust jacket. Perhaps within the novel, but most certainly within the presence of Mexican food, history, grandeur, violence, amour and tyranny are offered to the jaded.

—Richard Condon

Salsa de Chipotle

(Chipotle Chile Sauce)

From Tlaxcala comes a wonderful sauce that utilizes *chipotles*, or any type of smoked chile. Most commonly, *chipotles* are smoked red *jalapeños*. This is a table sauce served at room temperature to spice up any main dish, including meats and poultry.

10	dried *chipotle* chiles	½	cinnamon stick
4	*mulato* chiles; or substitute *anchos*	1	teaspoon Mexican oregano
	Hot water	½	teaspoon salt
½	onion, chopped	2	tablespoons olive oil
10	cloves garlic	4	tablespoons vegetable oil
1	tablespoon sesame seeds	½	cup vinegar
10	black peppercorns	1	cup water
10	cumin seeds		

Soak the chiles in hot water until soft, about 1 hour. Remove the seeds and stems.

In a food processor or blender, combine the chiles, onion, garlic, sesame seeds, peppercorns, cumin seeds, cinnamon stick, Mexican oregano, and salt and process to a paste.

Heat the olive oil and vegetable oil together in a saucepan and fry the paste over medium heat until it is aromatic, stirring constantly, for about 5 minutes. Add the vinegar and water, remove from the heat, and stir well.

Yield: About 2½ cups

Heat Scale: Hot

Salsa Negra

(Black Sauce)

From the state of Querétaro, this sauce is "black" because of the use of both *pasilla* and *mulato* chiles, which are quite dark in color. In a pinch, *ancho* chiles may be substituted. Serve this sauce over eggs or use it as an enchilada sauce. Some cooks do not like the raw aspects of this sauce, and cook it in oil or lard before using it in a recipe or serving it.

6	*pasilla* chiles, seeds and stems removed	½	small onion, chopped
1	*mulato* chile, seeds and stem removed	2	tablespoons olive oil
1	cup hot beef broth	1	clove garlic, crushed and chopped
			Salt to taste

On a griddle, toast the chiles on all sides, taking care not to burn them. Cut the chiles into strips and place them in the broth. Soak for about 1 hour.

　　Place the chiles and broth and the remaining ingredients in a food processor or blender and purée them until smooth, adding water if necessary to adjust the consistency.

Yield: About 2 cups

Heat Scale: Medium

Salsa Sabrosa Estilo Chihuahua

(Tasty Chihuahua-Style Sauce)

This sauce is designed to be served over cooked vegetables such as squash, corn, and beans. Even though it contains eggs, try it over breakfast eggs.

2	egg yolks	½	*ancho* chile, seeds and stem removed, puréed in ⅛ cup water (or a little more if necessary)
¼	cup vegetable oil		
	Juice of 1 lemon		
	Salt and pepper to taste	2	*serrano* chiles, seeds and stems removed, finely chopped; or substitute *jalapeños*
½	cup tomato juice		

In a small bowl, beat the egg yolks, adding the oil a little at a time. Then add the lemon, salt, pepper, tomato juice, and chile purée and stir well. Mix in the *serrano* chiles. Add more tomato juice if the mixture becomes too thick.

Yield: About 1 cup

Heat Scale: Mild

Mexican Chile Proverbs

"The chile is the same as the needle: equal sharpness."

"Don't be afraid of the chile, even though it's so red."

"We eat this food because our ancestors came from Hell."

"Small, but hot."

"If there's half a chile, look for half an onion."

Salsa Brava Tarahumara
(Tarahumara Bold Sauce)

Named after the rugged Tarahumara Indians of Chihuahua, this "ferocious" uncooked sauce uses three chiles and a variety of spices. It is great with meat, game, or turkey dishes

20	*cascabel* chiles, seeds and stems removed	10	black peppercorns
4	*guajillo* chiles, seeds and stems removed	3	cloves
		2	onions, chopped
10	*chiles de árbol*, seeds and stems removed	4	cloves garlic
		1	pinch ground cumin
	Water as needed	1	tablespoon Mexican oregano
1	cinnamon stick	2	cups vinegar
			Salt to taste

Place the chiles in hot water to soften them, about 60 minutes.

In a blender or food processor, combine half of the chiles, cinnamon, peppercorns, cloves, onion, garlic, cumin, and oregano, and 1 cup of vinegar and purée. Repeat with the remaining half of the ingredients. Combine the two batches and mix well, adding salt if desired. If your blender or food processor is large enough, this sauce can be made in one batch.

Yield: About 3 cups

Heat Scale: Hot

Salsa Verde Poblana

(Green Poblano Chile Sauce)

Also from Chihuahua, this tasty sauce can be used with enchiladas, or, interestingly enough, can be served over pasta, which is very popular in Mexico.

6   *poblano* chiles, roasted, peeled, seeds and stems removed

5   *serrano* chiles, seeds and stems removed

1   onion, chopped

4   tablespoons butter
    Salt to taste

1   cup cream, or more as needed

1   cup *añejo* (aged) cheese, grated; or substitute Romano

In a food processor or blender, combine the chiles and the onion and process into a paste.

Heat the butter in a saucepan and add the chile mixture. Cook for 5 minutes, stirring well. Season with salt to taste.

Remove the pan from the heat and add the cream and cheese, stirring until completely blended. Salt to taste. Add more cream if necessary to adjust the sauce to the desired consistency. This sauce can be heated gently.

Yield: About 2½ cups

Heat Scale: Medium

Salsa de Chile y Queso

(Chile–Cheese Sauce)

Often called "chili con queso" north of the border and made with processed cheese, this dish is far better if it is returned to its roots in Chihuahua. Serve Chile–Cheese Sauce over tortilla chips to make instant *chilaquiles*, or use it as a dip.

10	*serrano* chiles, stems removed; or substitute 7 *jalapeños*	2	onions, chopped
			Water as needed
3	medium tomatoes		Salt to taste
2	tablespoons lard or vegetable oil	½	pound Chihuahua cheese, grated; or substitute mild Cheddar

On a griddle, roast the chiles and tomatoes until slightly blackened. Place in a blender and purée.

    Heat the lard or oil in a frying pan. Fry the onion until transparent, about 5 minutes. Then add the chile–tomato sauce, a little water, and salt to taste. Bring the mixture to a boil, reduce the heat to medium, and add the cheese. Continue to heat the mixture until the cheese is melted.

Yield: About 2 cups

Heat Scale: Hot

Aperitivos Bravos
Bold Appetizers

_____

Appetizers are a Mexican tradition. In fact, eating between meals is not only allowed, it's encouraged. Some of the best foods we have ever had in Mexico have been *antojitos*, the "little whims" that are foods of the street. In no other place in the world have we ever seen such luscious tropical fruits, tangy popsicles, savory empanadas, or fresh fish tacos than in Mexico's little street stands, all manned by friendly cooks.

Appetizers, are, after all, first and foremost party foods and finger foods. We've assembled an impressive collection of both in this chapter; they are sure to give you a taste for tacos, or a craving for quesadillas. Sit back and enjoy this journey through the "little whims" of Mexico. We're certain you'll be up and cooking in no time!

Although there are dozens of chiles to choose from, many people often think of *jalapeños* when they think of Mexico. Our first recipe, *Aros de Jalapeño con Queso de Chorizo* (Jalapeño Rings with Chorizo Cream Cheese, page 48), presents this famous pod in Lula Bertrán's twist on onion rings. And speaking of chiles, *chipotles* to *poblanos* are the stars of our next four recipes: *Chipotles à la Cordobesa* (Chipotle Chiles Cordobesa-Style, page 49), *Chiles à la Norita* (Stuffed Ancho Chiles, page 50), *Chileajo* (Garlic Chile, page 52), and *Envueltos de Chiles Poblanos* (Poblano Chile Rolls, page 53). There might be more vitamin C in these recipes than in a whole pitcher of orange juice!

The next two recipes are wonderful for your vegetarian friends, or for those who are trying to cut down on their meat intake. *Coctel de Hongos* (Mushroom Cocktail, page 54) and *Chile con Queso Estilo Sonora* (Sonoran-Style Chile with Cheese, page 55), are easy to make and taste great!

And no party would be complete without our recipe for empanadas, *Carne Poco-Picaduras* (Mini-Meat Bites, page 56). After these unique *antojitos*, we turn to taco recipes, of which we have collected three different varieties. *Pescadillos* (Fish Tacos, page 57) are one of the healthiest choices you can make. Be sure to squeeze on a little lemon or lime to bring out the flavors. We also have *Taquitos Blancos y Negros* (White and Black Taquitos, page 58), and *Flautas con Crema* (Rolled Tacos with Cream Sauce, page 59) if you're in the mood for something a little richer.

Enchiladas are the perfect party food, as they serve many and are enjoyed by all. We searched far and long to find the following recipes. We promise that the *Enchiladas Estilo Querétaro* (Querétaro-Style Enchiladas, page 60) and *Papadazules* (Enchiladas with Pumpkin Seed Sauce, page 62) will produce a pleasant, pungent surprise for your guests.

Burros de Carne Machaca con Chile (Shredded Beef Burritos with Chile, page 63) launches our next set of lunch, brunch, or party recipes. We've also included two kinds of quesadillas, *Quesadillas de Flor de Calabaza* (Squash Blossom Quesadillas, page 64) and *Quesadillas Verdes de Nuevo León* (Nuevo León's Green Quesadillas, page 65), which have recently become incredibly popular in the United States. Feel free to add other chiles or ingredients to these cheesy delights to create your own favorites.

For every important occasion in Mexico, there are tamales. In fact, it is said that in pre-Conquest days, a young Aztec couple was considered married only when the person who arranged the marriage tied the bridegroom's cloak to the blouse of the bride, and the couple shared a dish of tamales. Our *Tamales de Picadillo de Pollo* (Chicken Picadillo Tamales, page 68) and *Chilehuates* (Tamales with Chile and Peanuts, page 66) may not be quite that important, but they are equally as good.

Our *Chilaquiles Caprichosos, à la Cerveza* (Whimsical Beer Casserole, page 69) is certainly as fun as it sounds, while the *Ensalada de Guacamole* (Avocado Salad, page 70) will be considered *muy excelente* by those who enjoy guacamole. And to top off this chapter of whimsical delights, we offer *Cuitlacoches Fritos.* (Fried Corn Fungus, page 71), which features the tasty "Mexican truffle" called *cuitlacoche.*

Aros de Jalapeño con Queso de Chorizo

(Jalapeño Rings with Chorizo Cream Cheese)

Our friend Lula Bertrán, from Mexico City, credits the invention of this recipe to her husband, Alberto. "He likes onion rings," she told us. "One day while eating them he said, 'Why don't you do this with chiles?'"

2	cups water	½	teaspoon baking powder
4	large *jalapeños,* roasted, peeled, seeds and stems removed, cut into rings	½	teaspoon salt
		½	cup milk
			Vegetable oil for deep frying
3	tablespoons vinegar	½	cup fried chorizo sausage
½	cup flour	½	cup cream cheese

Preheat the oven to 200 degrees F.

Place the water in a large saucepan. Heat the water on high until it boils. Next, add the *jalapeño* rings and vinegar to the boiling water and cook for 5 minutes. Remove from heat and cool. Drain the rings and pat dry.

Combine the flour, baking powder, salt, and milk in a bowl to make a batter. Dip the rings into the batter and fry in hot oil until they are crisp and brown. Drain on paper towels.

Combine the chorizo with the cheese to make a paste. Fill the rings with the paste, warm in the oven, and serve hot.

Serves: 4

Heat Scale: Medium

Chipotles à la Cordobesa
(Chipotle Chiles Cordobesa-Style)

This recipe for dangerous dip features *chipotles*, the designer chile of the '90s. *Chipotles* are actually smoked *jalapeños*, and are the favorite chile of Melissa, who loves their smoky, hot flavor.

4	cups water		¼	teaspoon thyme
4	ounces *chipotle* chiles, dried, stemmed and seeded		¼	teaspoon oregano
			1	bay leaf
1	cup packed brown sugar		1	cup sour cream
	Salt to taste		1	cup mayonnaise
2	cups white wine vinegar		1	tablespoon lemon juice
⅓	cup olive oil		1	bag of carrots (about 8), peeled and cut into sticks
4	pounds onion, chopped			
1	head of garlic, sectioned		1	stalk of celery, cleaned and cut into sticks
½	teaspoon salt			

Place the water, chiles, brown sugar, and salt in a saucepan and heat on low until the chiles rehydrate and the peels are easily loosened. Once the peels are removed, add the vinegar. Remove the pan from the heat and add the olive oil, onion, garlic, salt, thyme, oregano, and bay leaf. Store all but four of the chiles in glass jars in the refrigerator for later use. Purée the last four chiles in a blender, along with 2 tablespoons of the liquid. In a small bowl, mix together the puréed chiles, sour cream, mayonnaise, and lemon juice. Serve with the fresh vegetables of your choice.

Serves: 10 to 12

Heat Scale: Medium

Chiles à la Norita

(Stuffed Ancho Chiles)

Ancho chiles make some of the best stuffed appetizers that can be found. However, be careful to choose *anchos* that are fairly fresh. Look for chiles that are still bendable and whose aroma can be detected through their packaging.

Salsa

¼	cup vegetable oil	½	cup water
2	onions, finely chopped	¼	teaspoon Mexican oregano
2	tomatillos, finely chopped	2	tablespoons cilantro, chopped

To prepare the salsa, heat the oil in a saucepan and fry the onion. Then add the tomatillos, water, oregano, and cilantro. Let the mixture cook on high heat until the tomatillos are fully cooked, then set aside.

Stuffed Chiles

4	cups water		
6	large *ancho* chiles, stems and seeds removed	6	tortillas
		6	eggs, scrambled
13	ounces of aged cheese, such as Romano, sliced into 6 equal pieces	1	head lettuce, shredded or chopped
5	tablespoons butter	1	avocado, sliced
⅓	cup vegetable oil	7	ounces Cheddar cheese, grated

To prepare the chiles, pour the water into a large saucepan and bring to a boil. Place the chiles in the boiling water for 2 minutes to rehydrate them. Drain the chiles and carefully pat them dry on paper towels.

Fill each chile with a slice of cheese and set aside. In a large skillet, melt the butter over medium heat, then add the oil and turn the heat on high. Brown the chiles in the butter–oil mixture. Once they are browned, remove them from the oil, drain them on a paper towel, and place them on a platter.

Briefly dip the tortillas in the hot oil and place them on a separate plate. Place one chile on top of each tortilla, then top each with a spoonful of salsa and egg.

Decorate the plates with the lettuce, avocado slices, and grated cheese.

Serves: 4 to 6

Heat Scale: Medium

Mexican Truffles

Cuitlacoches are variously called "maize mushrooms," "corn smut," and "Mexican truffles," and these varied terms illustrate the fact that some farmers hate it, but chefs love it. Basically, it's a dark gray fungus *(Ustilago maydis)* that grows on corn and has become a gourmet delicacy in both Mexico and the United States. Although it infests corn and ruins some crops, some farmers in both countries are deliberately infecting their crops to harvest and can the fungus. While corn brings only pennies a pound, *cuitlacoches* can be sold for up to $2.00 a pound. It's used in tortilla casseroles, with zucchini to stuff tacos, and as a flavor base for sauces, soups, and meats. "It's the ugly duckling of the mushroom kingdom," commented *cuitlacoche* distributor Cristina Arnold, "but you don't consume it for its looks, you consume it for its earthy flavor."

Chileajo

(Garlic Chile)

This dish is the Mexican version of antipasto. We prefer the vegetables in this recipe steamed. However, the vegetables may also be served raw. We collected this recipe in Oaxaca, which is known for its fantastic *moles* and beautiful pottery as well as its uses of exotic, flavorful chiles such as the *chilcoxtle* and *guajillo*.

1¼ cups potatoes, peeled and cut into thin rounds

½ cup carrots, peeled and cut into small cubes

½ cup green beans, cut into small pieces

½ cup fresh peas, shelled

4 *chilcoxtle* chiles, seeds and stems removed, rehydrated in hot water and minced; or substitute *pasillas*

2 *guajillo* chiles, seeds and stems removed, rehydrated in hot water and minced; or substitute New Mexican

1 head of garlic, peeled

1 cup white vinegar

Salt to taste

8 ounces *asadero* cheese, grated (mozzarella may be substituted)

1 onion, sliced

Mexican oregano to taste

Steam the potatoes, carrots, green beans, and peas until they have reached the desired doneness, then chill in the refrigerator. Rinse the chiles in hot water and place them in a bowl with the garlic, vinegar, and salt. Remove the vegetables from the refrigerator, and arrange them in the center of a platter, then pour the chile mixture over the vegetables. Place the cheese and onion around the edges of the dish, sprinkle the oregano over the top, and serve.

Serves: 4 to 6

Heat Scale: Medium

Envueltos de Chiles Poblanos
(Poblano Chile Rolls)

Not surprisingly, the very best *poblano* chiles are grown in central Mexico. The heat scale for this pungent pod ranges from mild to snappy, depending on the growing conditions before it is picked. Choose the darkest colored *poblanos*, as they offer the best taste.

8	*poblano* chiles, seeds and stems removed, cut into strips	18	small flour tortillas
3	large tomatoes, grilled	3	tablespoons onion, chopped
3	cloves garlic, peeled and chopped	½	cup shredded Monterey Jack cheese
1	tablespoon water	1	avocado, pitted, halved, and sliced
8	squash blossoms, cleaned	1	*poblano* chile, seeds and stem removed, grilled, and sliced lengthwise
⅓	cup vegetable oil		

In a skillet, add the chiles, tomatoes, garlic, and water, then sauté. When the ingredients are cooked, stir in the squash blossoms, then remove the mixture from the stove and set aside.

In a separate skillet, heat the oil and quickly dip the tortillas into it, then remove and drain them on a paper towel. Fill the tortillas with equal amounts of the blossom mixture and onion, then roll each one up and place on a platter. Top the tortillas with your favorite salsa from Chapter 2, along with cheese, avocados, and chile strips, and serve.

Yield: 18 rolls

Heat Scale: Medium

Coctel de Hongos

(Mushroom Cocktail)

Who needs shrimp to create a great cocktail? Vegetarians and carnivores alike will enjoy this hot Mexican concoction. Feel free to substitute two fresh *habaneros* for the *serranos*.

1	pound mushrooms, cleaned	3	tomatoes, chopped
3	tablespoons water	6	*serrano* chiles, seeds and stems removed, finely chopped
1	clove garlic, peeled and chopped	½	cup tomato sauce
	Salt to taste	1	teaspoon hot sauce
3	tablespoons onion, chopped		Water

In a medium-sized saucepan, cook the mushrooms in water along with the garlic and salt for about 5 minutes. Add the onion, tomatoes, chiles, tomato sauce, and hot sauce, along with a little water, then serve in four shrimp cocktail glasses.

Serves: 4

Heat Scale: Medium

Chile con Queso Estilo Sonora
(Sonoran-Style Chile with Cheese)

Who could ask for a more perfect combination than chile and cheese? This recipe is a specialty of the Sonora area, which has millions of acres of agricultural land developed along the coastal plains.

¼	stick butter	3	*jalapeño* chiles, seeds and stems removed, minced
1	medium onion, chopped	¾	cup milk
2	tomatoes, chopped		Salt and pepper to taste
4	cloves garlic, finely chopped	1	cup grated Chihuahua cheese, or substitute mild Cheddar
5	*poblano* chiles, roasted, peeled, seeds and stems removed, chopped	2	tablespoons cilantro, chopped

Melt the butter in a skillet and sauté the onion, tomatoes, and garlic until the onions are translucent. Next, add the chiles, milk, salt, and pepper. Let this mixture cook for a few minutes so that the flavors blend, then add the cheese, stirring well.

Remove the mixture from the heat and place it in a glass bowl. Garnish with the cilantro. Serve with tortilla strips or chips for dipping.

Serves: 4 to 6

Heat Scale: Medium

Carne Poco-Picaduras

(Mini-Meat Bites)

This unique Mexican/Spanish appetizer can be filled with pork, beef, or chicken. These mini-bites of meat and corn masa are tiny ravioli-like masa pastries, which promise a savory salsa-covered sensation with every bite!

Mini-bites

1	pound ground beef		Salt to taste
1	onion, chopped	1	teaspoon baking powder
4	cups prepared masa	¼	cup vegetable oil

In a large skillet, fry the ground beef and onion until done.

In a separate bowl, mix the masa, salt, and baking powder, combining well. With this mixture, form 36 small masa rounds about the size of the bottom of a coffee cup.

Distribute ground beef and onion to each masa round and fold the rounds in half, sealing the ends.

Heat the oil in a skillet and fry the now semicircular mini-bites until done. Remove them from the oil and drain on paper towels.

Salsa

2	cups chopped tomatoes	3	*serrano* chiles, seeds and stems removed, finely chopped
¼	cup onion, chopped	½	cup grated Parmesan cheese

Mix the tomatoes, onions, and chiles together with the cheese in a small bowl.

Cover the mini-bites with the salsa and serve.

Yield: 36

Heat Scale: Medium

Pescadillos

(Fish Tacos)

One of the best appetizer treats you can ever taste is fresh fish tacos prepared in Yucatán.

½   cup vegetable oil

1   large onion, finely chopped

2   pounds large tomatoes, blanched and chopped

5   *serrano* chiles, seeds and stems removed, finely chopped

2½ pounds marlin (or your favorite seafood), cut into chunks

Chopped cilantro to taste

1   teaspoon oregano

Salt and pepper to taste

12 corn tortillas

¾   cup vegetable oil

1   lemon, cut into wedges

Heat the ½ cup of oil in a skillet and sauté the onions, tomatoes, and chiles. Add the marlin, cilantro, oregano, salt, and pepper. Cook until the fish flakes, then set aside.

Warm the tortillas and stuff them with the fish mixture.

Heat ¾ cup of oil in a separate skillet. Fry the stuffed tortillas until light brown, or until they have achieved the desired texture. Squeeze the lemon wedges over the fish in each taco and serve.

Yield: 12 tacos

Heat Scale: Medium

Taquitos Blancos y Negros

(White and Black Taquitos)

This recipe from the coastal city of Veracruz is often served with a variety of dipping sauces. Why not serve yours with some of the scintillating sauces from Chapter 2?

¼ cup butter

2 ears of corn, shucked, cleaned, and kernels removed

½ onion, chopped

2 *jalapeño* chiles, stems and seeds removed, chopped

1 pound black beans, cooked and mashed

½ cup vegetable oil

20 corn tortillas

2 cups mild Cheddar cheese, grated

2 cups cream

In a large saucepan, heat the butter and fry the corn until done. Add the onion, *jalapeños,* and beans, and cook until the moisture is almost gone. Set aside.

Heat the oil in a skillet and fry the tortillas briefly. Stuff the tortillas with the corn and bean mixture, then place them in a baking dish. Add the grated cheese and cream, cover, and bake at 300 degrees F for 10 minutes, or until the cheese has melted.

Serves: 8 to 10

Heat Scale: Mild

Flautas con Crema

(Rolled Tacos with Cream Sauce)

This recipe was collected from Guanajuato, which was founded by the Spaniards more than 400 years ago. This dish is also known as "disappearing tacos" since they disappear quickly when served at a party!

1	tablespoon cilantro, chopped	¾	cup oil
1	large tomato, chopped	30	tortillas
½	onion, chopped	1¾	pounds beef or pork, grilled and shredded
6	*serrano* chiles, stems and seeds removed, chopped	1	cup sour cream
2	medium avocados, peeled, pitted, and mashed		Cream to taste
1	tablespoon lemon juice	1	small head lettuce, chopped

In a medium-sized mixing bowl, combine the cilantro, tomato, onion, chiles, avocados, and lemon juice and mix well.

In a heavy skillet, heat the oil and fry the tortillas briefly, then drain on paper towels. Stuff the tortillas with the meat and roll. Next, return the rolls to the skillet and fry until crisp.

In a small bowl, mix the sour cream and cream together until blended, then serve over the flautas, along with the tomato/chile mixture. Top with chopped lettuce.

Yield: 30 flautas

Heat Scale: Medium

Enchiladas Estilo Querétaro

(Querétaro-Style Enchiladas)

This recipe calls for chile-infused vinegar, which has become fairly easy to find in the past few years. However, if you can't find any in your local hot shop or gourmet store, try one of the mail-order sources listed near the back of this book (see Mail-Order Sources and Retail Shops, page 279). This vinegar is also great as a marinade and stir-fry sauce.

2	cups water
10	*ancho* chiles, seeds and stems removed, chopped
2	cloves garlic, peeled and chopped
½	teaspoon oregano
2	cloves
½	teaspoon cinnamon
	Salt to taste
24	corn tortillas
5½	ounces chorizo, fried
3	potatoes, chopped into small pieces, cooked, and fried
4	carrots, chopped, cooked, and fried
1⅓	cups oil
¼	cup chile-infused vinegar
1½	cups *asadero* cheese, grated (a mild Cheddar cheese, or Monterey Jack, may be substituted)
1	onion, chopped
½	head lettuce, chopped

Pour the 2 cups of water into a large saucepan. Next, add the chiles, garlic, oregano, cloves, cinnamon, and salt and boil for 5 minutes. Remove the pan from the heat, transfer the mixture to a blender, and process it until smooth.

Place the tortillas on two large baking sheets with sides, and carefully put 1 tablespoon of the chile mixture onto the center of each tortilla. Combine the chorizo, potatoes, and carrots. Spoon some of the mixture on top of the chile paste on each tortilla.

Starting at one end, roll each tortilla into a cylinder and set aside. Pour the oil and chile-infused vinegar into a large skillet and heat until the oil is hot. Place the enchiladas in the oil and fry quickly until almost crisp. Drain the enchiladas on paper towels. Place the fried enchiladas on a platter and cover them with the cheese, onion, and lettuce and serve.

Yield: 24 enchiladas

Heat Scale: Medium

Differing Views on the Heat Scale

The Mexican says: "It's not hot."	*The foreigner understands:* "It's hot."
The Mexican says: "It's just a little hot."	*The foreigner understands:* "It's very hot."
The Mexican says: "It's mostly hot."	*The foreigner understands:* "Don't get near it. It's dangerous."
The Mexican says: "It's very hot."	*The foreigner understands:* "It burns."
The Mexican says: "It's very very hot."	*The foreigner understands:* "Abandon the establishment."

—Mexican Proverb

Papadazules

(Enchiladas with Pumpkin Seed Sauce)

Translated, the name of this filling appetizer means "food for the lords." It is said to have been first prepared by the Mayans for the Spaniards on the Yucatán peninsula.

Chiltomate

4	tomatoes, grilled and peeled	1	tablespoon butter or corn oil
1	*habanero* chile, stem and seeds removed, finely minced	1	onion, chopped
			Salt and pepper to taste

To prepare the *chiltomate*, grind the tomatoes and chile together with a mortar and pestle. Heat the butter in a skillet and sauté the onion, then add the tomato–chile mixture, and the salt and pepper. Mix well and set aside.

Pumpkin Seed Sauce

12	ounces pumpkin seeds, toasted and ground	1	bunch epazote, soaked in water and salt
		¼	cup olive oil

24 tortillas
10 eggs, boiled and chopped

In a small mixing bowl, liquefy the pumpkin seed along with the epazote and water until you create a salsa with a thick consistency. In a medium-sized frying pan, heat the oil over high heat. Quickly heat the tortillas in the oil, remove, and drain. Next, coat one side of the tortillas in the pumpkin seed salsa. Salsa side up, fill each tortilla with eggs and roll them. Arrange the tortillas on a plate and pour the rest of the salsa over them. Pour the tomato–chile sauce on top of the salsa and serve.

Yield: 24 enchiladas

Heat Scale: Hot

Burros de Carne Machaca con Chile

(Shredded Beef Burritos with Chile)

Originally, the beef in traditional *machaca* burritos was dried outside in the sun. However, we decided to dry out the beef in the refrigerator so that your dog won't have the opportunity to eat your dinner, and also to keep the beef at a healthy, consistent temperature. Please note that this recipe requires advance preparation.

2	cups beef arm roast, uncooked and finely shredded	3	tablespoons vinegar
2	tablespoons water	½	teaspoon oregano
3	cloves garlic, peeled and grated	½	teaspoon sugar
2	tablespoons vegetable oil		Salt to taste
2	tablespoons flour	6	flour tortillas
6	*pasilla* chiles, seeds and stems removed, lightly toasted and chopped		

Place the beef, uncovered, in a dish in the refrigerator and let it dry out for a couple of days. Once the beef is dry, add the water and garlic to the beef and mix together. Once this is blended, spice it to your liking and set it aside.

Heat the oil in a large skillet and add the beef mixture and flour, stirring constantly so it doesn't burn or stick. Once the mixture is heated through, add the chiles, vinegar, oregano, sugar, and salt.

Heat the tortillas and stuff them with the beef mixture, roll, and serve. Cut them in thirds for appetizer-size snacks.

Yield: 18 mini-burritos

Heat Scale: Medium

Note: Requires advance preparation.

Quesadillas de Flor de Calabaza
(Squash Blossom Quesadillas)

This recipe from Tlaxcala requires the use of a *comal*, which is a round, flat griddle on which tortillas are cooked. Traditional *comales* in Mexico are made of unglazed earthenware, and used over an open fire. If you do not have a *comal*, an electric skillet will also work.

2⅓ cups corn meal
     Water as necessary
3   tablespoons vegetable oil
1   onion, chopped
2   cloves garlic, peeled and
     chopped

2   *serrano* chiles, seeds and stems
     removed, sliced
12   squash blossoms, cleaned
     Epazote leaves to taste,
     chopped
     Salt to taste

In a bowl, moisten the corn meal with the water and 1 tablespoon of the oil until it reaches a thick, pasty consistency. Set aside.

In a skillet, heat the remaining oil and sauté the onion, garlic, chiles, squash blossoms, epazote, and salt, and set aside.

Using a tortilla press, form the masa into tortillas, and heat them on a *comal*; cook until done (about 3 minutes). When all of the tortillas are cooked (you should have about eight), spread an equal portion of the squash blossom mixture over each tortilla. Slice the tortillas into quarters and serve.

Yield: 32 slices

Heat Scale: Medium

Quesadillas Verdes de Nuevo León
(Nuevo León's Green Quesadillas)

These quesadillas earned their name from the *poblanos* that are cooked with the masa. This recipe is a favorite in the state of Nuevo León.

1	onion, finely chopped	½	cup cream
2	tablespoons vegetable oil	1⅓	cups corn masa
2	pounds pork ribs, cooked and boned	½	teaspoon baking powder
3	tomatoes, grilled and peeled	1	cup wheat flour
	Salt and pepper to taste	1	teaspoon salt
5	small *poblano* chiles, stems and seeds removed, grilled and peeled		Vegetable oil for frying

In a large skillet, fry the onions in 2 tablespoons oil until done. Add the rib meat and tomatoes, and cook over medium heat until the tomatoes liquefy. Season with salt and pepper and set aside.

In a medium bowl, mix the chiles with the cream. Add the masa, baking powder, flour, and salt. Mix well. Break the masa into eight small sections and roll out each on a floured surface. Place a small amount of the pork mixture in each one, then fold over to form the semicircular quesadillas and fry in oil in an electric skillet until done.

Yield: 8 quesadillas

Heat Scale: Mild

Chilehuates

(Tamales with Chile and Peanuts)

This dish is served in humid climates where the *cebollina* (wild onion) grows, which is what gives this dish its special flavor. *Chilehuates* are wonderful to include when you are serving an extensive menu of appetizers.

30	corn husks	6	*jalapeño* chiles, stems and seeds removed, chopped
1	pound butter		
2	pounds corn masa	4	tablespoons peanut oil
	Salt to taste	2	cups cooked black beans
3	teaspoons baking powder	4	ounces shelled peanuts, ground
4	*cebollinas* (green onions)	2	cups squash, cubed

Soak the corn husks overnight and drain the next morning.

Place the butter in a mixing bowl and beat with an electric mixture until it doubles in size. Add the masa slowly, beating constantly. Add the salt and baking powder. If necessary, you may add a small amount of cold water. Continue beating for 15 minutes or until a small piece will float in a glass of water.

With a mortar and pestle or in a blender, grind the *cebollinas* and chiles together. Place the mixture in a frying pan along with the peanut oil and sauté quickly. Next, add the black beans and peanuts to the mixture and stir. Add the squash and cook for 2 minutes or until most of the liquid has cooked off.

Spread the masa over each corn husk, add some of the bean mixture, then fold each husk over. Twist the ends of each husk, making sure they are closed. Place the folded husks in a steam cooker, cover, and cook for 45 minutes to 1 hour, or until the masa is easily removed from the husks.

Yield: 30 tamales

Heat Scale: Medium

Note: Requires advance preparation.

Presidential Dining

On June 29, 1962, a banquet in Mexico City given by President Adolfo López Mateos honored the visiting President of the United States, John F. Kennedy, and his wife. The menu that day reflected the international flavor of the capital:

Caviar
Consommé à la Madrilène
Red Snapper à la Veracruzana
Tournedos Rossini
Potatoes Dauphine
Mamey Glacé
Espresso coffee

Tamales de Picadillo de Pollo
(Chicken Picadillo Tamales)

This recipe is from Veracruz, which Cortez founded when he harbored there in 1519, before beginning his westward march to conquer the Aztecs.

1	large chicken	3	cloves
8	cups water	3	black peppercorns
	Salt to taste	2	cups corn meal
1	large onion, chopped	1	tablespoon chicken broth
4	*ancho* chiles, seeds and stems removed, chopped	½	cup vegetable oil
3	tomatoes	30	dry corn husks

In a large pot, boil the chicken in 8 cups water with the salt and onion until done. Remove the meat from the bones, chop it, and place it in a skillet along with the chiles, tomatoes, cloves, and peppercorns. Add more salt if necessary.

Place the corn meal in a separate bowl and moisten with chicken broth and oil until you create a thick masa.

Separate and soak the corn husks for about ½ hour and drain. Spread the masa on the individual husks, stuff with the chicken mixture, fold, and steam until done, about 45 minutes.

Yield: 30 tamales

Heat Scale: Mild

Chilaquiles Caprichosos, à la Cerveza
(Whimsical Beer Casserole)

This Michoacán recipe is perfect for just about any party, as it incorporates beer, one of the best known party beverages on Earth. Although Negro Modelo is our favorite, there are more than 20 varieties of beer brewed in Mexico, all of which are the perfect accompaniment to any of the hot and spicy foods in this chapter.

⅓ cup vegetable oil
12 tortillas
1 chicken breast, cooked, boned, and shredded
3 *serrano* chiles, stems and seeds removed, chopped

1 cup chopped tomato
1 Mexican dark beer
3 eggs
1 cup heavy cream
   Salt and pepper to taste
1 cup grated mild Cheddar cheese

Preheat the oven to 350 degrees F.

Heat the oil in a skillet and quickly dip the tortillas in the hot oil. Remove the tortillas and drain, then place them in a 9- by-13-inch baking dish. Cover the tortillas with the shredded chicken and set aside.

In a large bowl, mix the chiles with the tomato, beer, eggs, cream, salt, and pepper. Pour this mixture over the tortillas and bake for 30 minutes or until done. Sprinkle with grated Cheddar cheese and serve.

Serves: 6 to 8

Heat Scale: Medium

Ensalada de Guacamole

(Avocado Salad)

A native of the tropics, the avocado flourishes in the balmy weather of
Mexico. Although avocados have earned a reputation for being high in fat,
a half of one avocado has only 138 calories and is chock-full of vitamin C.

½	small onion, finely chopped	1	large tomato, skinned, seeded, and chopped
2	*serrano* chiles, stems and seeds removed, minced	¼	cup onion, chopped
1	teaspoon cilantro, finely chopped	1	tablespoon cilantro, chopped
⅛	teaspoon salt	2	teaspoons lemon juice
2	medium avocados	4	large lettuce leaves

Using a mortar and pestle, grind together the onions, *serranos,* finely chopped
cilantro, and salt until it resembles a paste, then set aside. Next, cut the avocados in half, remove the seeds, and scoop out the flesh into a separate bowl.
Add the paste to the avocado and mash together with a fork. Add the tomato,
onion, cilantro, and lemon juice, mixing to a thick, smooth consistency.
Arrange each lettuce leaf on a plate and spoon ½ cup of the guacamole on
each. Serve immediately with chips or tortillas.

Serves: 4

Heat Scale: Medium

Cuitlacoches Fritos

(Fried Corn Fungus)

Yes, we know this sounds a little scary to the uninitiated, but corn fungus is a delicacy well worth trying. It is available canned in Latin American grocery stores.

8	medium *cuitlacoches* (mushrooms may be substituted)	4	*serrano* chiles, stems and seeds removed, chopped
4	heaping tablespoons butter		Chopped epazote leaves to taste
1	medium onion, chopped		Salt to taste

In a medium frying pan on high heat, fry the *cuitlacoches* in the butter, then add the onion, chiles, epazote, and salt. Mix well, making sure the mixture doesn't stick. Turn the heat down and let it simmer for 15 to 20 minutes. This mixture can be served without accompaniment, or used to stuff tacos.

Yield: About 2 cups

Heat Scale: Hot

The *New* Mexican Cuisine

In 1995, there were 125 Kentucky Fried Chicken outlets in Mexico, closely followed by 72 McDonald's. In addition, there are numerous Burger King, Wendy's, T.G.I. Friday's, and Pizza Hut establishments, and even a Taco Bell or two!

Caldos, Guisados, Sopas y Pozoles
Soups and Stews

Today, soups in Mexico come in all varieties of colors, consistencies, and combinations, and it is unthinkable not to have at least one bowl a day. However, soup is not even mentioned by the early Spanish historians and chroniclers; the closest mention is of the thick stews that the Indians cooked in their large, clay *ollas*. Food historians believe that the soup course was introduced by the French and other European influences.

The traditional *comida* starts with a soup course, and is then followed by a *sopa seca*, a dry soup, which is a starchy dish containing rice, macaroni, noodles, or tortillas and is served between the starter and the entrée. There is an unbelievable variety of soups—from delicious clear broths to soups thick with vegetables, to hearty meat soups and stews that are literally a meal in themselves. The herbs and chiles, used judiciously and creatively, work together to really get one's taste buds started.

Even though our first soup recipes call for vegetables and chiles—no meat—the basis for these (and others to follow) is a good chicken stock. So, get out your stockpot and make a few gallons of rich chicken stock, freeze it, and you will be well on your way to creating excellent Mexican soups.

The first recipe, *Agua Chile* (Chile Water, page 77), is a simple peasant soup, spiced up by the addition of *chiltepines*. Chiles will spice up even the blandest of peasant diets, as this recipe, found in the mountain villages of Sinaloa, shows. Another simple, delicious recipe is *Consomé de Rajas* (Chile Strip Soup, page 78), which contains chicken stock and is richer than the Chile Water. The Veracruz style of *Sopa de Chiles Poblanos* (Poblano Chile Soup, page 79) is the richest version of these simple soups, with the addition of butter and evaporated milk.

Sopa de Calabacitas (Squash Soup, page 80) is another simple soup to make and has the traditional chicken stock as its base. It is light and spicy, with a touch of richness from the addition of the cheese at the end of cooking.

Since the avocado is native to Mexico, we thought it only fitting to include *Sopa Simple de Aguacate Estilo Querétaro* (Easy Avocado Soup, Querétaro Style, page 81), which is a lovely, velvety soup enlivened with *serrano* chiles. *Crema de Garbanzo con Chiles Chipotles* (Chickpea Soup with Chipotles, page 82) has an interesting blend of flavors; the nutty taste of the garbanzos (chickpeas) contrasts with the slightly smoky overtones of the *chipotle* chiles.

Veracruz-style *Xonequi* (Spinach and Black Bean Soup with Masa Balls, page 83) is a very substantial soup, with its little masa balls and black beans and a garnish of cheese. The longer cooking, more complicated stew, *Caldo Puchero*

(Pot of Vegetable Stew with Chiltepínes, page 86), is rich with New World vegetables, beans, and fiery little *chiltepínes.*

The next two soups incorporate corn tortillas. *Sopa de Tortilla con Chiles Pasillas* (Tortilla Soup with Pasilla Chiles, page 84) is one kind of *sopa seca* (dry soup) that is fairly rich with cream and cheese. *Sopa Tarasca* (Tarascan Soup, page 87) is also a substantial soup that contains three varieties of chile to give it a good depth of taste. *Caldo de Queso Estilo Sonora* (Sonoran Cheese Stew, page 88) is simple and basic in its ingredients—potatoes, cheese, and chiles. The *poblano* chiles are usually quite mild, but very tasty.

Susana Trilling's *Sopa de Ajo Estilo Rancho Aurora* (Rancho Aurora Garlic Soup, page 89) is redolent with two whole heads of garlic, which will ward off a cold as well as keep vampires away! The hot, cooked stock is poured over cubes of cheese and toasted bread, making a delectable cheese melt.

If the Spanish hadn't brought chickens to Mexico, we might never have enjoyed the most famous soup of the Yucatán peninsula, *Sopa de Lima* (Lime Soup, page 90), easy to make and also very easy to eat. The limes add a refreshing dash of taste to the chile–chicken stock, and the tortillas give it a pleasant crunch. An interesting chicken stew, *Mole de Olla con Epazote* (Mole with Epazote, page 92), has a powerful punch, with the incorporation of up to ten *chipotle* chiles. The chiles also impart a wonderful, slightly smoky taste to the dish.

Another important source of food for the early Indians, courtesy of the Spanish, was the pig. A wonderful, rich stew, *Chilorio al Estilo Sinaloense* (Sinaloa-Style Chilorio, page 93), is seasoned with pungent herbs and *pasilla* chiles, which add a raisin-infused flavor to the pork. *Frijoles con Puerco* (Beans with Pork, page 94) is not the usual "pork and beans." In traditional Yucatán style, this recipe incorporates epazote, shredded radishes, and *habanero* chile. A very different, but nonetheless delicious, dish is *Pozole al Estilo Sinaloense* (Sinaloa-Style Corn and Pork Stew, page 96). The longer you cook it, the better it gets! The dried slack corn in the recipe is better known as hominy, and with the addition of herbs and chiles, hominy need never be boring again. Variations of this dish are popular throughout Mexico; in fact, some restaurants set aside one night a week as "Pozole Night."

In the northern states of Mexico, with their plains and grasslands, beef reigns supreme. In fact, beef and wheat form an important basis of the cuisine. From northern Mexico and the Colima area comes *Sopa Seca de Adobo* (Dry Adobo Soup, page 98). In this recipe a rich beef broth is poured over toasted bread generously spread with a chile mixture containing garlic, juniper berries, herbs, and *ancho* chiles. *Chilatequile Estilo Puebla* (Puebla-Style Beef and Pork Stew with Vegetables, page 100), a full-bodied stew from the Puebla area, employs both fresh beef and dried beef. Squash, corn, and two types of dried chiles add depth and flavor to this dish.

We have included four beef stews, each from a different area. The variety of ingredients in these stews gives each one a particular taste and style. From Ciudad Guzmán comes *Guisado de Res con Pimientos Morrones Rojos* (Beef Stew with Red Peppers and Jalapeños, page 104). Mushrooms, herbs, and a dash of red wine liven up this elegant dish.

The influence of the Yucatán peninsula is evident in *Carne en Caldillo* (Yucatán-Style Beef Stew, page 102), with its combination of diverse flavors— roasted garlic, fresh mint, *xcatic* chiles, radishes, and orange juice. Grated or chopped radish is frequently used in this region. A popular stew in the northern states is *Caldillo Durangueño* (Durango Stew, page 106), flavored with tomatillos, onions, and chiles. Wheat flour tortillas would make a fine accompaniment for this hearty, hacienda-style food. The last beef stew recipe, *Caldo de Gato* (Oaxacan Beef Stew, page 105), comes from Oaxaca, the center of the southern highland region, an area of refined and complex meat dishes. The judicious use of *pasilla* chiles in this recipe doesn't overwhelm the accompanying ingredients.

The last recipe, *Chilpachole Veracruzano* (Veracruz-Style Shrimp Stew, page 108), is a type of shrimp stew that uses both dried and fresh shrimp; dried shrimp is very intense and adds a rich flavor. *Ancho* and *chipotle* chiles round out the flavors in this delicious dish.

Agua Chile
(Chile Water)

This recipe comes from our friend and guide to the north, Antonio Heras-Duran, who says it is one of the most basic *chiltepín* dishes known and is prepared only in the state of Sinaloa, where the *chiltepínes* produce fruit all year long. This simple soup is served in mountain villages, and everyone makes his own in a soup bowl.

2	*chiltepínes* (or more to taste), crushed	Pinch of Mexican oregano
1	garlic clove, peeled and chopped	Pinch of salt
¼	ripe tomato, diced	Boiling water

Add all of the ingredients, except the water, to a large soup bowl and mix together. Next, add the boiling water to the mixture until the desired consistency has been reached, and mash everything together with a large spoon.

Serves: 1

Heat Scale: Medium

Consomé de Rajas
(Chile Strip Soup)

Remembering the lush, green hills and verdant landscape, we can only reflect fondly on our travels to Morelia with its classic colonial architecture. This soup from Michoacán is spicy and clean to the palate, and is good to serve at a dinner party when richer foods will follow the soup course.

2	tablespoons vegetable oil		1	teaspoon salt
1	cup chopped onion		2	quarts chicken broth
2	cloves garlic, peeled and minced		2	teaspoons flour
1	cup chopped tomatillos		½	cup warm water
6	*poblano* chiles, roasted and peeled, seeds and stems removed, cut into strips			

Heat the oil in a large saucepan; add the onion and sauté for 1 minute. Next, add the garlic and tomatillos and sauté for 3 minutes. Add the chile strips and salt and continue to sauté for 2 more minutes.

Pour in the broth and bring the mixture to a boil, reduce the heat, and simmer for 5 minutes.

With a fork, mix the flour into the ½ cup warm water. Pour this through a fine sieve into the simmering soup and stir until the ingredients are blended. Simmer for 5 minutes. Serve hot.

Serves: 4

Heat Scale: Mild

Sopa de Chiles Poblanos
(Poblano Chile Soup)

This chile soup from Veracruz has a kind of smooth, easy heat, and the addition of the evaporated milk adds a touch of richness. Serve the soup with a salad from Chapter 8 for a light lunch or dinner.

6	*poblano* chiles, roasted, peeled, seeds and stems removed	1	tablespoon sweet (unsalted) butter
¼	onion	4	corn tortillas, cut into eighths, or substitute tortilla chips
3	cloves garlic, peeled		Oil for frying
1½	cups water	½	cup grated *manchego* cheese, or substitute pecorino Romano or Parmesan cheese
1	can evaporated milk		
2	beef bouillon cubes		
1	cup water		

Purée the chiles, onion, and garlic in a blender with ½ cup of the water. Pour this mixture into a small saucepan, add the milk, and heat slowly.

Dissolve the bouillon cubes in 1 cup of boiling water and add to the chile–milk mixture. Stir in the butter and simmer for 5 minutes, taking care that it does not boil.

Heat the oil in a small saucepan and fry the tortillas until they are crisp and then drain. Or, you can substitute tortilla chips.

Ladle the soup into warmed bowls and top with the tortillas and the grated cheese.

Serves: 4

Heat Scale: Mild

Sopa de Calabacitas

(Squash Soup)

Since this soup from Veracruz is light, serve it as a first course for a large dinner. The combination of squash and corn is very common in Mexican cuisine, as well as in certain parts of the American Southwest.

2	tablespoons butter	1	cup chopped tomato
2	tablespoons vegetable oil	1	cup whole corn kernels
1	pound chayote squash, cubed	½	teaspoon salt
1	cup chopped onion	1	quart chicken stock
3	*poblano* chiles, roasted, peeled, seeds and stems removed, diced	½	pound crumbled *queso fresco,* or substitute feta cheese (see note)

Heat the butter and the oil in a casserole pot; add the squash and the onion and sauté for 2 minutes, stirring often.

Add the chiles, tomatoes, corn, salt, and chicken stock and bring to a boil. Reduce the heat to a simmer, cover, and cook for 30 minutes, or until the squash is tender. Stir in the cheese and serve.

Serves: 5

Heat Scale: Mild

Note: Look for Cacique brand cheese in the grocery store; it is a U.S. company that manufactures Mexican-style cheeses.

Sopa Simple de Aguacate Estilo Querétaro

(Easy Avocado Soup, Querétaro Style)

Since the avocado tree is a native of tropical America, it is only fitting that we include a recipe that showcases its delicate taste. The preferred variety for this soup is the *Criollo,* which is mashed with its skin to impart a slight anise flavor.

3	avocados, *Criollo* (smooth-skinned) variety preferred	2	*serrano* chiles, seeds and stems removed
1½	quarts rich homemade chicken broth	1	teaspoon salt
		1	cup half-and-half cream

Garnishes:

Grated Chihuahua cheese, or substitute mild Cheddar

5   corn tortillas, cut into eighths, fried, and drained; or substitute packaged tortilla chips

If you are using *Criollo* avocados, do not peel them. Simply wash them, cut them in half, and remove the pits. Place the avocados in a blender along with 2 cups of the chicken broth, the chiles, and salt, and purée. (If you are using rough-skinned avocados, peel and split them, discard the pits, put them in a blender with 3 whole anise seeds and 2 cups of the chicken stock, the chiles, and salt, and purée.)

Pour the remaining broth into a medium-sized saucepan, heat just to the boiling point, add the puréed avocado mixture, the cream, and heat through.

Serve in warm soup bowls and garnish with the cheese and tortillas.

Serves: 5

Heat Scale: Medium

Crema de Garbanzo con Chiles Chipotles

(Chickpea Soup with Chipotles)

Chickpeas, also known as garbanzo beans, have a mild, nutty flavor. This delightful flavor is enhanced by the addition of chiles, chicken broth, and cream in this creamed soup from Sinaloa.

2½	cups cooked chickpeas (garbanzos)	2	tablespoons vegetable oil
4	cups chicken stock	¾	cup minced onion
2	*chipotle* chiles in *adobo* sauce (see Chipotle Chiles in Adobo Sauce, page 23)	1	teaspoon salt
		¼	teaspoon freshly ground white pepper
1	tomato, roasted and peeled	1	cup half-and-half cream

Garnish: ¼ cup chopped tomatoes

Coarsely chop ½ cup of the chickpeas and reserve. Place the remaining chickpeas in a blender with 2 cups of the chicken stock, the chiles, and the tomato and chop for 10 seconds.

Heat the oil in a small saucepan and sauté the onion for 2 minutes. Add the chickpea mixture from the blender, the reserved ½ cup of coarsely chopped chickpeas, the salt and pepper, and the remaining 2 cups of chicken stock. Bring the mixture to a low boil, reduce the heat, add the cream, and heat for 5 minutes. Do not let it boil.

Serve hot, and garnish each serving with some of the freshly chopped tomatoes.

Serves: 4

Heat Scale: Medium

Xonequi

(Spinach and Black Bean Soup with Masa Balls)

This soup from Veracruz is spicy and substantial and can be a meal in itself. The spinach, beans, chiles, and masa balls add a unique flavor and texture.

5	dry *chipotle* chiles, seeds and stems removed	2	cups rich homemade chicken stock
2	*ancho* chiles, seeds and stems removed	2	cups cooked and drained black beans
1	onion, cut into eighths	1⅓	cups corn masa
2	cloves garlic, peeled	1	teaspoon salt
2	cups water	¾	cup chopped cilantro
2	tablespoons vegetable oil	1½	cups crumbled *queso fresco,* or substitute goat cheese or feta cheese
6	tablespoons butter		
2	pounds fresh spinach, cleaned and coarsely chopped		

Lightly toast the chiles in a skillet for 2 to 3 minutes, but do not let them burn. Place the chiles in a blender with the onion, garlic, and 1 cup of water; chop coarsely and reserve.

Heat the oil and 2 tablespoons of the butter in a large casserole pot and pour in the chile mixture. Sauté this mixture for 10 minutes over low heat.

Bring the remaining cup of water to a boil in a saucepan, add the spinach, and cook for 1 minute. Pour the spinach and the cooking water into the simmering chile mixture. Add the chicken stock and beans, and salt to taste; bring this mixture to a low boil, then reduce to a simmer.

Mix the remaining butter into the masa, add the salt, and ¼ cup of the chopped cilantro. Shape the masa into ½-inch balls, bring the soup to a boil, and drop the balls into the soup. When the soup returns to a boil, reduce the heat to simmer and simmer for 3 minutes, or until the masa balls are tender.

Serve the soup hot and garnish with the remaining cilantro.

Serves: 6

Heat Scale: Hot

Sopa de Tortilla con Chiles Pasillas
(Tortilla Soup with Pasilla Chiles)

The only constant in this basic recipe from Chihuahua is the broth; all of the other ingredients—and there are many—may vary, depending on what's available and the cook's mood. The garnishes vary, too; it's all part of the fun of making and eating this soup!

4	*pasilla* chiles, seeds and stems removed	1	teaspoon salt
	Water as needed	¼	cup fresh cilantro
4	quarts rich homemade chicken broth	2	tablespoons vegetable oil
		½	cup cream
3	large tomatoes, peeled	3	dozen corn tortillas, cut into ¼-inch strips, fried and drained; or substitute 4 cups broken tortilla chips
2	onions, quartered		
2	cloves garlic, peeled		

Garnishes:

2	*pasilla* chiles, seeds and stems removed, lightly fried and coarsely ground in blender	1	cup crumbled cheese such as *panela*, feta, or mozzarella
1	cup avocados, peeled, pitted, and chopped		

Tear the 4 *pasilla* chiles into strips, cover with hot water, and rehydrate for 15 minutes.

Heat the chicken broth in a large casserole almost to the boiling point; reduce the heat to a simmer while you prepare the rest of the ingredients.

Put the rehydrated chiles in a blender, add the tomatoes, onions, garlic, salt, and cilantro and purée for 10 seconds.

Heat the oil in a small skillet, add the blended chile mixture, and sauté for 5 minutes. Stir this mixture into the simmering chicken broth, add cream, cover, and simmer for 30 minutes.

Cut the tortillas into strips. Fry the strips and distribute them to eight bowls. Ladle the simmering chicken–chile stock over the strips and garnish with the crushed *pasilla* chiles, avocado, and cheese.

Serves: 8

Heat Scale: Medium

In the Aztec Market, Part I

When the Spanish forces under Cortez arrived in Tenochtitlán (now Mexico City) in 1519, they were astounded by the size and complexity of the market at the great plaza of Tlatelolco. According to descriptions by Bernal Díaz del Castillo, it resembled a modern flea market, with thousands of vendors hawking every conceivable foodstuff and other products. The noise of the market could be heard 3 miles away, and some of the soldiers who had traveled to such places as Rome and Constantinople said it was the largest market they had ever seen. Every product had its own section of the market, and chiles were no exception; they were sold in the second aisle to the right. Sometimes chiles were used as a form of money to buy drinks or other small items.

Caldo Puchero

(Pot of Vegetable Stew with Chiltepínes)

Like most stews, this one takes a while to cook, about 4 hours. It is interesting because it contains a number of pre-Columbian ingredients, namely *chiltepínes*, corn, squash, potatoes, and beans. The spicy heat can be adjusted by adding or subtracting *chiltepínes*.

15	*chiltepínes*, or more to taste	3	green New Mexican chiles, roasted, peeled, seeds and stems removed, chopped
1	beef soup bone with marrow		
1	cup dried garbanzo beans	3	stalks celery, cut into 1-inch pieces
4	cloves garlic, peeled and chopped		
	Water as needed	2	large potatoes or sweet potatoes, cut into 1-inch cubes
1	acorn or butternut squash, peeled, seeds removed, and cut into 1-inch cubes	3	zucchini squash, cut into ½-inch slices
3	ears corn, cut into 2-inch rounds	1	onion, quartered
4	carrots, cut into 1-inch pieces	2	cups fresh string beans, cut into 1-inch pieces
1	head cabbage, quartered	½	cup minced fresh cilantro

In a large soup kettle combine the *chiltepínes*, soup bone, beans, garlic, and twice as much water as needed to cover. Bring to a boil, reduce the heat, and simmer for 1 hour.

Add the acorn or butternut squash, the corn, and more water to cover 1 inch above vegetables and simmer for 30 minutes.

Add the carrots and cabbage and simmer for 15 minutes.

Add the green chiles, celery, and potatoes and cook for 30 minutes.

Add the zucchini, onion, and string beans and simmer for 30 to 45 minutes, until everything is tender.

When ready to serve, remove the kettle from the heat, remove the soup bone, and add the cilantro.

Serves: 8
Heat Scale: Hot

Sopa Tarasca
(Tarascan Soup)

Many years ago, we went to Morelia, as well as Uruapan, where we visited the Tarascan weaving co-op and bought a small Tree of Life wool rug, which is a constant reminder of the pleasant days we spent there. The food was always great, and we tasted several versions of this soup. Some cooks make this soup with mashed beans and a garnish of crumbled chiles; however, in this recipe eggs are added, and chile is both in the soup and crumbled on top as a garnish.

1	*negro* chile, seeds and stem removed; or substitute *ancho*	1	teaspoon Mexican oregano
2	*ancho* chiles, seeds and stems removed	1	large onion, quartered
2	*guajillo* chiles, seeds and stems removed, or substitute New Mexican	2	large cloves garlic, peeled
		10	corn tortillas, cut into ¼-inch strips, fried, and drained
1	pound tomatoes, peeled and deseeded	4	eggs, beaten
		2	quarts chicken broth

Garnishes:

¼	cup minced onion	1	cup grated *Cotija* cheese, or substitute parmesan

Cut the chiles in half; put half of them in a blender and set the other half aside. Coarsely crush the chiles in the blender, pour into a bowl, and reserve.

Add the remaining chiles to the blender along with the tomatoes, oregano, onion, and garlic and purée the mixture and reserve.

Put the fried tortilla strips in a large bowl, cover with the beaten eggs, and toss. Add the puréed chile–tomato mixture and lightly toss with the tortillas.

Pour the broth into a large saucepan and bring to a boil. Reduce the heat to a simmer, and after 1 minute add the egg-coated tortilla–chile mixture. Simmer for 3 minutes. Serve in soup bowls and garnish with the chopped chiles, minced onion, and grated cheese.

Serves: 8
Heat Scale: Medium

Caldo de Queso Estilo Sonora
(Sonoran Cheese Stew)

Simple ingredients are combined to make this quick recipe from northern Mexico. Sonoran Cheese Stew is a flavorful soup, as well as being attractive to serve, with its flecks of red and green. Mexican cheeses are increasingly available in supermarkets, especially in the western parts of the United States.

2	tablespoons vegetable oil
1	tablespoon butter
4	cups cubed potatoes
1	large onion, sliced
2	scallions, sliced
1	cup peeled, chopped tomato
1	teaspoon salt

4	*poblano* chiles, roasted, peeled, seeds and stems removed, diced
1	quart milk at room temperature
2	cups warm water
3	cups Chihuahua cheese, grated; or substitute mild Cheddar
	Warm tortillas

Heat the oil and butter in a large skillet and sauté the potatoes for 7 minutes, until they start to brown. Add more oil, if they start to stick. Add the onion and scallions and sauté for 1 minute.

Transfer the sautéed mixture to a medium-sized saucepan, stir in the tomatoes, salt, chiles, and milk and bring the mixture to a low boil; add the water and stir.

When the mixture is hot, but not boiling, turn off the heat and stir in the cheese. Serve immediately with warm tortillas.

Serves: 6

Heat Scale: Mild

Sopa de Ajo Estilo Rancho Aurora

(Rancho Aurora Garlic Soup)

This recipe is from Susana Trilling, who owns the Seasons of My Heart cooking school in Oaxaca, Mexico. This recipe calls for *hoja santa*, an herb with large, fragrant leaves. Look for it in Latin markets or grow it in your garden. If unavailable, watercress is the best substitute.

2	heads garlic, peeled and thinly sliced		Salt and white pepper to taste
½	tablespoon butter	3	bay leaves
½	tablespoon olive oil	1	bunch celery leaves, coarsely chopped
1	large *hoja santa* leaf, cut into strips; or 1 bunch fresh watercress, chopped	20	toasted bread cubes
6	cups chicken stock	20	cubes *queso Oaxaqueño*, or substitute another melting cheese such as *queso blanco* or Monterey Jack
1	*de árbol* chile, left whole; or substitute a large *piquín*		

Garnish: grated Parmesan cheese

Sauté the garlic in the butter and olive oil in a soup pot until slightly browned, about 10 minutes. Add the *hoja santa* and sauté for 30 seconds. Add the stock, chile, salt, pepper, and bay leaves and simmer for half an hour. Remove the bay leaves and chile. Add the celery just before serving.

　　Place 5 cubes of bread and cheese in four individual soup bowls and ladle in the soup. Sprinkle with Parmesan cheese and serve.

Serves: 4 servings

Heat Scale: Mild

Sopa de Lima
(Lime Soup)

Even though this soup, and its many variations, is served all over Mexico, it is believed to have originated in Yucatán; it is Yucatán that provides the small, yellow, tart limes that give *Sopa de Lima* its particularly good flavor.

1	3-pound chicken, cut into 6 pieces	3	tablespoons chopped cilantro
3	quarts water	1½	cups chopped onion
2	teaspoons salt	2	tablespoons oil
3	cloves garlic, peeled and chopped	4	*serrano* or *jalapeño* chiles, seeds and stems removed, chopped
1	tablespoon Mexican oregano	1½	cups chopped tomatoes
		8	limes, thinly sliced

Garnishes:

8	corn tortillas, cut into eighths, fried and drained; or substitute tortilla chips	½	cup minced cilantro

Wash the chicken pieces and place them in a large casserole; add the water, salt, garlic, oregano, the 3 tablespoons of cilantro, and 1 cup of the onion and bring the mixture to a boil, skimming the foam from the top. Reduce the heat to a simmer, cover, and simmer for 30 minutes. Remove the chicken from the cooking liquid and set aside. Strain the broth through several thicknesses of cheesecloth, return the strained broth to a clean pot, bring to a boil, reduce the heat to a light rolling boil, and cook uncovered for 20 minutes to reduce the stock.

Remove the skin and bones from the chicken and discard. Coarsely shred the meat and reserve.

Heat the oil in a small skillet, add the remaining ½ cup onion, chiles, and tomatoes, and sauté for 3 minutes.

When the stock has reduced, stir in the shredded chicken, the sautéed tomato–chile mixture, and simmer for 15 minutes.

Serve the soup in large, heated soup bowls and garnish with tortilla chips and minced cilantro.

Serves: 8 to 10

Heat Scale: Medium

Early Mexican Cookbooks

1831:   *El Cocinero Mexicano* [The Mexican Cook], 3,000 copies

1872:   *La Cocinera Poblana* [The Pueblo Cook], by Narciso Bassols

1893:   *El Libro de Cocina* [The Cook Book], by Eduardo Rodríguez y Cía, 1,525 recipes

Mole de Olla con Epazote

(Mole with Epazote)

Mole is not only a sauce, but a thick soup. If you have a taste for *mole*, but very little time, try this quick and easy recipe from Tlaxcala. Serve the chicken with hot, cooked rice and an avocado salad.

5	tomatoes	1	3-pound chicken, cut into 6 or 8 pieces
8	to 10 *chipotle* chiles, seeds and stems removed	½	cup water
	Hot water as needed	½	cup chicken broth
2	cloves garlic, peeled	1	teaspoon salt
4	tablespoons oil	¼	cup chopped epazote

Roast the tomatoes until the skins blister; allow them to cool slightly and then peel and cut the tomatoes in half.

Tear the chiles into strips, cover with hot water, and rehydrate them for 20 minutes. Place the chiles and their soaking water into a blender, add the tomatoes and garlic, and purée until the mixture is smooth.

Heat 2 tablespoons of the oil in a small skillet, pour in the puréed mixture, and sauté for 5 minutes.

Heat the remaining oil in a medium-sized skillet, lightly brown the chicken, add the water, chicken stock, and salt and bring to a boil. Reduce the heat and simmer for 20 minutes, covered.

Pour the sautéed chile mixture over the chicken, cover, and simmer for 15 minutes. Add the epazote and simmer for 10 minutes more. Serve hot with cooked rice.

Serves: 6

Heat Scale: Medium

Chilorio al Estilo Sinaloense
(Sinaloa-Style Chilorio)

As with *mole*, *chilorio* can be two things at once—shredded pork with chile paste, or this rich pork stew from Sinaloa that is gently infused with the raisiny flavor of *pasilla* chiles and is laced with oregano, garlic, and coriander. Serve it with warm tortillas and a salad from Chapter 8.

3	pounds pork, cut into ¾-inch cubes		Hot water as needed
	Water to cover	½	teaspoon coriander seeds
1	onion, quartered	½	teaspoon cumin
1	teaspoon salt	1½	teaspoons Mexican oregano
4	large *pasilla* chiles, seeds and stems removed	¼	teaspoon salt
		5	cloves garlic, peeled
		3	tablespoons corn oil

Place the pork in a heavy, casserole pot and add just enough water to cover; add the onion and salt, and bring the mixture to a boil. Reduce the heat to a simmer and, as the meat simmers, skim the foam from the top and discard. Simmer, covered, for 1 hour. Remove the meat and drain it in a colander. Pour the broth into a heat-proof bowl and place the bowl in the freezer for a few minutes, to coagulate the fat. Remove the fat and discard it, reserving the broth.

Cover the chiles with hot water and rehydrate for 15 minutes. Put the chiles and the water into a blender or a food processor along with the coriander seeds, cumin, oregano, salt, and garlic and purée the mixture.

Sauté the chile mixture in a small skillet, over low heat, for 3 minutes and reserve.

Heat the corn oil in a large skillet, add the drained cubes of pork, and sauté the pork until the cubes are slightly browned. Add 1 or 2 tablespoons of the reserved broth if the cubes start to stick. Add the reserved sautéed chile mixture, ¼ cup of the reserved broth, and simmer for 10 minutes. Add more broth if the mixture gets too thick. Serve in warm soup bowls.

Serves: 6

Heat Scale: Mild

Frijoles con Puerco
(Beans with Pork)

This recipe is not your ordinary "pork and beans." The beans are cooked with a whole *habanero* chile, and *Chiltomate* (the roasted *habanero*–tomato sauce from Yucatán) spices it up even more, so this recipe is not for the faint-hearted. Even thought the recipe is long, it can be cooked in steps, and much of it can be done the day before serving.

2	pounds of dry black beans, washed and picked over Cold water as needed	1	pound pork ribs, cut into sections
10	cups hot water	1½	cups chopped onion
1	large, whole *habanero* chile	5	cups peeled, chopped tomatoes
¼	cup chopped epazote	3	tablespoons butter
2	tablespoons vegetable oil	4	cups rice
2	pounds pork, cut into 1-inch cubes	2	teaspoons salt

Garnishes:

½	cup shredded radishes	2	tablespoons (or more, to taste) of *Chiltomate* (page 27), or a favorite *habanero* hot sauce
¾	cup finely chopped cilantro		
4	lemons or limes, cut into eighths		

Cover the beans with cold water, bring to a boil, and boil gently for 2 minutes. Remove the beans from the heat, cover, and let the beans sit for 1 hour. Drain the beans in a colander, wash out the cooking pot, return the beans to the pot, and add 10 cups of hot water and the whole *habanero* chile. Bring this to a boil, and simmer (covered) for 1½ hours. Stir in the epazote and continue simmering for another 30 minutes, or until the beans are just tender.

Remove the whole *habanero* chile and discard. Reserve the cooking water as you drain the beans through a colander. Set the beans and the cooking water aside.

Heat the oil in a large casserole and sauté the pork cubes and the ribs; stir in 1 cup of the onion and sauté for 1 minute. Add 4 cups of the tomato, the reserved drained beans, and 1 cup of warm water, and cover and simmer for 1½ hours. Stir occasionally and add more water if necessary.

Heat the butter in a large saucepan; add the remaining ½ cup onion, remaining cup of chopped tomatoes, and sauté for 30 seconds; next, add the rice. Lightly brown the rice, about 2 minutes. Stir the rice to avoid burning.

Add 8 cups of the reserved bean liquid to the rice, salt, bring to a boil, reduce the heat to simmer, and cover and cook for 20 minutes.

Serve the rice with the cooked pork and beans and the garnishes. Sprinkle *Chiltomate,* or your favorite *habanero* hot sauce, on top.

Serves: 8 to 10

Heat Scale: Medium to Hot

Pozole al Estilo Sinaloense
(Sinaloa-Style Corn and Pork Stew)

This stew is common throughout northern Mexico and the American Southwest; it is always available, but even more so at Christmastime, because it is a traditional stew that is always simmering on the stove for guests. It is also a favorite dish in Jalisco and has endless variations. The corn in this dish is dried slack corn, also called hominy, and even though the stew takes a long time to prepare, it can be done in stages.

2 pounds *pozole* (dried corn, also available frozen which does not have to be rehydrated) Water as needed	¼ teaspoon freshly ground black pepper
	1 teaspoon freshly ground coriander seeds
4 *pasilla* or *guajillo* chiles	1½ teaspoons Mexican oregano
3 tablespoons vegetable oil	3 cups chopped onions
4 pounds pork ribs; or 2 pounds ribs and a 2-pound roast, cubed	10 cloves garlic, peeled and sliced
2 teaspoons salt	

Garnishes:

1½ cups chopped cilantro

2   cups finely shredded cabbage

1   cup minced onion

Place the *pozole* in a large plastic or ceramic bowl and cover with water. Put the *pozole* in the refrigerator overnight to rehydrate. Before going to bed, check the water level; if necessary, add more to cover the *pozole*.

   Put the chiles and enough water to cover in a medium-sized saucepan, bring to a boil, reduce the heat, and simmer for 10 minutes. Drain the chiles (reserving the water), and remove the seeds and stems. Place the chiles and the water in a blender and chop. Set aside or refrigerate overnight at this point.

Heat the oil in a large stockpot and sauté the meat for 2 minutes, and then sprinkle with the salt, black pepper, coriander, oregano, onions, and garlic and sauté for 3 minutes.

Drain and rinse the rehydrated corn and add it to the stockpot. Add the reserved chopped chiles, cover the mixture with warm water, and bring to a boil; reduce the heat to simmer, cover, and cook for 3½ hours, adding water to keep the mixture covered. Taste the mixture and add more salt as needed.

Serve the *pozole* in large soup bowls and garnish with the cilantro, cabbage, and onion. Warm tortillas make a nice addition.

Serves: 12 to 15

Heat Scale: Medium

Note: This recipe requires advance preparation.

Sopa Seca de Adobo
(Dry Adobo Soup)

Even though the terminology seems contradictory, a "dry soup" course consists of Mexican-style pasta or rice and, according to Diana Kennedy, it is served after the "wet soup" course. Juniper berries are commonly used by Mexican Indians in their cooking.

Beef Stock

2	pounds beef bones		1	teaspoon dried thyme
1	large beef marrow bone		½	teaspoon dried marjoram
3	carrots, sliced		¼	teaspoon freshly ground black pepper
1	cup chopped celery			
1	cup chopped tomato		2	quarts water
2	bay leaves		1	teaspoon salt

Place all of the ingredients in a heavy, large casserole pot, and bring the mixture to a boil; reduce the heat to a simmer, cover, and cook for 1½ hours. Pour the mixture through a colander and reserve the broth.

The Chile Mixture

6	*ancho* chiles, seeds and stems removed		1¼	teaspoons dried Mexican oregano
	Water as needed		4	whole cloves
3	cloves garlic, peeled		4	juniper berries
1	onion, cut into eighths		½	teaspoon salt
2	tomatoes, cut into quarters		3	tablespoons vinegar
6	whole black peppercorns		½	cup olive oil
20	slices good-quality, slightly dry white bread		½	pound grated *manchego*, Mozzarella, or Monterey Jack cheese

Garnishes:

Avocado, sliced	Onion rings, thinly sliced

Lightly roast the chiles in a dry pan over low heat. Cover the chiles with warm water and rehydrate for 15 minutes.

Place the chiles, garlic, onion, tomatoes, peppercorns, oregano, whole cloves, juniper berries, salt, and vinegar in a blender or food processor and purée. Pour this mixture into a small skillet and sauté over low heat for 3 minutes, stirring occasionally. Remove the skillet from the heat and set aside.

In another skillet, heat a small amount of the olive oil and fry the bread, adding just enough oil to toast each slice lightly.

Place a layer of bread in a 9-by-13-inch baking dish, spread some of the sautéed chile mixture over it, sprinkle with some of the cheese, and repeat the process until all of the ingredients have been used.

Gently pour the reserved broth over the layers of bread and chile mixture, until the broth almost reaches the top. Bake the mixture in the oven at 350 degrees F until the cheese has melted.

Garnish each serving with avocado and onion slices.

Serves: 8 to 10

Heat Scale: Mild

Chiles for the Spirit World

Among the descendants of the Mayas, chile is regarded as a powerful agent to ward off spells. For the Tzotzil Indians of the Chiapas highlands, chile assists in both life and death. The hot pods are rubbed on the lips of newborn infants and are burned during the funeral ceremonies of *viejos* ("old ones") to defeat evil spirits that might be around. The Huastec tribe of San Luis Potosí and Veracruz treat victims of the "evil eye" with chile peppers. An egg is dipped in ground chile, then rubbed on the victim's body to return the pain to the malefactor.

Chilatequile Estilo Puebla

(Puebla-Style Beef and Pork Stew with Vegetables)

The city of Puebla, in central Mexico, is beautiful and sophisticated, and full of superb food. *Chilatequile*, a regional dish from Puebla, is rich with different meats, textures, and New World vegetables. It is a meal in itself.

2	tablespoons vegetable oil	7	*ancho* chiles, seeds and stems removed
1	cup chopped onion	7	*guajillo* chiles, seeds and stems removed
3	garlic cloves, peeled and minced		Hot water as needed
¾	pound dried beef or jerky, torn into thin strips	2	cups chopped tomatillos
2	pounds pork ribs, cut into sections	2	cups whole corn kernels
		2	cups cubed squash (Hubbard or butternut)
1	2-pound beef roast	¼	cup chopped epazote
	Water as needed		

Garnishes:

3	limes, cut into eighths	1½	cups finely chopped onion

Heat the oil in a large stockpot and sauté the onion and garlic for 2 minutes. Add the dried beef, pork ribs, and beef roast and lightly brown. Cover with water, bring the mixture to a boil, partially cover, and reduce the heat to a simmer. Simmer for 2 hours, checking the water level to make sure the meats are still covered.

Tear the chiles into strips, cover with hot water, and rehydrate for 20 minutes. Pour the chiles and the water into a blender and coarsely chop them.

Place the tomatillos in a medium-sized skillet and sauté for 1 minute. Add the chopped chiles and simmer this mixture for 2 minutes and then set aside.

Remove the beef roast from the stockpot when it has finished cooking, draining any liquid back into the pot. Place the beef on a wooden cutting board to cool for a few minutes. Skim the fat from the stockpot. Trim the fat from the beef roast; then, using two forks, coarsely shred the meat and return the meat to the stockpot.

Add the reserved tomatillo–chile mixture to the pot, along with the corn and the squash, and simmer for 30 minutes, or until the squash is barely tender. Add the epazote and cook for 15 minutes more.

Serve the stew hot from the pot, and garnish each bowl with lime pieces and finely chopped onion.

Serves: 8 to 10

Heat Scale: Medium

Carne en Caldillo
(Yucatán-Style Beef Stew)

A taste treat from Yucatán, this stew is flavored with mint and garnished with radishes and cilantro doused with orange juice. The use of fruit juice, even in a garnish, is typical in Yucatecan cooking.

¾   cup finely chopped radish

¼   cup chopped cilantro

½   cup freshly squeezed orange juice

1   whole head of garlic

3   tablespoons vegetable oil

2   pounds beef, cut into ¾-inch cubes

1   cup chopped onion

1   green bell pepper, seeds and stems removed, diced

2   *xcatic* chiles, seeds and stems removed, chopped; or substitute yellow wax hot or banana chiles

3   cups chopped tomatoes

½   cup chopped cilantro

1½ teaspoons Mexican oregano

3   tablespoons chopped fresh mint; or 4 teaspoons dried mint

¼   teaspoon freshly ground black pepper
    Water as needed

3   tablespoons *Recado Rojo* (page 28)

2   cups cubed acorn squash

1   cup cubed chayote squash

Combine the radish, cilantro, and fresh orange juice in a ceramic bowl and let marinate while you prepare the stew.

Heat the oven to 400 degrees F. Cut off ¼ inch from the top of the head of garlic; wrap the whole head of garlic with aluminum foil and twist closed at the top. Bake for 45 minutes.

Heat the oil in a heavy casserole and sauté the beef for 2 minutes. Next, add the onion, bell pepper, and chiles and sauté for 2 minutes; add the tomatoes, cilantro, oregano, mint, and black pepper and mix. Cover the mixture with water, bring to a boil, reduce the heat to a simmer, cover, and simmer for 2 hours.

Mix the *Recado Rojo* into ½ cup water and add to the simmering meat.

When the garlic has finished baking, remove it from the oven and squeeze the contents of each clove into the simmering stew. Add the squash and continue cooking.

After 2 hours, check the tenderness of the meat and the squash. Cook longer if needed.

Serve the stew in heated, big soup bowls, and garnish with the marinated radish mixture.

Serves: 8

Heat Scale: Medium

Guisado de Res con Pimientos Morrones Rojos

(Beef Stew with Red Peppers and Jalapeños)

We thank Jay Lewis for obtaining this recipe for us from Gonzalo Cardenas. Gonzalo Cardenas lives in beautiful Ciudad Guzmán, the sister city of Lake Havasu City, Arizona, where Dave was a judge the Hava-Salsa Challenge. This beef–vegetable stew can be made hotter simply by adding more *jalapeños*.

2	tablespoons vegetable oil	6	mushrooms, sliced
1	pound beef, cubed	2	tomatoes, peeled and chopped
2	tablespoons butter	4	bay leaves
1	large onion, sliced	⅛	teaspoon dried marjoram
1	carrot, sliced		Salt and pepper to taste
1	slice bacon, chopped	1	beef bouillon cube
1	stalk celery, sliced	1¼	cups boiling water
1	red *jalapeño*, seeds and stem removed, minced	2	tablespoons red wine
1	red bell pepper, sliced		

Heat the oil in a skillet, brown the beef, and place it in a casserole dish.

Heat the butter in the skillet and fry the onion, carrot, bacon, and celery for 3 minutes, then add them to the casserole dish, along with the *jalapeño*, bell pepper, mushrooms, tomatoes, bay leaves, marjoram, salt, and pepper.

Dissolve the bouillon cube in the 1¼ cups boiling water and pour this over the beef and vegetables. Add the wine.

Cover the casserole and bake for 1½ hours at 350 degrees F. Remove the bay leaves and serve.

Serves: 4

Heat Scale: Mild

Caldo de Gato

(Oaxacan Beef Stew)

This mysteriously named ("cat stew") hot pot from Oaxaca contains several New World ingredients—squash, tomatoes, and chile. Chayote squash is usually available in major grocery stores or Latin American specialty markets. Serve this stew with warm flour tortillas.

3	tablespoons vegetable oil	2	cups cubed potatoes
2	pounds beef, cubed	3	cups chopped tomatoes
1	pound beef bones	2	cups cooked chickpeas (garbanzos)
1	cup chopped onion		
	Water to cover	3	tablespoons chopped cilantro
2	cups sliced carrots	1	teaspoon salt
3	cups cubed chayote squash	7	*pasilla* chiles, seeds and stems removed, finely ground
1	cup corn		

Garnish: thin slices of lemon

Heat the oil in a large, heavy casserole pot; brown the cubed beef and the bones. Reduce the heat slightly, add the onions, and sauté them for 1 minute. Add enough water to cover the meat, bring the mixture to a boil, reduce the heat, cover, and simmer for 2 hours.

Add the carrots, squash, corn, and potatoes and cook for 20 minutes, or until the potatoes are almost done. Add the tomatoes, cooked chickpeas, cilantro, salt, and ground *pasilla* chiles and simmer for 15 minutes, adding more water if necessary. Remove the bones

Serve the stew in large, warmed bowls, and garnish with thin slices of lemon.

Serves: 6

Heat Scale: Medium

Caldillo Durangueño

(Durango Stew)

"Hot and spicy" describes this recipe from beautiful, quaint Durango. Serve this *caldillo*, or stew, on football or soccer days; you can double the recipe and prepare it the day before. It can simmer for hours during the game, and this only intensifies the flavor. Serve it with warm tortillas or fresh bread, and plenty of cold Mexican beer.

6	*poblano* chiles, roasted	3	cloves garlic, peeled and minced
2½	pounds beef roast	1	cup chopped onion
1½	teaspoons salt	½	teaspoon Mexican oregano
3	cups water	½	teaspoon ground cumin
4	cups hot water	3	tablespoons chopped cilantro
½	pound tomatillos, cut into quarters		

Peel the chiles and remove the stems and seeds. Place the chiles on wire racks, put the racks on cookie sheets, and slide the sheets into the oven (heated to 250 degrees F) for 1 hour.

Place the beef in a shallow pan and sprinkle with the salt. Using something blunt-edged, such as a meat tenderizer mallet or a hammer covered with plastic wrap, pound the salt into the meat and let the meat dry out slightly at room temperature, about 2 hours.

In a large saucepan heat 3 cups of water to the boiling point and add the tomatillos; reduce the heat to a simmer, add the garlic, onion, oregano, cumin, and cilantro and simmer for 30 minutes, partially covered. Remove from the heat and set aside.

Place the oven-seasoned chiles in a heat-proof bowl and cover with the remaining 1 cup of hot water. Rehydrate for 10 minutes, and then drain (reserving the water); dice the chiles, and add the chiles and the reserved water to the cooked tomatillo–onion mixture.

Cut the beef into ½-inch cubes; heat the oil in a large, heavy casserole, add the beef, and sauté for 5 minutes. Add the remaining 3 cups of hot water and bring the mixture to a boil. Reduce the heat to a simmer, add half of the chile mixture, cover, and simmer for 1 hour. Next, add the remaining chile mixture, cover, and simmer for 1 hour. Serve hot.

Serves: 5

Heat Scale: Mild to Medium

Chilpachole Veracruzano
(Veracruz-Style Shrimp Stew)

The use of dried shrimp in this recipe intensifies the flavor. Dried shrimp and epazote are available in Latin and Asian markets; there is no substitute for epazote, with its unique, pungent flavor. Serve the shrimp stew over cooked rice and garnish with lemon or lime slices.

8 cloves garlic, unpeeled	3 tablespoons vegetable oil
2 *chipotle* chiles, seeds and stems removed	3 cups water
	8 dried shrimp
2 *ancho* chiles, seeds and stems removed	¼ cup epazote
	2 pounds fresh shrimp, shelled and deveined
1 onion, cut into eighths	
3 tomatoes, peeled and cut into quarters	

Wrap the unpeeled cloves of garlic in aluminum foil and roast them in the oven at 400 degrees F for 30 minutes. When they are cool enough to handle, squeeze the garlic cloves out of their skins and into a blender.

In a dry skillet, lightly roast the chiles for 2 minutes, taking care not to burn them. Add the chiles to the blender along with the onion and tomatoes and purée the mixture.

Heat the oil in a medium skillet. Pour in the puréed chile–tomato mixture, and cook over medium low heat for 1 minute. Next, add the water, dried shrimp, and epazote and simmer for 3 minutes.

Add the fresh shrimp and simmer the mixture for an additional 5 minutes, or until the shrimp are cooked. Add more water if the mixture becomes too thick. Serve immediately.

Serves: 4

Heat Scale: Medium

Carnes con Chiles
Highly Spiced Meats

M eat (*carne*) plays an important role in the Mexican diet, with pork being the most favored, and accessible, variety by far. The Aztec hunted wild boar, but it was the Spaniards who brought the domesticated pig to Mexico; they are credited with the popularity of pork, which has grown steadily since its introduction. One quality that has certainly helped foster the pig's high profile is its willingness to eat just about anything, from garbage to grain. Literally no part of the pig is thrown away—the feet are pickled, the neck and tail are used to flavor soups, the head is used in *pozole*; there are even uses for the snout! In honor of this incredible creature, we invite you to pig out on our first seven meat recipes, each featuring pork, of course.

Chorizo con Chiltepínes (Chiltepín Chorizo, page 112) and *Longaniza con Chiles Guajillos* (Pork Sausage with Guajillo Chiles, page 113) are the first of our tasty treats. Although making your own chorizo takes a little bit of work, there is simply nothing like fresh Mexican sausage scrambled with an egg and rolled in a tortilla.

Our next two recipes were inspired by the Mayas, and collected in Yucatán, where some of the most spectacular Mayan ruins still exist. *Chilorio Sorpresa* (Pork Surprise, page 116) features two kinds of chile, as well as the citrus flavoring of orange juice. *Cochinita Pibíl* (Pork Cooked by the Pibíl Method, page 114) is one of the most famous dishes from Yucatán, and is a staple on almost every menu in that region of Mexico.

Mexico is a land of changing environments. Active volcanoes still exist in places such as Sinaloa, where we collected our *Soufflé de Chilorio* (Pork Soufflé, page 117) recipe. And yet there are incredible tropical regions, too, that supply the pineapples and mangos that are featured in *Mango de Puerco* (Pork with Mango, page 118). Our final pork dish, *Bistec de Cerdo con Chiles Pasillas* (Pork Steaks with Pasilla Chiles, page 119) is simple yet delicious.

Mexico consists of a series of high valleys ringed by mountain peaks. Our first beef recipe, *Machaca Estilo Norteño* (Northern-Style Shredded Beef, page 124) is prepared in the Sierra Madre, one of the most famous mountain ranges of the country. Films, books, and now recipes have been created in honor of its majestic beauty.

Chile Pepper contributor Susana Trilling, who owns the Seasons of My Heart cooking school in Oaxaca, Mexico, contributed many incredible *mole* recipes to this book, such as *Chichilo Oaxaqueño* (Oaxacan Chichilo, page 120). Three other beef recipes that any carnivore is sure to enjoy are *Carnero Asado con Jitomate y Chile* (Roasted Beef with Tomatoes and Chile, page 122),

Puntas de Filete Estilo Norteño (Northern-Style Points of Beef, page 125), and *Filete en Salsa de Oregano* (Fillet in Oregano Sauce, page 126).

Mexico is the Mecca of any true chilehead. As the home to so many exotic kinds of chile (see our Glossary of Mexican Chiles, page 259), the flavors and combinations are almost infinite! *Carnitas con Chile Negro* (Steak with Black Chile, page 127) features the *chile negro,* which is also known as the *morelia.* Our next two recipes, *Bistec con Salsa de Cacahuetes* (Beef with Peanut Sauce, page 128) and *Res à la Cerveza* (Beef with Beer, page 129), present the perfect opportunity to try out a bottle or two of the many excellent Mexican beers available. From Dos Equis with a little lime and salt, to ice-cold Negro Modelo, you can't go wrong.

Our last six recipes are somewhat eclectic. *Lengua en Chile Pasilla* (Beef Tongue with Pasilla Chiles, page 130) is a Mexican favorite, although each cook is known to have his or her own special way of preparing this delicacy. Small deer are plentiful in Yucatán, where we collected the recipe for *Pipián de Venado* (Venison in Pipián Sauce, page 131). *Chiles Anchos Encaramelados con Picadillo en Salsa de Aguacate* (Caramelized Ancho Chiles with Picadillo in Avocado Sauce, page 132) is the masterpiece of Lula Betrán, who says the key to this unusual dish is to make sure the orange juice is absorbed by the anchos.

And who doesn't like meat dishes smothered in mushrooms? *Hongos y Costillas Estilo Mexicano* (Mexican-Style Mushrooms and Ribs, page 134) is exactly that, although it also packs a punch with the addition of a pod or two. And speaking of pods, no Mexican cookbook would be complete without a recipe for *Chiles Rellenos con Res y Pasa* (Beef and Raisin-Stuffed Chiles, page 135), one of our favorite versions of chiles rellenos. Finally, we round out this chapter with *Cabrito y Res con Chiles Anchos* (Braised Goat and Beef with Ancho Chiles, page 136). Your guests will love the interesting taste of this hot and spicy dish.

Chorizo con Chiltepínes

(Chiltepín Chorizo)

There are as many versions of chorizo in Mexico and the American Southwest as there are of enchiladas. Essentially, it is a hot and spicy sausage that is served with eggs for breakfast, as a filling for tostadas or tacos, or mixed with refried beans. This Sonoran version is spicier than most, and, in addition, it is served crumbled rather than as patties.

1	pound ground lean pork	¼	teaspoon freshly ground black pepper
15	to 20 *chiltepínes*, crushed		
1	cup red New Mexican chile powder	½	teaspoon Mexican oregano
		3	tablespoons white vinegar
1	tablespoon chile seeds (from *chiltepínes* or other chiles)	4	cloves garlic, minced
		1	teaspoon ground cloves
¼	teaspoon salt		

Combine the pork with the rest of the ingredients, mix well, and let sit at room temperature for 1 or 2 hours, or in the refrigerator overnight. (It keeps well in the refrigerator for up to a week. Or, freeze the chorizo in small portions and use as needed.)

Fry the chorizo until it is well browned.

Serves: 4

Heat Scale: Hot to Extremely Hot

Longaniza con Chiles Guajillos

(Pork Sausage with Guajillo Chiles)

The art of sausage making is still alive and well in Jalisco, where one would be lucky to be offered a sampling of a *señora's* homemade sausage. While making sausage is not too difficult, please be careful to keep it refrigerated and to clean all working areas well, in order to avoid any spoilage.

8	*guajillo* chiles, toasted, stems and seeds removed, and crushed; or substitute New Mexican	½	teaspoon ginger
		1	teaspoon Mexican oregano
		2	tablespoons lemon juice
		2	tablespoons orange juice
1	cup vinegar		Salt to taste
6	cloves garlic, minced	2½	pounds pork, ground or minced
5	cloves, crushed		Sausage casings for stuffing
20	black peppercorns, crushed		
½	teaspoon cumin		
½	teaspoon ground cinnamon		

In a large mixing bowl, place the crushed chiles in the vinegar along with the garlic, cloves, peppercorns, cumin, cinnamon, ginger, oregano, lemon juice, orange juice, and salt. Mix the ingredients well and combine them with the meat, stirring well. Cover the meat mixture and refrigerate for 24 hours.

Clean the sausage casings well, then stuff with the meat mixture, using a funnel. Refrigerate just the amount you plan to use in the next day or two, and freeze the rest.

Yield: 50 sausages

Heat Scale: Medium

Cochinita Pibíl
(Pork Cooked by the Pibíl Method)

This pre-Columbian dish is probably the best known food of the Mayas, according to Jeff and Nancy Gerlach, who collected this recipe on one of their many trips to Yucatán. It is one of the most popular entrées of this area, and is on virtually every menu. This dish is traditionally served with warmed corn tortillas, black beans, *cebollas encuridas* (marinated onions), and *habanero* salsa.

10	whole black peppercorns	2	pounds lean pork, cut in 1½- to 2-inch cubes
¼	teaspoon cumin seeds		Banana leaves or aluminum foil
5	cloves garlic		
3	tablespoons *Recado Rojo* (see recipe, page 28); or substitute achiote paste	3	*xcatic* chiles, stems and seeds removed, cut in strips; or substitute banana or yellow wax hot chiles
1	teaspoon dried Mexican oregano	1	large purple onion, sliced
2	bay leaves		
⅓	cup bitter orange juice, or substitute ⅓ cup lime juice, fresh preferred		

Place the peppercorns and cumin seeds in a spice or coffee grinder and process to a fine powder. Add the garlic and grind again.

In a bowl combine the spice mixture, *Recado Rojo*, oregano, bay leaves, and orange juice. Pour the marinade over the pork and marinate for 3 hours or overnight.

Cut the banana leaves in pieces to fit a roasting pan. Soften the leaves by passing them over a gas flame or by holding them over an electric burner for several seconds until the leaves begin to turn light green. Remove the center ribs from the leaves and use for tying. Lay a couple of these ribs that are long enough to tie around the pork along the bottom of the pan. Line the pan with the banana leaves or foil.

Place the pork, including the marinade, on the leaves and top with the chiles and onion. Fold the banana leaves over and tie with the strings. Cover the pan and bake in the oven at 325 degrees F for 1½ hours.

Serves: 4 to 6

Heat Scale: Mild

Note: Advance preparation required.

The *Mole* Home Page

Mole is such a popular sauce and dish that it even has its own Web site on the Internet, complete with recipes. Web site organizer Bob Nemerovski commented: "Some refer to *Mole Poblano* as the National Dish of Mexico. But there are many, many *moles,* including Green Mole with Tomatillos, Green Mole with Pumpkin Seeds, Orange-Red Mole, Red Mole, Yellow Mole, and the famous peasant soup, *Mole de Olla.* To some, *mole* is a sauce poured on enchiladas and heated up in a microwave. To others, *mole* is a turkey (or chicken) stew. To me, *mole* is my expression of passion for cooking, especially cooking with chiles. It is a tribute to seventeenth-century tradition while it allows me to create a new dish every time I make it." The address of the *Mole* page is:

http://www.slip.net/~bobnemo/mole.htm

Chilorio Sorpresa

(Pork Surprise)

You will be surprised how tender the pork becomes in this excellent recipe from Playa del Carmen. The Mayas used wild boar for this dish, until the Spanish introduced domesticated pigs.

2	pounds pork meat, cubed	1	teaspoon oregano powder
	Water as needed	¼	teaspoon cumin powder
1	tablespoon salt	1	teaspoon black pepper
1	cup orange juice	¼	cup vinegar
6	*ancho* chiles, stems and seeds removed	½	cup beef broth
1	*pasilla* chile, stem and seeds removed	2	tablespoons pork lard, or substitute shortening
5	cloves garlic	1	small onion, sliced
1	small onion, chopped	2	squash, sliced and lightly boiled

Place the meat in a skillet with a little water, salt, and orange juice and cook, covered, until the meat is tender, about 45 minutes. Shred the meat and set aside.

Place the chiles, garlic, onion, oregano, cumin, pepper, vinegar, and beef broth in a blender; blend until smooth and set aside.

In a separate skillet, heat the lard and fry the meat and chile mixture together until blended. Serve with the onion and squash.

Serves: 6 to 8

Heat Scale: Medium

Soufflé de Chilorio
(Pork Soufflé)

This dish is served for both lunch and dinner in Sinaloa, but we see no reason why it wouldn't make a great breakfast when served with fruits, such as mangos, bananas, and pineapples, on the side.

3	tablespoons butter	¼	cup Parmesan cheese, grated
3	tablespoons flour	4	*chipotle* chiles in *adobo* sauce (see recipe on page 23)
1	cup milk		
1	cup *chilorio* (stewed and shredded pork, as prepared in *Chilorio Sorpresa,* page 116)		Salt and pepper to taste
		4	egg yolks
		5	egg whites
½	cup Gruyère cheese, grated		

Melt the butter in a saucepan and mix in the flour. Once the flour is dissolved, remove the pan from the burner. Add the milk little by little until the mixture becomes thick. Return the pan to the burner on low heat, and add the *chilorio*, cheeses, chiles, salt, and pepper. Stir until the cheeses have melted, then remove from heat.

In a bowl, beat the egg yolks until they become foamy and pale yellow. Stir in the chile–cheese mixture.

In another bowl, beat the egg whites until they form stiff peaks. Fold them into the egg yolk and chile–cheese mixture.

Gently pour the mixture into a greased soufflé pan and bake for about 20 minutes in an oven preheated to 300 degrees F, or until the soufflé has risen and is firm and golden brown. Serve immediately.

Serves: 4 to 6

Heat Scale: Medium

Mango de Puerco

(Pork with Mango)

This recipe was collected in Colima, where many artists from around the world gather to paint the surrounding mountains and the nearby ocean. Colima is the home of Mexico's second highest active volcano. Serve this recipe with one of the rice dishes in Chapter 8.

8	green *guajillo* chiles, toasted, seeds and stems removed; or substitute New Mexican Pinch coriander seeds, roasted	¼	cup vinegar Salt and pepper to taste
2	cloves garlic	4	pounds pork meat, cut into 1½-inch cubes
1	tablespoon cilantro	4	ripe mangos, peeled, pitted, and cubed
1	pinch cumin, ground	1	onion, sliced
2	cloves, ground	6	radishes
1	cinnamon stick		Sliced pineapple
½	teaspoon fresh ginger, grated	1	head lettuce, shredded

In a blender, combine the chiles, coriander, garlic, cilantro, cumin, cloves, cinnamon, ginger, and vinegar. Season with salt and pepper to taste and purée.

Place the pork in a baking dish and pour the chile mixture over the pork; top the entire mixture with the mango cubes. Bake for about 1 hour at 275 degrees F or until done. Garnish with the onion, radishes, sliced fruit, and lettuce.

Serves: 6 to 8

Heat Scale: Medium

Bistec de Cerdo con Chiles Pasillas

(Pork Steaks with Pasilla Chiles)

We collected this recipe in Zacatecas, which is also known as the "pink city." The town received this name because of the pink sandstone used to build most of the homes in the area. The sloping town is 8,200 feet above sea level. Parts of it are so steep that steps cut into the sides of the canyon, instead of streets, are the only way to get around.

4 *pasilla* chiles, roasted, seeds and stems removed, and soaked in hot water	Vinegar to taste
1 large clove garlic	1 teaspoon salt
1 teaspoon oregano	8 pork steaks
	Vegetable oil as needed for frying

Place the chiles, garlic, oregano, vinegar, and salt in a blender and blend until smooth.

Pound the steaks, cover with the chile sauce, and let them sit for about 2 hours.

Heat a little oil in a skillet and fry the steaks. Serve with *Ensalada de Guacamole* (page 70).

Serves: 4 to 8

Heat Scale: Medium

Note: Advance preparation required.

Chichilo Oaxaqueño
(Oaxacan Chichilo)

Susana Trilling, of the Seasons of My Heart cooking school in Oaxaca, observes: "Here is the legendary seventh *mole* from Oaxaca, my friend Celia's famous *mole chichilo*."

The Meat and Beef Stock

1½ pounds beef bones with meat; meat cut off the bones into 1-inch cubes

2   quarts water

1   onion, chopped

8   cloves garlic

1   bay leaf

1   *chile de árbol*, or substitute large *piquín* or *santaka* chile

5   whole peppercorns

2   carrots, chopped

2   stalks celery, chopped

1   whole clove

1   whole allspice berry

½   pound pork butt, cut in 1-inch cubes

Chile Purée

5   *chilhuacle negro* chiles, stems and seeds removed (save the seeds), or substitute *anchos*

6   *guajillo* chiles, stems and seeds removed (save the seeds), or substitute dried red New Mexican chiles
    Hot water as needed

1   corn tortilla, torn into strips

1   sprig fresh oregano

1   sprig fresh thyme

2   allspice berries

1   whole clove

1   teaspoon cumin seeds

1   2-inch stick cinnamon, Mexican preferred

Tomato Purée

4   large tomatoes, quartered

3   fresh tomatillos, halved

1   small onion, roasted

1   clove garlic

2	chayotes (or substitute zucchini), sliced thin	3	tablespoons lard or vegetable oil
½	pound green beans, chopped		Salt to taste
5	small potatoes, peeled and quartered	2	or 3 avocado leaves, chopped or substitute bay leaves

Garnishes: sliced onion and lime slices

Meat and beef stock: In a large stockpot, cover the beef bones with cold water, bring to a boil, and boil for 20 minutes, skimming off any foam that forms. Lower the heat and add the onion, garlic, bay leaf, *chile de árbol*, peppercorns, carrots, celery stalks, clove, and allspice berry and cook for 5 minutes. Add the beef and pork cubes, lower the heat, and simmer, covered, for 1 hour. Strain the stock, cool in the refrigerator and skim off any fat that rises to the top.

Chile purée: Toast the chiles in a large frying pan or *comal*, turning them once until darkened, but not burned. Place the chiles in a bowl and cover with hot water to soak for ½ hour to soften.

Toast the tortilla strips on the *comal* until they blacken and remove them. Toast the reserved chile seeds on the *comal* until the seeds are blackened. Remove the seeds and place them in water to soak. Change the water after 5 minutes, and soak again for another 5 minutes. Drain.

Drain the chiles and place in a blender or food processor along with the tortilla strips, blackened seeds, oregano, thyme, allspice, clove, cumin, cinnamon, and a little water and purée to a paste.

Tomato purée: Roast the tomatoes and tomatillos on the *comal* until soft, and remove them. Then roast the onion and garlic. Place them in the blender and purée.

Bring 3 cups of the reserved stock to a boil and add the chayotes, beans, and potatoes. Reduce the heat and simmer until the potato is easily pierced with a fork. Drain and reserve the vegetables.

Heat the lard or oil in a heavy pot or *cazuela* and fry the chile purée. Add the tomato mixture and fry for a couple of minutes. Stir in just enough of the beef stock to thin the mixture and salt to taste. Toast the avocado leaves and add.

Add the vegetables and meat to the *mole* and heat through. Garnish the *mole* with the sliced onion and lime and serve.

Serves: 4 to 6
Heat Scale: Medium

Carnero Asado con Jitomate y Chile
(Roasted Beef with Tomatoes and Chile)

This is the perfect fiesta food, in quantities large enough to offer nice-sized help-ing for 20 or so guests. We suggest that you add a few tamales from Chapter 3, as well as some flan for dessert, and you'll have an authentic party straight from Mexico City.

2	5-pound rump roasts
	Water as needed
4	cups vinegar
3	*ancho* chiles, stems and seeds removed, toasted, rehydrated, and minced
3	*poblano* chiles, stems and seeds removed, roasted, peeled, and chopped
5	ripe tomatoes, chopped
1	head garlic, crushed and chopped
1	cup white wine
	Cloves to taste

	Cumin to taste
	Thyme to taste
	Marjoram to taste
1	bay leaf
	Oregano to taste
	Salt to taste
4	ounces ham, sliced
4	ounces bacon or salt pork, chopped
	Lemon juice to taste
1	large onion, sliced
40	tortillas

Place the beef in a large stockpot and cover with the water and vinegar. Add the chiles, tomatoes, garlic, wine, spices, and salt; let marinate for a few hours, covered, in the refrigerator.

Remove the meat from the pot and place it in a roasting dish, along with the strained ingredients from the pot, ladling the chiles over the roasts. Place the ham and bacon on top of the roasts and insert a meat thermometer into the thickest part of the meat. Cook in the oven at 350 degrees F for 1 hour and 45 minutes, or until the meat thermometer reads 180 degrees F. Remove from the oven and squirt lemon juice over the top of the roasts.

Place the roast beef on a platter and cut into slices. Serve with onion slices, tortillas, and the salsa of your choice from Chapter 2.

Serves: 20

Heat Scale: Medium

Note: Advance preparation required.

One Man's Meat Is Another Man's Tamale

Armadillo, venison, fish and other less identifiable animals are also sold pre-cooked, most commonly in markets and small towns with a strong Indian influence. In southern Mexico you may be offered *tepescuintle.* It is a delicious meat, even if it is from the agouti, a raccoon-sized rodent. I've yet to meet a hungry carnivore who didn't love it.

—Carl Franz

Machaca Estilo Norteño
(Northern-Style Shredded Beef)

The word *machaca* derives from the verb *machacar*, to pound or crush, and that description of this meat dish is apt. The shredded meat is often used as a filling for burritos or chimichangas and is sometimes dried. Serve the meat wrapped in a flour tortilla along with shredded lettuce, chopped tomatoes, grated cheese, and sour cream, which will reduce the heat scale.

3   pound arm roast
    Water to cover
10 to 15 *chiltepínes*, crushed
1½ cups green New Mexican chile, roasted, peeled, with stems and seeds removed, and chopped

1   cup tomatoes, peeled and chopped
½   cup onions, chopped
2   cloves garlic, minced

Place the roast in a large pan and cover with water. Bring to a boil, reduce the heat, cover, and simmer until tender and the meat starts to fall apart, about 3 or 4 hours. Check it periodically to make sure it doesn't burn, adding more water if necessary.

Remove the roast from the pan and remove the fat. Remove the broth from the pan, chill, and remove the fat. Shred the roast with a fork.

Return the shredded meat and the defatted broth to the pan, add the remaining ingredients, and simmer until the meat has absorbed all of the broth.

Serves: 6 to 8

Heat Scale: Hot

Puntas de Filete Estilo Norteño
(Northern-Style Points of Beef)

This recipe is a northern Mexico specialty. All of us love this style of cuisine, and are lucky enough to have an excellent authentic northern Mexican restaurant in Albuquerque, where we live. If we don't have time to cook, the restaurant El Norteño is a great second choice.

¼	cup corn oil	4	*serrano* chiles, stems and seeds removed, sliced into rings
½	cup olive oil	6	beef fillets, cut into 1½-inch cubes
1	large onion, sliced		
2	cloves garlic		Salt and pepper to taste
2	green bell peppers, sliced		
2	red bell peppers, sliced		

Heat the oils in a skillet, then add the onion and fry until soft. Add the garlic, bell peppers, and chiles and fry for another 5 minutes; then add the meat and salt and pepper to taste. Cook until done, stirring constantly. Serve with a bean dish from Chapter 8.

Serves: 6

Heat Scale: Medium

In the Aztec Market, Part II

The chile seller . . . sells mild red chiles, broad chiles, hot green chiles, yellow chiles, smoked chiles, small chiles, tree chiles, those like beetles. He sells hot chiles, the early variety, the hollow-based kind. Separately he sells strings of chiles, chiles cooked in an *olla,* fish chiles, white fish chiles.

—Bernardino de Sahagún

Filete en Salsa de Oregano
(Fillet in Oregano Sauce)

From Sinaloa, this recipe features oregano, a member of the mint family. Mexican oregano offers a much stronger flavor than Italian or Mediterranean oregano, so remember that a little goes a long way!

2	tablespoons butter		1	*poblano* chile, roasted, peeled, stem and seeds removed
3	tablespoons vegetable oil		1	cup cream
2	pounds beef medallions		2	tablespoons minced onion
2	cups fresh Mexican oregano leaves, ground			Salt and pepper to taste
1	cup chicken broth			Fresh Mexican oregano leaves for decoration

Heat 1 tablespoon butter and the oil in a skillet and cook the beef to taste. Once cooked, set aside and keep warm.

In a blender, combine the oregano leaves with the broth, chile, cream, and onion and purée. Strain the mixture, then heat the remaining butter and cook the sauce for about 25 minutes, adding salt and pepper to taste, stirring constantly.

Serve the sauce over the medallions and decorate with oregano leaves.

Serves: 6

Heat Scale: Mild

Carnitas con Chile Negro

(Steak with Black Chile)

This recipe features a variety of *poblano* that is grown exclusively in Querétaro, Michoacán. These *morelia* pods dry to a dark, almost black color, and thus are called *chiles negros.* If they are unavailable, substitute the darkest *poblano* chiles. Serve this with a rice dish from Chapter 8.

6   tomatillos, roasted

10   *chiles negros,* roasted, peeled, stems and seeds removed (reserve the seeds)

2   cloves garlic

¼   cup olive oil

2   pounds flank steak, cut into ½-inch cubes

½   cup chopped cilantro

1   pinch cumin

Salt to taste

Tortillas

In a blender, combine the tomatillos, chiles, and garlic and process until coarsely chopped.

    Heat the olive oil in a skillet, then fry the tomatillo mixture for about 10 minutes, stirring constantly. Then add the meat, cilantro, cumin, and salt and simmer for 30 minutes. Serve, decorated with the chile seeds, and with tortillas on the side.

Serves: 4 to 6

Heat Scale: Medium

Bistec con Salsa de Cacahuates
(Beef with Peanut Sauce)

The central Mexican state of San Luis Potosí has a thriving cattle industry, and is a big grower of the agave plant, from which *mezcal* and tequila are produced. This dish is easy to prepare, which we think is great—it leaves ample time to enjoy a margarita or two beforehand.

½	*bolillo* (Mexican roll)			Salt and pepper to taste
	Vegetable oil as needed		½	cup peanuts, peeled
6	beef steaks		4	*chipotle* chiles in *escabeche* (canned)
1	onion, sliced			
2	cloves garlic		2	tomatoes, roasted, peeled, and chopped
1	tablespoon cilantro			
1	tablespoon oregano		½	cup water

Garnish: 2 avocados, sliced

Heat the oil in a skillet and fry the roll until hard, then crumble. Set the bread crumbs aside.

In the same oil, fry the steaks, onion, garlic, herbs, salt, and pepper.

In a separate pan, fry the peanuts until brown, then remove them. To the same pan, add the chiles and tomatoes and cook for about 10 minutes. In a blender, combine the tomato mixture, peanuts, bread crumbs, and ½ cup water and purée. Return this sauce to the pan and cook for about 15 minutes, stirring constantly. Serve the sauce over the steaks, garnished with the avocado slices.

Serves: 4 to 6

Heat Scale: Medium

Res à la Cerveza

(Beef with Beer)

Norma de Cardenas contributed this casserole of sorts. The beer adds an exciting flavor when combined with the chiles. Although it's not altogether authentic, Melissa likes to top this dish with a little sour cream.

2	tablespoons vegetable oil	1	tablespoon flour
2	onions, chopped	2	tablespoons tomato paste
2	carrots, sliced	⅔	cup Mexican beer
½	cup mushrooms, sliced		Salt and pepper to taste
2	*pasilla* chiles, stems and seeds removed, chopped	1	teaspoon thyme
1	pound beef, cubed	1	bay leaf

Heat the oil in a skillet and fry the vegetables and chiles for about 5 minutes, then remove them from the burner and set aside.

Flour the beef cubes, heat a little oil in a skillet, and brown them. Add the vegetables, tomato paste, beer, salt and pepper, and herbs to the meat and place the mixture in a casserole dish. Bake for 1½ hours at 350 degrees F. Remove the bay leaf and serve. Decorate with toasted bread triangles, and a dollop of sour cream if you wish.

Serves: 6 to 8

Heat Scale: Mild

Lengua en Chile Pasilla

(Beef Tongue with Pasilla Chiles)

According to Elisabeth Lambert Ortiz, tongue is one of the all-time favorite Mexican foods. This recipe is a tribute to the one ingredient that has created so many wonderful dishes. Serve this with a rice dish from Chapter 8.

1	beef tongue	3	tomatoes, roasted and peeled
	Water as needed	4	cloves garlic
2	tablespoons vegetable oil	1	small onion, chopped
3	*pasilla* chiles, stems and seeds removed		Salt to taste
	Hot water as needed	1	teaspoon cumin
1	pound pork sausage, chopped		

Cook the tongue in a covered pot with a little water for about 1 hour.

Heat the oil in a skillet and fry the chiles, then add a little hot water and continue to cook for about 10 minutes. Remove from the skillet and set aside.

In the same skillet, fry the sausage. Remove and set aside.

In a blender, combine the chiles, tomatoes, garlic, and onion and purée. Strain the mixture. Remove the excess grease from the skillet and add the tomato mixture and salt to taste and cook for about 10 minutes. Add the cumin, cover, and cook for another 10 minutes over low heat.

Remove the skin and grease from the tongue, then slice and add to the salsa mixture. Add the sausage and cook for another 10 minutes and serve.

Serves: 4

Heat Scale: Medium

Pipián de Venado

(Venison in Pipián Sauce)

Yucatán, with its spectacular beauty and wealth of native ingredients, has long been the home of some of the most interesting cooking in Mexico. This recipe features venison in a pumpkin sauce—a rich combination with a Mayan heritage.

½ cup pumpkin seeds

3 *ancho* chiles, stems and seeds removed

1 cup hot water
  Pepper to taste

2 tablespoons *Recado Rojo* (page 28)

2 cloves garlic

2 cups water

2 pounds venison, cut into 1-inch cubes

1 small bunch epazote
  Salt and pepper to taste

4 tomatillos, chopped

1 tablespoon cornstarch

½ cup water

Toast the pumpkin seeds and chiles, then rehydrate the chiles in 1 cup hot water for about 30 minutes.

Grind the seeds, chiles, pepper, *Recado Rojo*, and garlic with a mortar and pestle, then dilute the paste in 2 cups of water.

Strain the mixture, place it in a skillet, and cook over medium heat for 15 minutes. Add the venison, epazote, and salt and pepper to taste. Cook for about 10 minutes, then add the tomatillos.

Dilute the cornstarch in ½ cup water and add to the stew. Continue to cook over low heat until the venison is tender, removing any grease that collects on the surface.

Serves: 6 to 8

Heat Scale: Medium

Chiles Anchos Encaramelados con Picadillo en Salsa de Aguacate

(Caramelized Ancho Chiles with Picadillo in Avocado Sauce)

"This is one of my top creations regarding chiles," says Lula Betrán. The key to this recipe is the absorption of the orange juice into the skin of the *anchos*, making the chiles soft enough to eat. Make sure you choose *anchos* that are still pliable; if they are hard as a brick, they will need to be steamed first. The presentation of the chiles is elegant on the light green avocado sauce.

The Chiles

6	medium *ancho* chiles, stems left on	½	cup vinegar
1½	cups orange juice	1	teaspoon salt
½	cup grated *piloncillo* (raw sugar), or substitute molasses		

The Picadillo

3	tablespoons vegetable oil	1	medium tomato, chopped
1	small onion, chopped fine	2	teaspoons minced cilantro
1	clove garlic, minced	5	*serrano* chiles, seeds and stems removed, minced
½	pound ground beef	½	teaspoon Mexican oregano
½	pound ground pork		Salt to taste
¼	cup raisins		

Avocado Sauce

3	tomatillos, husks removed	1	avocado, peeled
2	tablespoons chopped onion	1	teaspoon lime juice
2	*serrano* chiles, seeds and stems removed, halved	⅛	teaspoon sugar
1	clove garlic	½	teaspoon salt
1	tablespoon chopped cilantro	½	cup half-and-half

The chiles: Take each *ancho* by the stem and, using scissors, cut a T-shaped incision that extends across the shoulders of the chile and about two-thirds down the pod. Carefully remove the seeds and membrane. In a saucepan, bring the remaining ingredients to a boil. Add the cleaned *anchos* and cook at a low boil for 15 minutes, turning once (carefully). Remove from the heat and let cool. Remove the *anchos*, clean off any remaining seeds, and drain on paper towels.

The picadillo: Heat the oil and sauté the onion and garlic. Add the beef and pork, turn the heat to high, and brown thoroughly, stirring often. Drain nearly all the fat and liquid from the meat mixture. Add the remaining picadillo ingredients and cook over medium heat, uncovered, about 15 to 20 minutes.

Avocado sauce: Combine all of the sauce ingredients in a food processor and purée. Add more half-and-half if necessary; the sauce should be just thin enough to pour. Strain the sauce and heat in a saucepan, but do not boil.

To assemble dish carefully stuff the *anchos* with the picadillo and place each one on a plate. Heat the plates in the oven or in the microwave. Drizzle the avocado sauce over each *ancho*, add side dishes, and serve.

Yield: 6 servings

Heat Scale: Medium

The Hidden Cache of Chiles

Mexico City, 1910. Elegant Mexicans eat in French. They prefer the *crêpe* to its poor relation of native birth, the corn tortilla. *Oeufs en cocotte* to the humble [*huevos*] *rancheros.* They find *béchamel* sauce more worthy than guacamole, that delicious but excessively indigenous mixture of avocados, tomatoes, and chile. Faced with foreign peppers or Mexican chiles, the gentry rejected the chile, although later they sneak back to the family kitchen and devour it secretly, ground or whole, side dish or main dish, stuffed or plain, unpeeled or naked.

—Eduardo Galeano

Hongos y Costillas Estilo Mexicano
(Mexican-Style Mushrooms and Ribs)

Mushrooms have been gathered in the wild since ancient times, but they have been cultivated only since the eighteenth century. They are very popular in Mexican cuisine, and there are several Mexican cookbooks devoted to them.

¾   cup mushrooms

2   tablespoons vegetable oil

8   cloves garlic, whole

3   onions, chopped

1½ pounds pork ribs

3   *poblano* chiles, roasted, stems and seeds removed, sliced

1   bunch epazote

1   pound tomatoes, roasted and puréed

Salt and pepper to taste

Clean the mushrooms well with a mushroom brush.

In a large skillet, heat the oil and fry the garlic, onions, and mushrooms together for about 10 minutes.

Add the ribs, chiles, epazote, tomatoes, and salt and pepper. Cook over low heat until done, for about 1 hour.

Serves: 4 to 6

Heat Scale: Medium

Chiles Rellenos con Res y Pasa

(Beef and Raisin-Stuffed Chiles)

This recipe was collected in Aguascalientes, which means "hot water" when translated. The town received this name because it is close to thermal springs, promising everyone a hot time in town tonight! This stuffed chile recipe is unusual in that the chiles are not battered and fried. Thus the pure taste of roasted chiles shines through.

1	pound beef	10	olives, chopped
1	clove garlic, chopped	20	raisins, chopped
½	teaspoon salt	10	almonds, peeled and chopped
1	tablespoon vegetable oil		Salt to taste
½	onion, chopped	6	*poblano* chiles, roasted, peeled, seeds removed
1	cup chopped tomato		
1	tablespoon vinegar	½	cup cream

Garnish: cilantro leaves

Cook the meat, along with the garlic and salt, in a large pot with water to cover. Once the meat is cooked, remove it from the pot and chop it into small pieces.

Heat the oil in a skillet, and sauté the onion until soft. Add the tomato and vinegar and fry a while longer. Then add the meat and stir. Add the olives, raisins, almonds, and salt to taste. Stuff the chiles with this mixture and place in the oven on a greased cookie sheet. Bake at 350 degrees F for 10 minutes. Heat the cream in a pan and drizzle the cream evenly over each chile as it is served. Garnish with the cilantro leaves.

Serves: 6

Heat Scale: Mild

Cabrito y Res con Chiles Anchos

(Braised Goat and Beef with Ancho Chiles)

Goat is often saved for celebrations in Mexico, such as a baptism or wedding. Baby goats, or kids as they are called, offer the most tender, succulent meat imaginable. This recipe from Nayarit includes beef and is flavored with *ancho* chiles. Serve it with the side dish of your choice from Chapter 8.

5 *ancho* chiles, toasted, stems and seeds removed	½ cup vinegar
2 pounds tomatoes, chopped	½ cup dry red wine
1 pinch powdered ginger	2 bay leaves
8 black peppercorns	2 pounds goat meat, cut into 1-inch cubes
5 cloves garlic	2 pounds beef, cut into 1-inch cubes
½ teaspoon cumin	Tortillas
2 whole cloves	

In a food processor or blender, combine the chiles, tomatoes, ginger, peppercorns, garlic, cumin, cloves, and vinegar and purée in batches. Transfer to a bowl and add the wine and bay leaves. Place the goat and beef in a large baking pan, and pour the chile mixture over it. Bake, covered, at 250 degrees F for 2 hours, or until done and the meat is falling apart.

Serve with tortillas and the salsa of your choice from Chapter 2.

Serves: 8 to 10

Heat Scale: Medium

Pato y Pollo Picante

Peppered Poultry

The Spaniards came to the New World in search of gold, but they also found a cuisine that would have a much larger impact on the world than all the riches of their dreams. Corn, beans, tomatoes, pumpkins, and, of course, chiles, were but a few of the crops that the Spaniards and Portuguese would pass along on their travels to remake the tastes of the world. According to Marilyn Tausend, "The true dawn of Mexican cuisine began when the Spanish allowed the subjugated Indians to have domesticated animals." Thus enters the chicken, whose ascent into popularity has been nothing short of spectacular. But before there were chickens in Mexico, the indigenous people depended on ducks.

We begin this chapter with three duck recipes, which are of Aztec heritage. *Pato Asado con Tequila y Salsa Chipotle* (Roasted Duck with Tequila and Honey Chipotle Sauce, page 140) is the creation of Chef John Gray, from the Ritz-Carlton in Cancún. *Pato Mulato con Piñones* (Roasted Duck with Piñons and Mulato Chiles, page 141) features the sweet and rich pine nut, and our *Pato con Chiles Habaneros* (Duck with Habanero Chiles, page 145) is sure to heat things up a bit.

The Náhuatl word *molli* means a sauce made with chiles. This introduces our next four recipes, including the most famous *mole*, *Mole Poblano con Pollo* (Mole Poblano with Chicken, page 142), along with *Mole Negro Oaxaqueño* (Oaxacan Black Mole, page 146), *Mole Coloradito Oaxaqueño* (Oaxacan Little Red Mole, page 148), and *Mole de Arroz* (Rice Mole, page 152) from Jalisco. SusanaTrilling supplied the recipes for all but the last mole, which she collected from friends, relatives, and *señoras* in Oaxaca.

Tropical and fertile, the Yucatán peninsula offers a veritable treasure trove of interesting ingredients from which to choose. We've pick two representative poultry recipes from the area: *Pollo en Escabeche Estilo Yucateca* (Shredded Chicken Yucatán Style, page 150) contributed by Marta Figel, and *Pollo Pibíl* (Pibíl-Style Chicken, page 153), which is chicken wrapped in banana leaves and steamed.

Our next recipe, *Pollo con Salchichas en Chile Chipotle* (Chicken and Sausage with Chipotle Chiles, page 154) is a hearty dish, full of smoke and fire. You may want to try our two nutty chicken dishes, *Gallina en Nogada* (Hen in Walnut Sauce, page 155) and *Almendrado Oaxaqueño* (Almond Chicken Oaxacan Style, page 156), as they both marry texture and taste to make excellent dishes.

What spice is a member of the lily family and closely related to the onion? It's the garlic, of course, which is the main ingredient of *Ajo–Comino de Gallina* (Garlic and Cumin Chicken, page 157) and *Chileajo de Pollo* (Chicken with Chile and Garlic, page 162). These recipes are sure to chase off vampires and colds alike!

Barbecued chicken makes its entrance next with two rustic recipes, *Pollo Barbacoa* (Barbecued Chicken, page 158) and *Barbacoa de Pollo y Chiles* (Barbecued Chicken with Chiles, page 160). You'll find that the Mexican barbecue technique is very different from what may be your weekend ritual of throwing a few chicken breasts on the grill.

Tart and sweet, these next fruity recipes are intensely *enchilado,* or "enchilied," as the Mexicans would say. From *Pechugas en Salsa de Chipotle con Piña* (Chicken Breasts in Chipotle–Pineapple Sauce, page 163) to *Pollo en Frutas* (Chicken with Mixed Fruit, page 164) and *Pollo con Limón y Cascabella* (Chicken with Lemon and Cascabel Chiles, page 165), we've covered our sweet bases with the best of the tropics.

Our final three recipes are memorable. *Pollo en Chile Verde* (Green Chile Chicken, page 166) is full of spirit and chiles, and our *Gallina Rellena con Chiles Chipotles* (Stuffed Chicken with Chipotles, page 168) may just change the turkey ritual of Thanksgiving. And finally, your neighbors are going to wish they were invited to your *fiesta* when they smell the *Pollo Enchilado* (Grilled Chile–Chicken, page 167) cooking on your grill. You can either torture them, or invite them over for a Mexican feast—it's up to you!

Pato Asado con Tequila y Salsa Chipotle

(Roasted Duck with Tequila and Honey Chipotle Sauce)

This recipe was contributed by John Gray, chef at the Ritz-Carlton in Cancún. This dish is an excellent example of the sophisticated flavors that can be created with seemingly simple ingredients and one pan.

2	tablespoons olive oil
6	shallots, coarsely sliced
½	cup raisins
1	tablespoon sugar
¼	cup balsamic vinegar
1	cup port wine
¾	cup chicken stock

2	*chipotle* chiles, rehydrated in warm water, seeds and stems removed, chopped
¼	cup tequila
¼	cup honey
1	whole duck

Preheat the oven to 300 degrees F.

Add the olive oil and shallots to a very hot saucepan. Sauté until golden, stirring constantly, then add the raisins and sugar. Allow the sugar to dissolve and lightly caramelize; do not allow it to burn. Add the balsamic vinegar and the port wine, then reduce until thickened and about ¼ cup of the liquid remains.

Add the chicken stock to the reduced sauce, mix well, and add the *chipotles*. Let the sauce stand for 10 to 15 minutes, then strain (the less time the peppers are in the sauce, the lighter the *chipotle* flavor). Add the tequila and honey to the sauce, return to the heat, and keep just warm, stirring occasionally.

In a roasting pan roast the whole duck for 45 minutes, uncovered. Debone the duck, remove the skin, and cover the meat with the sauce. Serve with rice or polenta and julienned vegetables or asparagus.

Serves: 4 to 6

Heat Scale: Medium

Pato Mulato con Piñones

(Roasted Duck with Piñons and Mulato Chiles)

In Mexico, nuts are often used as a thickening agent for sauces. The pine nuts in this recipe from Chihuahua help to coat the duck and keep in the juices that make the meat tender. Serve this with a rice or bean dish from Chapter 8.

1	cup water		½	cup water
1	sprig fresh rosemary		3	tablespoons honey
4	cloves garlic		½	teaspoon soy sauce
2	black peppercorns		1	teaspoon corn oil
2	cups *piñones* (pine nuts)		1	duck
4	*mulato* chiles, stems and seeds removed			

Preheat the oven to 350 degrees F.

Heat 1 cup water in a saucepan and cook the rosemary, garlic, peppercorns, and nuts for about 10 minutes. Remove the rosemary sprig, transfer the mixture to a blender, and purée. Reserve.

In the blender, combine the chiles and ½ cup water and purée. Remove to a saucepan, add the honey, soy sauce, and oil, and cook for about 5 minutes, stirring constantly. Add the nut purée and adjust the consistency by adding water if necessary. Over low heat, cook the sauce until it is thick enough to cling to the duck.

Place the duck in a roasting pan and cover it with the sauce. Baste the duck with the sauce and roast, uncovered, at 350 degrees F for 1½ hours or until done. Continue basting while roasting.

Serves: 4 to 6

Heat Scale: Medium

Mole Poblano con Pollo
(Mole Poblano with Chicken)

This recipe is from our friend and *Chile Pepper* author Jim Peyton, who has written two books on the foods of the border country. He says that as with most Mexican dishes, there are probably as many recipes for *mole poblano* as there are cooks who have prepared it. According to Jim, the *mole* recipe presented here is an amalgamation that is about as elaborate as this recipe gets in terms of the number of different ingredients.

2	to 3 tablespoons vegetable oil	1	to 2 cups chicken broth
4	chicken breasts, boneless and skinless, cut in half	1	tablespoon sugar
	Spice mixture (recipe follows)	1	ounce Mexican or bittersweet chocolate
	Chile paste (recipe follows)		

Garnish: 2 to 3 tablespoons sesame seeds

Make the spice mixture and chile paste (recipes follow).

Heat the oil in a skillet and quickly brown the chicken breasts; remove and keep warm.

Add the chile paste to the skillet and simmer for 5 minutes. Next, add the spice mixture and continue simmering for an additional 5 minutes. Stir in enough chicken broth to produce a sauce that just coats a spoon—about as thick as a thin milkshake.

Add the sugar and chocolate to the sauce and stir to dissolve. Return the chicken breasts to the skillet and simmer, uncovered, for 5 to 10 minutes or until just cooked through.

Garnish with the sesame seeds and serve.

Variation: To prepare *mole* enchiladas, simply wrap shredded chicken in corn tortillas that have been softened in hot oil, top with the sauce and garnish, and heat at 350 degrees F for 10 minutes

Serves: 4

Heat Scale: Mild

Spice Mixture

4	fresh tomatillos, husks removed	3	tablespoons pumpkin seeds
3	tablespoons vegetable oil	2	tablespoons peanuts
1	tomato, roasted and peeled	2	tablespoons almonds
½	teaspoon coriander seeds	2	tablespoons raisins
½	teaspoon chile seeds	3	tablespoons prunes
3	tablespoons sesame seeds	1	3-inch piece plantain, or substitute a banana
¼	teaspoon anise	½	corn tortilla
2	whole cloves	½	piece white bread
½	inch stick cinnamon	1	to 2 cups chicken broth, homemade preferred
¼	teaspoon whole black peppercorns		

Fry the tomatillos in 1 tablespoon oil until just soft, about 5 minutes; drain and place in a blender. Add the tomato.

Toast the seeds, anise, cloves, cinnamon, and peppercorns in a heavy skillet over low heat, stirring constantly, until the sesame seeds just begin to brown—about 3 to 5 minutes. Allow the seeds to cool, then grind them to a fine powder in a coffee or spice grinder. Add the powder to the tomatillos and tomato.

Fry the pumpkin seeds in 1 tablespoon oil until they puff up. Be careful, as they will pop and spatter as they brown. Drain and add to the blender.

In 1 tablespoon oil, fry the nuts, raisins, and prunes for about 2 minutes or until the raisins are puffed. Remove and add to the blender.

Fry the plantain until it begins to brown. Remove and add to the blender.

Finally, fry the tortilla and bread until the tortilla is softened, adding more oil if necessary. Remove, drain, and coarsely chop. Add to the blender.

Blend the spice mixture, adding just enough chicken broth to make a thick paste. Transfer the paste to a bowl.

Yield: 2 to 3 cups

(continues)

Chile Paste

1   dried *mulato* chile, stem and
    seeds removed

1   dried *ancho* chile, stem and
    seeds removed

2   *pasilla* chiles, stems and seeds
    removed

1   tablespoon vegetable oil
    (optional)

1   *chipotle* chile, stem removed

Either fry the chiles (except the *chipotle*) in a little oil or toast them in the oven at 250 degrees F until they just begin to brown and become fragrant, taking care that they do not burn.

Place the toasted chiles and the *chipotle* in 2 cups hot water and soak for 15 minutes or until soft. Place the chiles, and a little of the water they were soaking in, in a blender and purée to a paste. Strain the paste.

Yield: ¾ cup

Heat Scale: Medium

Secrets of *Mole*

A *mole* recipe is not something dashed off on a file card and handed to an appreciative dinner guest. It is a family treasure, and in some cases a family secret. A visitor certainly can ask for the recipe and the flattered cook may begin ticking off the ingredients on the fingers of both hands, sometimes two or three times over. But ask the cook to specify proportions of ingredients and the steps to create the *mole,* and the conversation suddenly can become vague.

—William Stockton

Pato con Chiles Habaneros
(Duck with Habanero Chiles)

You may never taste anything quite as snappy as this specialty from Yucatán. The *habanero* actually brings out the flavor of the duck, especially when combined with four strong spices. Serve this dish over rice, with fried plantains on the side.

2	large ducks, cut up in pieces	2	cloves
1	medium onion, sliced	2	bay leaves
2	cloves garlic	1	sprig fresh thyme
	Water to cover	1	sprig fresh oregano
6	pounds tomatoes, roasted	1	heaping tablespoon butter
2	*habanero* chiles, seeds and stems removed, minced		Salt to taste

Place the duck, onion, and 1 clove of garlic in a large pot and just cover it with water. Boil at high heat for about 1 hour, or until the duck is tender.

Combine the tomatoes with the chiles, cloves, bay leaves, thyme, oregano, and remaining clove of garlic in a blender and purée. In a saucepan, fry this mixture in the butter for 20 to 30 minutes, stirring constantly. Add the duck pieces and continue to cook at a low temperature for about 30 minutes. Add salt to taste and serve.

Serves: 6 to 8

Heat Scale: Extremely Hot

Mole Negro Oaxaqueño
(Oaxacan Black Mole)

This recipe is from Susana Trilling, *Chile Pepper* author and owner of the Seasons of My Heart cooking school in Oaxaca. She wrote: "Eliseo, my favorite chile vendor in the largest *mercado* in Oaxaca, told me that there are more than sixty varieties of chiles that are grown only in the state of Oaxaca and nowhere else in Mexico! I have suggested substitutions here to reflect varieties more commonly available north of the border. You can use oil instead of lard, but the flavor will change dramatically. In our pueblo, people use turkey, which is traditional, and also add pork meat and a piece of beef to enhance the flavor."

1   whole chicken, cut into eight serving pieces

6   cups chicken stock

5   *chilhuacle negro* chiles, stems and seeds removed (save the seeds); or substitute *ancho* chiles

5   *guajillo* chiles, stems and seeds removed (save the seeds); or substitute dried red New Mexican chiles

4   *pasilla* chiles, stems and seeds removed (save the seeds)

4   *mulato* chiles, stems and seeds removed (save the seeds); or substitute *ancho* chiles

2   *chipotle* chiles, stems and seeds removed (save the seeds)

1   medium white onion, quartered

6   cloves garlic

2   tablespoons whole almonds

2   tablespoons shelled and skinned peanuts

2   to 4 tablespoons lard or vegetable oil

2   teaspoons raisins

1   slice of bread (challah or egg type is best)

1   small ripe plantain, sliced; or substitute a banana

½   cup sesame seeds

2   pecan halves

1   1-inch cinnamon stick, Mexican preferred

2   whole peppercorns

2   whole cloves

2   medium tomatoes, chopped

5   fresh tomatillos, chopped

½   teaspoon dried oregano

½   teaspoon dried thyme

1   avocado leaf (omit if not available); or substitute bay leaf

1   bar (or to taste) Mexican chocolate, Ibarra preferred

Salt to taste

Plenty of fresh tortillas

Simmer the chicken in the stock until tender, about ½ hour. Remove the chicken and keep warm, reserving the stock.

In a large frying pan or *comal,* toast the chiles, turning often until darkened, but not burned; or, as some Oaxaqueñas prefer, fry the chiles in lard. Place the chiles in a bowl and cover with hot water to soak for ½ hour to soften. Remove the chiles and place in a blender or food processor and purée, adding a little of the chile water if necessary, to form a paste. Remove from the blender and set aside.

In the same frying pan or *comal,* roast the onion and garlic cloves until slightly browned; remove. Next, toast the almonds and peanuts slightly; remove. Finally, toast the chile seeds, taking care to make them dark but not burned.

Heat 2 tablespoons of lard in the skillet and fry the raisins until plumped; remove and drain on paper towels. Next, fry the bread until browned; remove and drain. Repeat with the plantains. Add more lard if necessary, lower the heat, and fry the sesame seeds slowly, stirring often. When they are slightly browned, add the pecans and brown; remove and drain.

Toast the cinnamon, peppercorns, and cloves lightly in a dry pan. Cool and grind in a *molcajete* or spice grinder.

In a food processor or blender, purée the nuts, bread, sesame seeds, and pecans in small batches; remove. Add the onion, garlic, and plantain and purée; remove. Finally, purée the tomatoes and tomatillos.

In a large *cazuela,* or heavy pot, heat the remaining lard and fry the chile paste, stirring constantly so it will not burn. When it is "dry," add the tomato purée and fry until the liquid has evaporated. Add the ground spices, the nut–bread mixture, the puréed onion mixture, and the oregano and thyme.

Heat, stirring constantly, to a simmer and add the chocolate to the *mole.* Toast the avocado leaf for a second. Slowly add some of the reserved chicken stock to the *mole* until the mixture is just thick enough to lightly coat a spoon; salt to taste. Continue to simmer for 5 minutes, return the chicken to the *mole* and heat through.

Serve with plenty of sauce and hot tortillas.

Serves: 4 to 6

Heat Scale: Hot

Mole Coloradito Oaxaqueño
(Oaxacan Little Red Mole)

This recipe is also from Susana Trilling. She notes that there are still many *señoras* in the small pueblos who insist on using their *molcajetes* for the tedious grinding of the ingredients for this celebrated dish!

1	whole chicken, cut into eight serving pieces	4	tablespoons lard or vegetable oil
6	cups chicken stock	1	small French roll, sliced
5	*ancho* chiles, stems and seeds removed	1	small plantain, or substitute a banana
2	*guajillo* chiles, stems and seeds removed; or substitute dried red New Mexican chiles	2	tablespoons raisins
	Hot water as needed	¼	cup sesame seeds
		10	whole almonds
5	whole peppercorns	2	medium tomatoes, quartered
5	whole cloves	3	sprigs fresh marjoram or oregano
2	2-inch cinnamon sticks, Mexican preferred	1	bar (or to taste) Mexican chocolate, such as Ibarra
1	white onion, peeled and quartered	1	or 2 avocado leaves, or substitute bay leaves
10	cloves garlic		

Simmer the chicken in the stock until tender, about ½ hour. Remove the chicken and keep warm; reserve the stock.

In a large frying pan or *comal*, toast the chiles, turning often until darkened but not burned. Toast the *guajillos* a little longer because of their tougher skins. Place the chiles in a bowl and cover with hot water to soak for ½ hour to soften. Remove the chiles and place in a blender or food processor and purée, adding a little of the chile water if necessary; strain.

Lightly toast the peppercorns, cloves, and cinnamon sticks in a dry pan or *comal*. Cool and grind in a *molcajete* or spice grinder.

In the same pan, roast the onion and garlic cloves until slightly browned. Cool and place in a blender or food processor and purée with a little water. Remove and set aside.

Heat 2 tablespoons of the lard in the pan until smoking hot, and fry the bread until lightly brown; remove and drain on paper towels. Fry the plantain on both sides until browned; remove and drain. Quickly fry the raisins; remove. Lower the heat and add the sesame seeds, stirring constantly for a couple of minutes, then add the almonds and continue to fry until both are well browned. Remove, drain, and combine with the bread, plantain, and raisins, reserving a bit of the sesame seed for garnish. Place in a blender or food processor and purée, adding a little water if necessary. Remove and set aside.

Wipe out the skillet with a cloth and add 1 tablespoon of lard. When hot, add the tomatoes and fry well. Place in a blender or food processor and purée until smooth; remove.

Heat the remaining tablespoon of lard in a *cazuela*, or heavy pot, until smoking. Add the chile purée and fry, stirring constantly, so it will not burn. It tends to splatter about, so be careful! Fry for a couple of minutes, add the tomato purée, the ground spices, and the marjoram, and heat through. Stir in the bread mixture and continue to heat, stirring constantly. Add the chocolate and avocado leaves, thin with the reserved chicken stock, and continue to simmer for 30 minutes.

Add the chicken, adjust the salt, and heat through. Serve with black beans, rice, and tortillas.

Serves: 4 to 6

Heat Scale: Medium

Pollo en Escabeche Estilo Yucateca
(Shredded Chicken Yucatán Style)

Marta Figel, writing in *Chile Pepper* about Isla Mujeres, collected this fiery, fantastic chicken recipe. Your guests will enjoy it even more if you serve it with a round of margaritas from Chapter 9. The drinks won't cut the heat, but may help you forget how hot it is!

10	peppercorns		Water
¼	teaspoon ground oregano	1	teaspoon salt
½	teaspoon salt	½	teaspoon ground oregano
2	cloves garlic, peeled and crushed	1	*xcatic* chile, stem and seeds removed; or substitute yellow wax hot
1	tablespoon vinegar		
2	large red onions	1	*habanero* chile, stem and seeds removed
2	heads garlic		
	Juice of 3 bitter (Seville) oranges, or mix 1 cup lime juice with ½ cup orange juice	2	*serrano* chiles, stems and seeds removed
			Flour tortillas
3	pounds chicken legs and thighs		

Place the peppercorns, oregano, and salt in a spice or coffee grinder and grind to a powder. Combine this powder with the garlic and vinegar and make a paste. Set aside.

Roast one of the onions and both heads of garlic in the oven at 350 degrees F for 20 minutes. Let cool.

Peel the remaining onion, slice it into rings, and marinate it in the bitter orange juice.

Place the chicken in a stockpot with water to cover, add the salt and oregano, and simmer until the chicken is tender, about 30 minutes.

Drain the chicken, reserving the broth, and transfer it to an oven-proof dish. Add the peppercorn paste, 2 tablespoons of the bitter orange juice, and bake uncovered at 350 degrees F until golden brown, about 30 minutes.

Peel the roasted onion and garlic and combine them with the reserved chicken stock. Add the chiles and simmer for 5 minutes. Add the marinated onion, bring to a boil, and remove from the heat immediately.

Drain the broth and reserve both the broth and the chiles and onions. Separate the chiles from the onions and coarsely chop them.

Skin the chicken and shred the meat from the bones. Add the chopped chiles and the onions to the chicken and mix well. Reduce the stock by boiling to 1½ cups and add it to the chicken mixture until the mixture is moist but not soupy.

Serve the chicken with *Salsa Xcatic* (page 000) on the side.

Serves: 4

Heat Scale: Hot

A Mexican Chile Prayer

Sun of salsas, burning on the tongue, sky of feelings, eulogy of the seasonings, dream of the aromas, triumphant of the spices, honor of the palate; master of the *molcajetes,* soul of the *metates,* forger of the casseroles, celebrated sting of the meat, brightest of the fruits, passion and glory of corn; anchor of epazote, key to *guajolote,* splendor and enthusiasm of the fruits, summer of the tamarind, you're notable, delight of the jicama, shining capsule and vital to immortal enjoyment; consort to the pumpkin seed, sire to all moles, blazing flaming fruit, our daily chile; illuminate every field, blaze every meal, adorn every emergency, nourish every urge, patron of the tortillas, infuse body and soul; gold of the *nopales,* crest of the onion, friend of the tomato, brother of the blood of beans, let us enjoy your taste, enlighten us now and always with your fire. Amen.

Mole de Arroz

(Rice Mole)

This recipe was collected in Jalisco, where cooks combine *pasillas, cascabels,* and pickled *jalapeños* to form their trilogy of chiles. This is certainly one of the more simple *mole* recipes we've come across. It's also very good.

1	chicken, sectioned	4	tablespoons vegetable oil
	Water to cover	1	teaspoon cumin
2	medium onions, sliced	6	black peppercorns
	Salt to taste	4	cloves garlic, crushed
1½	cups rice, cleaned and soaked	4	tomatillos (green tomatoes), chopped
4	*pasilla* chiles, seeds and stems removed		Salt to taste
3	*cascabel* chiles, seeds and stems removed		

Garnishes:

½   to 1 head lettuce, shredded
    Pickled *jalapeños* to taste

Place the chicken parts in a pan, cover with water, and add the onions and salt to taste. Cook the chicken until it is tender, 45 minutes to 1 hour. Once cooked, remove the chicken from the broth, keep it warm, and set the broth aside.

Measure the broth to 3 cups, adding more water if necessary. Cook the rice in the broth until done, stirring occasionally to make sure it doesn't stick.

In a separate pan, fry the chiles in a little oil, then add the cumin, peppercorns, garlic, and green tomatoes until the chiles become soft. Remove to a blender and purée, then return to the pan. Add the rice and cook for a few minutes.

Serve the rice with the chicken and decorate with the lettuce and pickled *jalapeños.*

Serves: 6

Heat Scale: Medium

Pollo Pibil

(Pibil-Style Chicken)

This recipe was contributed by our friends Nancy and Jeff Gerlach, who have traveled extensively in Mexico. Although they were served this dish on both sides of Mexico, it does come from Yucatán, where it is available in nearly every restaurant. In Cancún, they even saw *pollo pibil* take-out stands! *Pibil* refers to the method of cooking marinated meats wrapped in banana leaves in a rock-lined pit. Banana leaves are abundant in the central *mercado* in Cozumel, but since they are rare in the United States, use aluminum foil instead. Bitter (or Seville) oranges are also hard to find, but mixing orange, grapefruit, and lime juices makes an acceptable substitute. Please note: This recipe requires advance preparation.

¼	cup *Recado Rojo* (see recipe, page 000)	1	medium onion, sliced
2	tablespoons lime juice	3	*xcatic* or banana chiles, chopped; or substitute yellow wax hot
1	tablespoon orange juice		
1	tablespoon grapefruit juice	2	tablespoons vegetable oil
4	chicken breasts	4	large banana leaves or aluminum foil

Mix the *Recado Rojo* with the fruit juices. Marinate the chicken in the mixture for 4 hours or overnight in the refrigerator.

Sauté the onion and chiles in 1 tablespoon of the oil until soft.

Brush the banana leaves or aluminum foil with oil. Place one chicken breast in the center, pour ¼ of the marinade over the chicken, and top with the onion mixture. Fold the foil over and tightly secure the seams.

Place the packages on a pan, and bake for 1 hour at 350 degrees F.

Remove the foil and drain off any excess liquid. Serve with onion salsa, refried black beans, and *Habanero* salsa.

Serves: 4

Heat Scale: Mild

Note: Requires advance preparation

Pollo con Salchichas en Chile Chipotle
(Chicken and Sausage with Chipotle Chiles)

This hearty dish offers a smoky taste that comes from both the sausages and the *chipotles*. You might like to start this dish with *Salad de Guacamole* (page 000). If you can't find *chipotles* en adobo in cans, rehydrate dried *chipotles* in hot water.

	One 2-pound chicken, sectioned	½	clove garlic
	Water to cover	2	tablespoons vegetable oil
1	clove garlic	1	medium onion, sliced
1	small onion	5	slices sausage
1	pound tomatoes, chopped		Salt to taste
4	*chipotle* chiles in adobo, chopped		

In a large pan, cover the chicken with water, add the garlic and onion, and cook over high heat until the chicken is tender, about 45 minutes.

In a separate pan, cook the tomatoes, then add the chiles and garlic.

Fry the sliced onion in the oil and add the tomato mixture. Cook over low heat for about 10 minutes. Add the chicken, sausage, and salt to taste. Cook over low heat for another 10 minutes and serve with rice.

Serves: 4 to 6

Heat Scale: Hot

Gallina en Nogada

(Hen in Walnut Sauce)

This recipe requires you to grind spices in a coffee grinder or spice mill. If you have a coffee grinder, don't worry about removing the leftover spices after you're done. Simply grind white rice in the grinder and then wipe out with a wet paper towel. The rice will remove all spices, ensuring you won't have chile coffee!

6	tablespoons butter	2	onions, peeled and quartered
1	piece white bread	4	*ancho* chiles, seeds and stems removed, rehydrated in hot water
¼	cup peanuts, peeled		
¼	cup walnuts	¾	cup chicken broth
1	stick cinnamon	1	large chicken, separated and cooked for 45 minutes in 3 cups of water with salt and pepper to taste
2	cloves		
3	*piquín* chiles, stems removed		
2	cloves garlic		

Heat the butter in a skillet and fry the bread, peanuts, and walnuts for about 5 minutes. Remove and purée in a food processor or blender. Reserve.

In a spice mill, combine the cinnamon stick, cloves, and *piquín* chiles and grind to a powder. Combine this powder with the garlic, onions, *ancho* chiles, and chicken broth in a food processor or blender and purée.

Transfer to a saucepan, add the puréed nuts and cooked chicken parts, and let this cook until the flavors blend. Serve over white rice.

Serves: 6 to 8

Heat Scale: Hot

Almendrado Oaxaqueño
(Almond Chicken Oaxacan Style)

The Oaxaca market place is famous for its incredible selection of chiles and other locally grown produce. This recipe features the *ancho* chile, which is the dried version of the *poblano*. Serve with a side dish from Chapter 8.

1	medium chicken, sectioned Salt and pepper to taste Corn oil as needed for frying	1	medium onion, peeled and chopped
3	*ancho* chiles, stems and seeds removed	6	black peppercorns
½	cup almonds	3	cloves
4	tomatoes, roasted, peeled, and seeded	1	cinnamon stick
2	cloves garlic	½	*bolillo* (or small French roll), in crumbs
		2	tablespoons sugar
		4	cups chicken broth

In a large skillet, salt and pepper the chicken and fry it in the oil, making sure it doesn't burn or stick. Remove the chicken from the pan and drain.

In the same grease, fry the chiles, all but 2 tablespoons of the almonds, tomatoes, garlic, onion, peppercorns, cloves, cinnamon stick, and bread crumbs. Pour the mixture into a blender and blend until smooth. If necessary, add a little broth. Return the mixture to the pan and cook at a low temperature. Add the chicken, sugar, and chicken broth and cover. Cook at a low temperature until the chicken is tender. Before serving, add the remaining almonds.

Serves: 4 to 6

Heat Scale: Medium

Ajo–Comino de Gallina

(Garlic and Cumin Chicken)

This recipe from Hidalgo calls for nine cloves of garlic. We know what you're thinking—that's a lot of garlic! But in Mexico, garlic has been used for centuries to fight infections, stimulate the immune system, reduce high blood pressure, and cleanse the system of harmful substances. All that and it tastes good, too!

1	large chicken, sectioned		2	*pasilla* chiles, stems and seeds removed, rehydrated in hot water
	Salt			
1	onion		8	cloves garlic
1	clove garlic		½	teaspoon cumin
	Water to cover		¼	cup butter for frying
5	*ancho* chiles, stems and seeds removed, rehydrated in hot water			

Cook the chicken with the salt, onion, and garlic, with water to cover, in a large pot.

Grind the chiles with the garlic and cumin in a mortar and pestle, then fry it with the butter for about 5 minutes, stirring constantly.

Add the chicken and some of the broth and let it cook until the flavors marry. Serve with white rice.

Serves: 4 to 6

Heat Scale: Medium

Barbacoa de Pollo

(Barbecued Chicken)

The Mexican *barbacoa* has much more in common with the Hawaiian luau than with the Americanized version of barbecue, which has come to mean cooking meat over hot coals with a tangy sauce. In Mexico, the meat is wrapped in agave leaves or banana leaves, or corn husks if the first two are not available.

8	*guajillo* chiles, stems and seeds removed, or substitute red New Mexican chiles	3	black peppercorns
2	*chipotle* chiles, stems and seeds removed	2	bay leaves
2	*ancho* chiles, stems and seeds removed	2	cups vinegar
2	tablespoons cumin	4	pounds uncooked chicken meat, chopped
2	heads garlic	10	corn husks
			Red chile powder
			Salt to taste

Place the chiles on a baking sheet and toast them in the oven at 200 degrees F; then soak them in hot water until they become soft.

Put the chiles in a blender along with the cumin, garlic, peppercorns, and bay leaves. After blending, place this mixture in a bowl, add the vinegar, and mix well.

Place the chicken in a deep dish and cover it with the chile mix and salt to taste, then let it marinate overnight in the refrigerator so that the meat absorbs the flavors.

Place the marinated chicken in the corn husks and sprinkle with a little ground chile, then wrap well and tie the ends.

Place the wrapped meat in a skillet with a little water, or in a steamer; cover and cook at low temperature for 1 or 2 hours, or until done.

Serve with lettuce, avocado, and Green Pipián Sauce from Chapter 2 (see page 000).

Serves: 8

Heat Scale: Medium

Note: Requires advance preparation

What Kind of Chile Goes with Mexican Cockatoo, Anyway?

The proper way to cook a cockatoo is to put the bird and an axehead into a billy and boil them until the axehead is soft. The cockatoo is then ready to eat.

—Anonymous

Barbacoa de Pollo y Chiles
(Barbecued Chicken with Chiles)

This barbecue recipe is created Puebla style, which includes the use of *anchos* and *guajillos*, as well as cinnamon and both avocado and banana leaves. Please note that bay leaves may be substituted for the avocado leaves, and that this recipe requires advance preparation.

6	*ancho* chiles		3	cloves garlic
6	*guajillo* chiles			Salt and pepper to taste
	Water		2	tablespoons olive oil
10	black peppercorns		1	large chicken, sectioned
5	cloves			Avocado leaves
½	teaspoon cumin seeds			Banana leaves
½	teaspoon dried oregano		2	limes, sliced
1	cinnamon stick			

Garnishes:

1	head lettuce, shredded		1	avocado, peeled, pitted, and sliced
1	onion, sliced			

Toast the chiles in the oven at 200 degrees F, then remove and soak them in a large pot with water to cover.

Grind the peppercorns, cloves, cumin, oregano, cinnamon stick, garlic, salt, and pepper in a mortar and pestle, and transfer to a skillet. Fry briefly in the oil to release the flavors.

Place the chicken in a separate container, and cover with the spice mixture. Let the chicken marinate for about 12 hours in the refrigerator.

Place an avocado leaf on each piece of chicken, then wrap each piece individually in a banana leaf, and tie closed.

Bake or steam the chicken until done. Serve individually, sprinkled with lime juice and garnished with lettuce, onion, and avocado.

Serves: 4 to 6

Heat Scale: Medium

Note: Requires advance preparation

Chileajo de Pollo

(Chicken with Chile and Garlic)

This pungent fried chicken will make your kitchen smell heavenly—that is, if you love chiles and garlic the way we do! If you're feeling really exotic, substitute 1 dried *habanero* for the *guajillos* for a hot heat treat.

1	chicken, separated into pieces		Hot water as needed
2	cloves garlic	1	loaf white bread, sliced and dried
1	piece onion		
	Water to cover	10	black peppercorns
	Salt to taste	1	clove
7	*ancho* chiles, stems and seeds removed	½	tablespoon oregano
		1	stick cinnamon
6	*guajillo* chiles, stems and seeds removed	2	cloves garlic
		¼	cup vegetable oil

Cook the chicken, garlic, and onion with water to cover in a large pan for about 45 minutes, then set aside.

Place the chiles in hot water and soak until soft.

Grind the chiles, bread, peppercorns, clove, oregano, cinnamon stick, and garlic together in a mortar and pestle, or a food processor or blender. Transfer the mixture to a large saucepan and fry in a little oil until cooked.

Add the chicken and a little broth to the chile mixture, making a thick sauce, then cover the pan and simmer the ingredients at low temperature long enough for the flavors to blend.

Serves: 4

Heat Scale: Medium

Pechugas en Salsa de Chipotle con Piña

(Chicken Breasts in Chipotle–Pineapple Sauce)

Pineapples thrive in the tropical terrains of Mexico. This fruity-hot dish was collected in Mazatlán. Mazatlán, while full of college students and tourists, is still home to fine traditional Mexican cooking.

1½ pounds tomatoes, cooked and peeled	Salt and pepper to taste
1 medium onion	2 tablespoons vegetable oil
2 cloves garlic	3 chicken breasts, boned and pounded
4 *chipotle* chiles in *adobo* (available in cans; or rehydrate dried *chipotles* in hot water)	1 can pineapple in heavy syrup
	1 cup chicken broth

Combine the tomatoes, onion, garlic, chiles, salt, and pepper in a food processor and pulse until just blended.

In a large pan, fry the mixture in the oil. When done, add the chicken, pineapple, and chicken broth.

Cook uncovered, until done, about 40 minutes. Stir occasionally. Serve with white rice, or a spiced rice from Chapter 8.

Serves: 4 to 6

Heat Scale: Medium

Pollo en Frutas

(Chicken with Mixed Fruit)

Mango is the featured fruit in this mild but wild dish. This dish is especially popular in Chiapas, where the Mayan city of Palenque now lies in ruins. Serve this with a bean dish from Chapter 8.

1	chicken, sectioned	½	cup tomatoes, chopped
	Salt to taste	½	cup potatoes, cubed
1	bay leaf	1	ripe mango, cubed
	Thyme to taste	8	prunes
	Mexican oregano to taste	2	tablespoons raisins
2	tablespoons vinegar	8	olives
1	chayote, cubed; or substitute zucchini	1	*ancho* chile, seeds and stems removed, rehydrated in hot water and chopped
3	carrots, peeled and cubed		
1	small onion, chopped		

Clean the chicken and season with the salt, pepper, herbs, and vinegar. Let it marinate for 15 minutes in a large pot in the refrigerator.

Next, add the remaining ingredients to the chicken and cook over medium heat for 45 minutes to 1 hour or until done, stirring occasionally.

Serves: 4 to 6

Heat Scale: Mild

Pollo con Limón Cascabella

(Chicken with Lemon and Cascabel Chiles)

This tart dinner treat from the city of Culiacán makes for a wonderful luncheon item or early evening supper. The addition of *cascabels* provides heat and nutty depth of flavor. This recipe is excellent served either hot or cold. Note that it requires advance preparation.

	One 2-pound chicken, sectioned	1	onion, chopped
8	lemons, juiced	3	*cascabel* chiles, stems and seeds removed, crushed
	Salt to taste		Pinch of cumin
4	tablespoons olive oil		Avocado leaves; or use bay leaves
	Two 8-ounce cans stewed tomatoes		
4	cloves garlic, chopped		

Marinate the chicken with the lemon juice and salt for about 2 hours in a bowl in the refrigerator. Next, fry the chicken in the olive oil in a large skillet until golden brown and somewhat crispy, about 20 minutes. Drain the chicken on paper towels and set aside.

In a separate pan, combine the tomatoes, garlic, onion, chiles, and cumin and cook for about 10 minutes. Add the chicken to the chile mixture with enough water to cover the top of the chicken. Top with avocado (or bay) leaves and cook at a low temperature for 20 minutes, or until all the flavors have combined. Remove the avocado leaves and serve with white rice or fried plantains.

Serves: 4 to 6

Heat Scale: Medium

Note: Requires advance preparation

Pollo en Chile Verde

(Green Chile Chicken)

It's easy to see how this traditional Mexican recipe from the state of Chihuahua received its name; more than half of the ingredients are green, including both *poblanos* and *serranos*, which offer high heat when combined.

14	tomatillos, chopped	½	medium onion
4	*serrano* chiles, stems and seeds removed	1	small bunch cilantro
2	*poblano* chiles, stems and seeds removed	1	chicken, sectioned
			Salt and pepper to taste
2	cloves garlic	½	cup hot water

Cook the tomatillos in a large saucepan and set aside.

Grind the chiles, garlic, onion, and cilantro together in a blender. Add the chile mixture to the tomatillos, then add the chicken parts and salt and pepper to taste. Add the hot water to the skillet and cook over medium heat for 1 hour 15 minutes, or until done. Serve with white rice.

Serves: 4 to 5

Heat Scale: Medium

Pollo Enchilado

(Grilled Chile–Chicken)

This recipe was collected in Querétaro, where we were happy to find a Mexican recipe that is low in fat and high in flavor. This chicken is also wonderful cubed and served in tortillas, fajita style, with a sauce from Chapter 2. Note that this recipe requires advance preparation.

2	cloves garlic, peeled	1	teaspoon Mexican oregano, dried
6	*ancho* chiles, toasted, seeds and stems removed, chopped	2	cloves
3	*de árbol* chiles, toasted, seeds and stems removed	½	teaspoon cumin
			Salt and pepper to taste
3	*cascabel* chiles, toasted, seeds and stems removed	1	chicken, sectioned
			Lettuce leaves
¾	cup apple cider vinegar		Avocado slices
2	tablespoons vegetable oil		Tortillas
1	sour (Seville) orange, juiced; or substitute 1 orange and 1 lime		

In a blender, combine the garlic, chiles, vinegar, oil, orange juice, oregano, cloves, cumin, salt, and pepper and process until it is thoroughly blended. Marinate the chicken in this mixture overnight.

Roast the chicken over hot coals until done. Or, bake uncovered in the oven at 400 degrees F for 40 minutes. Serve with lettuce and avocados and warmed tortillas.

Serves: 4 to 6

Heat Scale: Medium

Note: Requires advance preparation

Gallina Rellena con Chiles Chipotles

(Stuffed Chicken with Chipotles)

The Spaniards first tasted turkey in Mexico, however, we're sure this stuffed recipe will rival any turkey dish around. Although this dish requires a bit of work, it is well worth the trouble.

Filling

3	tablespoons vegetable oil	8	olives, chopped
2	cloves garlic	6	capers, chopped
½	onion, chopped	2½	cups raisins, chopped
7	ounces ground pork	3	*chipotle* chiles in adobo (available in cans; or rehydrate dried *chipotles* in hot water), chopped.
4	ounces ground ham		
2	medium tomatoes, chopped		
3	cloves garlic, chopped		
4	bunches parsley, chopped		

Chicken

1	large chicken		Pinch of Mexican oregano
6	cups water	1	sprig thyme
1	head garlic		Salt and pepper to taste
½	onion	3	*chipotle* chiles in adobo, chopped
6	tablespoons vinegar		
2	bay leaves	3	tablespoons oil

Filling: In a large skillet, heat the oil and fry the garlic and onion until soft. Add the pork and ham and cook over high heat for about 10 minutes, stirring often. Add the tomatoes and remaining ingredients for the filling and continue to cook for about 20 minutes, stirring often.

Chicken: Stuff the chicken with the filling and set aside. In a stockpot, heat the water and add the garlic, onion, vinegar, bay leaves, oregano, thyme, salt, and pepper. When this mixture comes to a boil, add the stuffed chicken and cook for about 25 minutes or until done.

Combine the chopped chiles with a few teaspoons of adobo sauce, and fry in oil over medium heat. Remove from the fire.

Transfer the chicken to a roasting pan. Pour the chile mixture over the chicken, then bake in a preheated oven at 350 degrees F for 20 minutes.

Serves: 6 to 8

Heat Scale: Medium

Mexican Mole Sayings

"Don't tell me you ate *mole* without wiping your mustache."

"When you grind and grind, not even the *metate* is left."

"There is no *mole* if there's no *metate.*"

"If you didn't put chile in it, don't pretend to know."

"*Mole, mole,* give them *mole.*"

"You are the sesame seed of my *mole.*"

Mariscos Maravillosos
Scorching Seafood

The Mexican coastlines of the Pacific, the Sea of Cortez, the Gulf of Mexico, and the Caribbean yield an amazing quantity and variety of fish and seafood. Early in the morning, the market stalls are piled high with the fresh catch, and, in a few hours, the fresh fish, shrimp, and shellfish are finding their way into restaurants and homes. Most of the fish used in the following recipes are available in the United States; for those not as readily available we have suggested substitutes so it will be easy to prepare the recipes.

The first recipe, from the elegant Ritz-Carlton Hotel in Cancún, is *Mero Estilo Tik en Xic* (Whole Grouper "Tik in Xic," page 175). The fish is marinated in citrus juice, spiked with the regional *habanero* chiles, and grilled. Chef Gray's second recipe is certainly one of divine inspiration. Salmon steaks are dressed with a mixture of shallots, *pasilla* chiles, and balsamic vinegar in *Salmon Estilo Ritz-Carlton Cancún* (Salmon with Smoked Tomato and Pasilla Chile Vinaigrette, page 176). From Tabasco we present the simple but tasty *Pescado Empapelado* (Fish Baked in Foil, page 177); the fish is spiced, baked, and served with a smooth green salsa. *Makum* (Baked Chile-Spiced Snapper, page 178), from Campeche, is a flavorful dish enhanced with roasted garlic, lemon juice, and *güero* chiles.

An *escabeche* dish is one that first is marinated in an acid base and then cooked. The recipe *Escabeche de Marlin* (Pickled Marlin, page 180) is very typical of Baja, as it is served with the vegetables on top. Even though both *escabeches* and *ceviches* are popular in Mexico, the dish that most norteamericanos are familiar with is *ceviche*. Some food historians maintain that *ceviche* was originally created in Peru; however, if that is true, then Mexican cooks have raised it to culinary perfection. The citrus juice "cooks" the fish or the seafood (precipitating the albumen in the fish, turning it white and firm) and has the same effect as boiling.

The first recipe in this fine tradition is *Ceviche de Mojarra* (Sunfish Ceviche, page 181), from Chiapas. The fish is marinated and then spiced with cilantro, *jalapeños*, and garlic. *Ceviche de Palapa Adriana—Estilo Acapulquito* (Acapulco-Style Ceviche from Palapa Adriana, page 182) is a favorite of those who eat at the popular restaurant, Palapa Adriana, in La Paz. The *ceviche* is drained slightly and then served on crisp tortillas. *Serrano* chiles add the flavorful heat in this recipe.

Fresh clams are a gastronomic orgasm for those who love them. The recipe for *Ceviche de Almejas Estilo Baja* (Clam Ceviche from Baja, page 183) comes from a "clam picker" in Baja who says this is the only way to eat clams. The heat and spice come from the hot sauce that the consumer chooses to put on his pure, marinated clams. Served with a warm tortilla, this is dinner! Another interesting recipe from Baja is *Almejas à la Mexicana* (Mexican-Style Clams, page 184), in which the clams are slightly cooked with flavorful *serrano* chiles. Serving these clams over chile-flavored pasta is our idea of heavenly food.

The recipe from Jalisco, *Ostiones Frescos en Escabeche* (Pickled Fresh Oysters, page 185), is heated up with the fire of *jalapeño* chiles and further infused with garlic, lemon juice, and olive oil. Serve this fiery fare over shredded greens for an interesting luncheon dish. The last *ceviche* recipe, from Yucatán, *Ceviche de Caracol del Mar* (Conch Ceviche, page 186), is heated up with the *habanero* chiles of the region. Just don't tell your dinner guests that this delightful, spicy concoction served over hot tortilla strips is roughly translated into English as "sea snails."

Two crab recipes are included for those chileheads who like to work for their meal, that is, dig into the shells and get the meat out. The *Chiles Rellenos de Jaiba* (Crab-Stuffed Chiles, page 187) from Sinaloa are lightly herbed, seasoned with smoky *chipotle* chiles, and served with a smooth salsa. Spicy *serranos* play a starring role in *Jaiba à la Veracruzana* (Veracruz-Style Crab, page 188); these are usually served in crab shells, but if you use crab leg meat, just serve them in porcelain ramekins.

Shrimp . . . ah, shrimp. Great, fresh Mexican shrimp cannot be matched. Shrimp is used in tacos, rellenos, and empanadas (turnovers). Fresh shrimp is found in abundance on the coasts of Mexico, and it is used in every imaginable way. In addition, the dried, pungent variety is used all over Mexico. Historical sources say that the Emperor Moctezuma and his royalty consumed fresh shrimp from the coast, brought to him by a series of runners.

Tacos Rellenos de Camarón (Shrimp Tacos, page 189) from Campeche is a delicious stuffing for tortillas, spiced with chiles and topped with pickled onions. Chiles are the stuffing mechanism for *Chile Rellenos de Camarón* (Shrimp-Stuffed Poblanos, page 190) from the Veracruz area. The mixture is flavored with green olives, garlic, capers, and tasty *serrano* chiles. Serve them hot, covered with the salsa!

Ancho chiles star in the next shrimp recipe, *Camarón en Chile Rojo* (Shrimp in Red Chile, page 192), which is a favorite in the Mexico City area. The shrimp is cooked with epazote, *ancho* chiles, and served with tiny potato cubes. The *Empanadas de Camarón* (Shrimp Turnovers, page 194) from Nayarit are incredibly delicious and very rich in flavor. The empanadas are infused with garlic, *de árbol* chiles, and herbs. *Camarones Adobados Estilo de Baja* (Adobo Shrimp Baja Style, page 196) is one of the area's primo dishes. The shrimp is spiced with *ancho* and *pasilla* chiles and is flavorful beyond belief. Another recipe, *Camarones*

Adobados Estilo Veracruz (Adobo Shrimp Veracruz Style, page 197), employs more vinegar and uses *pasilla* chiles in abundance. It is also cooked on top of the stove, rather than in the oven.

    Chiles Rellenos de Mariscos (Seafood-Stuffed Poblano Chiles, page 200) hails from Quintana Roo, as evidenced by the use of *xcatic* and *habanero* chiles. Even though these chiles pack a lot of heat, the seafood mixture is tempered with a light white sauce and stuffed into the milder *poblano* chiles. *Barbacoa de Langostinos* (Barbecued Langostinos, page 198), is not lobster, but a type of freshwater crustacean similar in taste to crayfish. This elegant dish is loaded with garlic and several types of chiles, and spiced with cumin, cinnamon, and cloves.

There's a Fungus in Mexico City!

Perhaps the most innovative dish I tried in my Mexican haute cuisine tastings was the *cuitlacoche* ravioli at Isadora, a dish that symbolized the philosophical flaw in the Mexican haute cuisine's culinary theory. To read the words "*cuitlacoche* ravioli" on a menu is to marvel at the stunning combination of cultures, languages, and cooking styles. *Cuitlacoche* is a highly prized fungus that grows on ears of corn under certain wet conditions. The combination of the quintessential delicacy of the Indo-American corn culture and the semolina pasta of the European wheat cuisine made for interesting symbolism, but boring eating. *Cuitlacoche* has an incredibly smooth texture that needs the foil of something crisp. It might have worked on toast points, but the ravioli was too close in texture to the filling. The result was a gloppy mouthful of cheap pasta that masked the exotic flavor and texture of the delicate *cuitlacoche*.

—Robb Walsh

Mero Estilo Tik en Xic

(Whole Grouper "Tik in Xic")

We thank Chef John Gray of the Ritz-Carlton Hotel in Cancún for this recipe. The *habanero* chile adds just a little heat to the fish dish. As in many Cancún resorts, the guests are "gently" introduced to the flaming chiles of the area; many of these tourists have probably never eaten chiles before, so the chefs tend to use a light and judicious hand with them. Serve this with a rice dish and salad from Chapter 8.

2 pounds whole grouper, butterflied	2 cloves garlic, chopped
1 cup *Recado Rojo* (see recipe, page 28)	1 medium onion, sliced
	1 medium tomato, sliced
1 cup orange juice	2 tablespoons finely minced *habanero* chiles
½ cup water	Salt to taste
¼ cup plus 2 tablespoons fresh lemon juice	Banana leaves for steaming
¼ cup plus 2 tablespoons vinegar	

Marinate the whole butterflied grouper in a mixture of *Recado Rojo*, orange juice, water, lemon juice, vinegar, and garlic for 1 hour. Cover the fish with the slices of onion and tomato, sprinkle the chiles on top, and then lightly salt the fish.

Layer a grill with banana leaves. Place the fish on the leaves and layer heavily with more leaves, covering the entire grill. Bake at 325 degrees F under the leaves for 20 minutes per pound.

Serves: 4

Heat Scale: Medium

Salmon Estilo Ritz-Carlton Cancún

(Salmon with Roasted Tomato and Pasilla Chile Vinaigrette)

Here John Gray presents another of his terrific fish recipes. The *pasilla* chiles and the balsamic vinegar add a spicy and herbal edge to the grilled salmon. Chef Gray suggests serving this dish with mashed potatoes with *serrano* chiles and roasted onions.

½	cup shallots, finely chopped		Pinch of basil to taste
½	cup dried *pasilla* chiles, seeds and stems removed, julienned	1	cup plus 2 tablespoons balsamic vinegar
1	medium tomato, peeled	2	cups olive oil
	Salt and pepper to taste	4	salmon steaks

To prepare the dressing, roast the shallots and *pasilla* chiles in a skillet until the shallots are golden. Roast the tomato in a skillet for 5 minutes; then deseed and dice it. Add the tomato to the chiles and shallots. Add salt and pepper to taste; this seasons the tomatoes instead of the dressing. Allow the mixture to sit for 5 minutes, then add the basil, balsamic vinegar, 1¾ cups of the olive oil, and additional salt and fresh-cracked pepper to taste.

Brush the salmon with olive oil and grill the steaks for 3 to 5 minutes per side. Arrange the finished salmon on a heated platter and cover with the reserved vinaigrette.

Serves: 4

Heat Scale: Mild

Pescado Empapelado
(Fish Baked in Foil)

This recipe from Tabasco is a deceptively easy dish to make, and it takes only a few minutes to prepare. The garlic and salsa infuse the fish and give it a wonderful flavor. Serve the fish with warm tortillas and a salad from Chapter 8.

6	cichlid (or sunfish) fillets; or substitute a freshwater fish such as perch, pan fish, or bass	10	green *serrano* or *jalapeño* chiles, roasted, peeled, stems and seeds removed, coarsely chopped
5	cloves garlic, minced	1	large thinly sliced onion
½	teaspoon salt	2	cloves garlic, minced
¼	teaspoon freshly ground black pepper	¼	cup water
3	tablespoons vegetable oil	6	large spinach leaves

Wash the fillets and blot them dry with paper towels. Spread the garlic over the fillets, and then sprinkle with salt and pepper.

To make the salsa, heat the oil in a saucepan and add the chiles, onion, and garlic. Sauté until the onion softens and wilts, about 1 to 2 minutes. Stir in ¼ cup water and remove the mixture from the heat.

Place a fillet on a spinach leaf, spoon some cooked salsa on top, wrap the spinach (envelope style) around the fillet, and then wrap the fillet in a piece of aluminum foil. Repeat the procedure for the remaining fillets.

Place the wrapped fillets in a large, glass baking dish and bake in the oven at 325 degrees F for 20 minutes, or until the fish is flaky.

Serves: 4 to 5

Heat Scale: Hot

Note: To reduce the heat in this recipe, simply use fewer chiles.

Makum

(Baked Chile-Spiced Snapper)

For fish and garlic lovers, this recipe from Campeche is the one to cook. The roasted garlic and onion, along with the cumin, vinegar, and chiles, add a burst of flavor.

2	medium onions, cut in half
8	cloves garlic, unpeeled
1	teaspoon butter
2	tablespoons dry white wine
½	teaspoon ground achiote
1	teaspoon Mexican oregano, dried
1½	teaspoons ground cumin
5	whole cloves, ground in a processor
1	teaspoon whole black peppercorns, ground in a spice mill
3	large *jalapeño* chiles, roasted, peeled, seeds and stems removed

½	cup olive oil
¼	cup fresh lemon juice or lime juice
½	cup vinegar
½	teaspoon salt
1	large banana leaf
4	8-ounce snapper or grouper fillets
3	tomatoes, sliced
4	*güero* chiles, seeds and stems removed, chopped; or substitute yellow wax hots

Place the onions and garlic in a small, oven-proof, glass-covered casserole dish (or use a terra cotta garlic roaster). Dot them with the butter, and pour in the wine. Roast in the oven at 400 degrees F for 50 minutes, or until the cloves are soft. Carefully squeeze the cloves out of their peels and place them in a blender along with the onion.

Add to the blender the achiote, oregano, cumin, ground cloves, ground black peppercorns, chiles, oil, lemon juice, vinegar, and salt and purée until the mixture is smooth.

Lightly oil a shallow baking pan, spread the banana leaf in it, and pour half of the puréed mixture over the banana leaf. Arrange the fish fillets in a single layer toward the middle of the leaf, and pour the remaining purée over the fish.

Arrange the tomatoes and the chiles over the purée, wrap the leaf over the mixture, and secure the leaf with a toothpick.

Bake the fish at 350 degrees F for 25 minutes, or until the fish is tender.

Serves: 4

Heat Scale: Medium

The First New World Restaurant

The first inn and restaurant in North America was opened in Mexico City on December 1, 1525. A settler by the name of Pedro Hernández was authorized by the mayor and city council: "They grant a license for setting up an inn at his houses where he can receive those who may come here, and may also sell them wine and meat and other necessary things." The proprietor was required to list the rates for his services, and overcharging was punished by a fine of four times the overcharge.

Escabeche de Marlin

(Pickled Marlin)

The pickling in this recipe from Baja California comes from the addition of pickled *jalapeños* and vinegar. Serve the fish hot and accompany it with salad and rice dishes from Chapter 8, and a tamale appetizer from Chapter 3.

2	pounds fresh marlin, cleaned and cut into 6 fillets; or substitute tuna	¼	teaspoon freshly ground black pepper
	Water to cover	3	tablespoons vegetable oil
2	cups chopped onion	2	cloves garlic, minced
2	cloves garlic, sliced	1	cup sliced red bell peppers
2	bay leaves	2	cups sliced carrots
1	teaspoon Mexican oregano, dried	1	cup thawed peas
1	tablespoon whole black peppercorns	4	pickled *jalapeño* chiles, sliced
1	teaspoon salt	¾	cup white wine vinegar
		3	tablespoons reserved fish broth

In a large pot, cover the fish with water and add 1 cup of the onion, sliced garlic, bay leaves, oregano, peppercorns, salt, and ground black pepper, and bring the mixture to a light boil. Reduce the heat to a simmer, cover, and simmer for 15 minutes, or until done. Remove the fish and keep warm. Reserve the cooking broth.

Heat the oil in a medium-sized skillet and sauté the minced garlic, remaining cup of onion, red peppers, and carrots for 4 minutes. Add the peas, *jalapeños*, vinegar, and reserved fish broth and simmer for 2 minutes.

Arrange the fish on heated dinner plates and spoon the vegetable mixture over the fish.

Serves: 6

Heat Scale: Medium to Hot

Ceviche de Mojarra

(Sunfish Ceviche)

This spicy *ceviche* from the southern state of Chiapas can be served on fresh greens for lunch or as a light dinner, accompanied by warm tortillas. Any of the fish substitutions will work equally well in this dish. Serve this with a salad from Chapter 8.

2	pounds cichlid or sunfish fillets, or substitute freshwater fish such as bass, perch, or pan fish	1	teaspoon salt
1½	cups fresh lemon juice	¼	teaspoon freshly ground black pepper
4	*jalapeño* chiles, stems and seeds removed, minced	½	cup cilantro, chopped
1	cup red (or sweet) onion, chopped	3	tablespoons olive oil
2	cups tomatoes, peeled, seeded, and chopped	2	cloves garlic, minced
		½	cup green olives, chopped
		3	tablespoons mayonnaise

Cut the fish into 1-inch pieces and place them in a shallow glass baking dish (such as Pyrex). Pour the lemon juice over them and sprinkle with half of the minced *jalapeños.* Marinate the fish for 1 hour in the refrigerator. Next, pour the fish and the marinade into a colander and let it drain for a few minutes. Carefully place the fish in a glass bowl and set aside.

In a small bowl, mix together the onion, tomatoes, salt, pepper, cilantro, olive oil, garlic, and the remaining *jalapeños.* Pour this mixture over the fish and mix gently.

Mix the green olives and mayonnaise together in a small bowl.

Serve the marinated fish on fresh greens with a dollop of the olive–mayonnaise mixture.

Serves: 4 to 5

Heat Scale: Hot

Ceviche de Palapa Adriana–Estilo Acapulquito

(Acapulco-Style Ceviche from Palapa Adriana)

This recipe is from Kathy Gallantine, who told about her search for the best ceviche in *Chile Pepper* magazine. "If you wish to try Acapulquito-Style ceviche at Palapa Adriana," she wrote, "a restaurant on the Malecón in La Paz, Baja California Sur, you must specially request it. The ceviche listed on the menu is served without peas, carrots, and *serrano* chiles. Serve this dish for a light lunch or a light dinner on hot nights when you don't even want to turn on an oven!"

1½	pounds of any white fish fillet, chopped	¼	cup canned peas
8	Mexican (or Key) limes, juiced	¼	cup cooked carrots, finely diced
2	*serrano* chiles, stems and seeds removed, minced	2	teaspoons fresh cilantro, minced
1	tomato, finely chopped		Salt and black pepper to taste
½	onion, finely chopped	8	to 10 corn tortillas, fried flat and very crisp

Place the chopped fish in a shallow container. Pour the lime juice over the fish, cover and refrigerate the mixture for about 2 hours, stirring occasionally, until the fish is opaque.

Just before serving the *ceviche*, stir in the chiles, tomato, onion, peas, carrots, and cilantro. Add salt and pepper to taste. With a slotted spoon, heap the *ceviche* onto the crisp tortillas and serve.

Serves: 3 to 4

Heat Scale: Mild

Variation: Use tiny cocktail shrimp or sliced bay scallops in place of the white fish. Reduce the marinating time to 30 minutes or less.

Note: Requires advance preparation.

Ceviche de Almejas Estilo Baja

(Clam Ceviche from Baja)

This recipe came from *Chile Pepper* author Kathy Gallantine. She collected it from Antonio Seja Torrez, a clam picker in Baja. Every day at low tide, Antonio crawls through the mangroves and collects 500 *pata de mula* "clams," which are really mussels. He carries them several miles to the dock at Magdalena Bay, where he sells them for 10 pesos apiece. His daily earnings come to about $2 U.S. About enough to buy a kilo of beans, he says cheerfully. Try this recipe with true clams, but be prepared to pay a much higher price for them!

	Bottled Mexican hot sauce (to taste), or a sauce from Chapter 2		Juice of 6 to 8 Mexican (Key) limes
24	whole clams, removed from their shells		Salt and black pepper to taste
1	onion, chopped	¼	bunch fresh cilantro (optional)
1	tomato, chopped	2	pounds crushed ice (optional)

Combine all of the ingredients except the cilantro and the ice. Put the *ceviche* in a covered container and refrigerate it until it is well chilled. Serve it immediately, or let the flavors marry and serve it up to 3 days later.

To serve the *ceviche* Guaymas style, save the clam shells and scrub them well. Fill four to six shallow bowls or plates with crushed ice. Nest the half shells into the ice and heap them with the *ceviche*. Then garnish each plate with a sprig of cilantro.

Variation: Use freshly shucked oysters in place of the clams. Omit the tomato and add an 8-ounce can of sliced water chestnuts, and half of a red bell pepper, seeds removed, and chopped.

Serves: 4 to 6

Heat Scale: Varies depending on the type and amount of hot sauce used

Almejas à la Mexicana
(Mexican-Style Clams)

Since the Baja California coastline is thousands of miles long, it's no wonder that everyone partakes of the wonderful varieties of fish and seafood. Serve these spicy clams over an equally spicy pasta, or a rice dish from Chapter 8.

6	dozen clams	¼	cup chopped cilantro
1	cup water	2	teaspoons salt
1	cup dry white wine	½	teaspoon freshly ground black pepper
½	cup olive oil		*Cotija* cheese (or substitute Parmesan), grated
1	large onion, chopped		
3	cups peeled and chopped tomatoes		
5	*serrano* chiles, seeds and stems removed, chopped		

Thoroughly clean the clams.

Put all of the remaining ingredients except the cheese in a large stock-pot, bring the mixture to a light rolling boil, and reduce the heat to a simmer. Add the clams, cover, and steam until the shells open, about 10 minutes. Discard any unopened shells. Serve the clams with the sauce ladled over them and a little cheese grated on top.

Serves: 6 to 7

Heat Scale: Medium

Variation: Serve the clams over a spicy, cooked pasta covered with a warm tomato salsa.

Ostiones Frescos en Escabeche

(Pickled Fresh Oysters)

If you are fond of oysters, you will love this dish from Jalisco—just make sure the oysters are fresh. There are many myths surrounding oysters, including their supposed aphrodisiac qualities. Some oystermen claim that they can tell the sex of oysters and say that females should be fried and males should be stewed!

30	fresh oysters, shucked and washed	¼	cup vinegar
½	cup white wine	¼	teaspoon freshly ground black pepper
¼	cup fresh lemon juice	4	*jalapeño* chiles, seeds and stems removed, thinly sliced
½	teaspoon salt	⅓	cup olive oil
	Water to cover		Shredded mixed greens
1	cup chopped onion		
3	cloves garlic, minced		

Garnish: avocado slices

Place the oysters in a medium-sized saucepan, add the wine, lemon juice, salt, and enough water just to cover. Bring the mixture to a light boil, reduce the heat to a simmer, and cook for 3 minutes. Drain the oysters, place them in a ceramic bowl, and set aside.

Bring 2 cups of water to a boil, turn off the heat, add the onion, and let it sit in the hot water for 2 minutes. Next, drain the onion and add it to the oysters, along with the garlic, vinegar, ground black pepper, chiles, and olive oil. Toss the mixture lightly to distribute the ingredients. Chill for 4 hours and serve on shredded greens with slices of avocado and warm tortillas or toasted garlic bread.

Serves: 4

Heat Scale: Hot

Note: Requires advance preparation.

Ceviche de Caracol del Mar

(Conch Ceviche)

This dish is one where you get to beat the daylights out of the conch with a meat tenderizing mallet! If you don't, you'll still be chewing it 3 years from now. It is tough, but it is also extremely tasty, much like abalone. Serve this dish from Yucatán on chopped mixed greens and include some grated radish. Garnish with warm corn chips and lime slices.

1	pound fresh conch, pounded to tenderize and cut into bite-size pieces	¼	cup chopped cilantro
¼	cup fresh lime juice	1	cup peeled and choppped tomato
¾	cup fresh lemon juice	¼	cup olive oil
1	*habanero* chile, seeds and stem removed, minced	1	teaspoon salt
1	cup finely chopped onion	¼	teaspoon freshly ground black pepper

Put the cut-up conch in a shallow glass pan and cover with the lime and lemon juices. Marinate in the refrigerator for 5 hours. Drain the conch and place it in a mixing bowl.

Add the chile, onion, cilantro, tomato, olive oil, salt, and black pepper, mix, and serve.

Serves: 3 to 4

Heat Scale: Hot

Note: Requires advance preparation.

Chiles Rellenos de Jaiba

(Crab-Stuffed Chiles)

The use of *chipotle* chiles in this recipe from Sinaloa adds a smoky dimension to the taste of the crab. We recommend the meat from freshly cooked crab legs, but if they are unavailable, good-quality canned crab meat can be substituted. But nothing beats fresh crab!

4	tomatoes, roasted, peeled, and chopped	2	cups cooked, shredded crab
1	cup chopped onion	½	cup minced onion
½	cup chicken broth	1	teaspoon dried Mexican oregano; or 2 teaspoons fresh, minced
½	cup water		
3	*chipotle* chiles in *adobo* sauce (available in cans), diced	2	tomatoes, peeled, deseeded, and chopped
½	teaspoon salt	2	to 3 tablespoons chicken broth
¼	teaspoon freshly ground black pepper	½	cup flour
8	green chiles (*poblanos* or New Mexican), roasted, peeled, seeds removed	3	egg whites, stiffly beaten
		1½	cups corn oil

To make the salsa, put the tomatoes, chopped onion, chicken broth, water, *chipotle* chiles, salt, and pepper in a small saucepan. Bring the mixture to a boil, then lower the heat and allow the mixture to simmer while you stuff the chiles.

In a small bowl, mix together the crab, onion, oregano, and tomatoes. If the mixture seems dry, add 1 tablespoon of the chicken stock at a time. Stuff the chiles with this mixture.

Dredge the stuffed chiles in the flour, dip them into the egg whites, and then deep fry them in the oil for 2 minutes per side, or until golden brown. Drain them on paper towels.

Arrange the rellenos on a warm dinner plate and top with the warm salsa.

Serves: 4

Heat Scale: Medium

Jaiba à la Veracruzana

(Veracruz-Style Crab)

Another delicious recipe from beautiful Veracruz! If fresh, whole crabs are not available, cook crab legs, remove the meat, and then serve the final mixture in individual, oven-proof serving dishes (preferably shell-shaped). This entrée is easy to prepare and makes an elegant presentation.

12	fresh whole crabs, cooked, meat removed, and shells reserved; or substitute 3 pounds freshly cooked crab legs	2	tablespoons minced parsley
¼	cup olive oil	½	teaspoon salt
1	cup minced onions	¼	teaspoon freshly ground black pepper
3	cloves garlic, minced	¾	cup coarsely chopped green olives
1½	cups peeled, chopped tomatoes	⅔	cup dry bread crumbs
4	*serrano* chiles, seeds and stems removed, minced	1	egg, thoroughly whisked

Garnishes:

Thinly sliced lemons or limes

Minced parsley

Coarsely chop the crab meat and set aside.

Heat the oil in a medium-sized saucepan and sauté the onions and the garlic for 1 minute. Add the tomatoes, chiles, parsley, salt, and black pepper and sauté for another minute, stirring and tossing the mixture.

Next, mix in the reserved crab, olives, and bread crumbs. Mound this mixture into lightly oiled crab shells or oven-proof, shell-shaped ramekins.

Pour about 1 teaspoon of the whisked egg and a few drops of olive oil over each portion. Place the shells on a baking sheet and bake in an oven preheated to 350 degrees F for 20 minutes, or until golden. Garnish and serve immediately.

Serves: 6 to 8

Heat Scale: Medium

Tacos Rellenos de Camarón
(Shrimp Tacos)

Since fresh shrimp is found in abundance, shrimp tacos are popular with locals and tourists alike on all coasts of Mexico. They are sold as street food, as well as appearing on menus at the finest restaurants. Here is a particularly tasty taco treat from Campeche.

5	*ancho* chiles, seeds and stems removed	1	onion, finely chopped
2	tomatoes, peeled and deseeded	1	*habanero* chile, seeds and stems removed, minced
1	onion, chopped	1½	cups finely chopped, cooked potatoes
¼	teaspoon salt	½	teaspoon salt
	Corn oil, as needed to fry tortillas		Freshly ground black pepper to taste
18	tortillas		
2	tablespoons olive oil	2	cups thinly sliced onion, soaked in ½ cup vinegar
2	cups uncooked finely chopped shrimp	5	cups finely shredded lettuce
2	tomatoes, crushed		

Place the *ancho* chiles, tomatoes, chopped onion, and salt in a food processor and process until the mixture is a smooth purée. Set the mixture aside.

Heat the corn oil in a deep-sided skillet. Dip each tortilla in the *ancho* chile–tomato mixture, then fry it for a few seconds on each side, draining on paper towels. Place the tortillas on a platter.

Heat the 2 tablespoons of olive oil in a medium-sized skillet and add the shrimp, tomatoes, finely chopped onion, *habanero* chile, and potatoes. Lightly fry the mixture for 2 minutes, until the shrimp is cooked. Add salt and pepper to taste. Stuff this mixture into the tortillas and roll up each tortilla.

Drain the onion–vinegar mixture thoroughly and sprinkle it over the tortillas, along with the shredded lettuce.

Serves: 6

Heat Scale: Medium to Hot

Chiles Rellenos de Camarón

(Shrimp-Stuffed Poblanos)

This relleno recipe from Veracruz makes a very sophisticated presentation. The unique combination of ingredients, from slightly salty to herbal to spicy, transforms the flavor of the shrimp. Serve this with a rice dish from Chapter 8.

2	pounds fresh shrimp, peeled and cleaned	2	*serrano* chiles, stems and seeds removed, minced
	Water to cover	½	cup minced parsley
1¼	cups onion, chopped	3	tablespoons capers
3	cloves garlic, minced	½	teaspoon oregano
2	tablespoons olive oil	8	*poblano* chiles, roasted, peeled, and seeds removed
½	cup green olives, chopped		

Salsa

2	tablespoons olive oil	1	clove garlic, minced
1	pound peeled, deseeded, chopped tomatoes (about 4½ cups)	½	cup chopped onion
		1	tablespoon tequila

Place the shrimp in a saucepan, cover with water, add ¼ cup of the chopped onion, one-third of the minced garlic, and bring the mixture to a boil. Turn down the heat and simmer for 2 minutes. Remove the shrimp and chop them coarsely. Reserve 1 cup of the shrimp broth.

Heat the olive oil in a large skillet and sauté the remaining onion and garlic for 1 minute. Add the green olives, *serrano* chiles, parsley, capers, oregano, and reserved shrimp, and sauté for 30 seconds.

Stuff the *poblano* chiles with this mixture, place in an oiled baking dish, and set aside.

To make the salsa, heat the olive oil in a large saucepan and add the tomatoes, garlic, and onion and sauté for 2 minutes, adding enough of the reserved shrimp broth to give the salsa a heavy pouring consistency. Stir in the tequila and sauté for 30 seconds.

Pour the sauce over the stuffed chiles, cover the mixture with foil, and bake at 325 degrees F for 15 minutes, or until the rellenos are hot.

Serves: 4

Heat Scale: Medium

Ceviche Lore

I love *ceviche*, but some of my friends won't even taste it because they think it's raw fish. It's true that *ceviche* is not cooked fish; however, it's not raw, like the fish in sashimi and sushi. When you cook fish, the protein muscle fibers coagulate. This is a chemical process which changes the fish from soft and slightly translucent to firm and opaque. The fish in *ceviche* is also firm and opaque but the same chemical process is accomplished by marinating it in lime juice, in the refrigerator. *Ceviche* is "cold-cooked" fish.

Will marinating fish eliminate parasites? Deep-sea fish are relatively free of parasites, but fresh fish and fish such as salmon, that spend part of their lives in fresh water, may be contaminated with roundworms or tapeworm larvae. Cooking fish with heat kills these parasites, but marinating in lime juice may not. When in doubt, freeze the fish, keeping it at zero degrees Fahrenheit for three days. This will kill the parasites making the defrosted fish safe to be eaten cold-cooked or raw.

—Kathy Gallantine

Camarón en Chile Rojo
(Shrimp in Red Chile)

The *ancho* chiles in this recipe from the state of México do not overpower the delicate flavor of the shrimp; instead, they add just a bit of heat and color. Serve this dish with warm tortillas, a chopped lettuce and tomato salad, and minted fresh fruit for dessert.

6	*ancho* chiles, stems and seeds removed		Water for shrimp
	Water for soaking	½	teaspoon salt
2	cloves garlic	¼	teaspoon freshly ground black pepper
1	medium onion, coarsely chopped	¼	cup coarsely chopped epazote
3	medium tomatoes	2	potatoes, peeled and cut in small cubes
2	tablespoons vegetable oil		
1	pound fresh whole shrimp		

Toast the chiles in a hot dry skillet for 1 minute, tossing constantly so they do not burn. Place the chiles in a heat-resistant bowl, cover with water, and soak for 15 minutes. Next, drain the chiles and reserve the water.

Put the drained chiles in a small blender along with the garlic and onion, and purée the ingredients. Add more of the soaking water, if necessary, to form a smooth paste. Set this mixture aside.

Roast the tomatoes by holding them over a gas flame until they blister; or gently roll them in a small, dry saucepan until they start to blister. Remove the skins, crush them between your fingers, and add them to the heated vegetable oil in a saucepan. Sauté the tomatoes for 30 seconds and then add the reserved chile mixture, and sauté for 30 seconds; remove the pan from the heat and reserve.

Wash the shrimp, place them in a small saucepan, cover with water, and add the salt, pepper, and epazote. Bring the water to a boil, reduce the heat to a simmer, and cook for 2 minutes. Remove the shrimp from the water (reserve the cooking water) and, when they are cool enough to handle, clean them and cut in half lengthwise.

Cook the potatoes in the shrimp water for 10 minutes, or until they are tender (reserve 1 cup of the water) and then drain the potatoes. Add the sliced shrimp and potatoes to the chile mixture and toss to blend. Heat the mixture to serve.

Serves: 3

Heat Scale: Mild

Empanadas de Camarón
(Shrimp Turnovers)

This recipe features both fresh and dried shrimp. These spicy empanadas from Nayarit are served hot with the warm salsa on top. Prepare the salsa first, so that the flavors can blend. Serve with a citrus fruit salad.

Salsa

1   tablespoon olive oil

2   cups peeled and chopped tomatoes

6   tomatillos, husks removed, coarsely chopped

2   cloves garlic, minced

3   *serrano* chiles, stems and seeds removed, minced

3   *de árbol* chiles, stems and seeds removed, crushed

½   teaspoon salt
    Water as needed

¼   cup chopped cilantro

Heat the olive oil in a small saucepan and then add the tomatoes, tomatillos, garlic, and *serrano* chiles, and sauté for 2 minutes. Stir in the crushed *de árbol* chiles and salt, and check the thickness of the mixture. Add enough water to make a nice, thick, spoonable salsa. Simmer the mixture for 1 minute and remove from the heat. Stir in the cilantro and set aside.

Shrimp Filling and Tortillas

2   pounds fresh shrimp
    Water to cover

1   *ancho* chile, seeds and stem removed, broken into several pieces

½   teaspoon salt

2   cloves garlic

¾   teaspoon Mexican oregano

¾   cup minced, sautéed onion

2   tablespoons minced cilantro

2   tablespoons dried shrimp

4   cups corn flour
    Corn oil or canola oil as needed

Wash the shrimp in cold water. Place them in a large, heavy pot and cover with cold water. Add the *ancho* chile, salt, garlic, and oregano, and bring the mixture to a boil; reduce the heat and simmer for 3 minutes, or until the shrimp turn pink. Remove the shrimp, reserve the water, and allow the water to cool. Remove the shells and finely chop the shrimp. Mix the shrimp with the sautéed onion and cilantro and set aside.

Strain the cooled, reserved cooking water, add the dried shrimp, and purée the mixture in a blender. Pour the puréed mixture into a large bowl and add the corn flour a little at a time, stirring thoroughly after each addition, until the mixture has a very thick, pasty consistency. Scoop out about ¼ cup of the dough, roll it into a ball, flatten it, and roll it out until it is ⅛ inch thick and about 6 inches in diameter. Continue this procedure with the remaining dough.

Heat the oil, ½ inch deep, in a large skillet to the sizzling point.

While the oil is heating, stuff each tortilla with several tablespoons of the minced shrimp mixture, roll, and seal the outer edge with a little water.

Fry the stuffed tortillas for 30 seconds on each side, remove, and drain on paper towels.

Arrange several stuffed tortillas on a warm dinner plate and top with the reserved salsa.

Serves: 6 to 7

Heat Scale: Hot

Denial of Chile

Chiles were as significant when they were absent as when they were present. The concepts, familiar to Europeans, of fasting and penance were widespread in Mesoamerica, and without exception the basic penance was to deny oneself salt and chile.

—Sophie Coe

Camarones Adobados Estilo de Baja
(Adobo Shrimp Baja Style)

If you can't find *mulato* chiles, substitute an extra *ancho* or *pasilla* chile. Serve this chile shrimp from Baja California with hot, cooked rice and complement the dish with sautéed baby vegetables.

2	dozen large, fresh shrimp	1	onion, cut into eighths
1	*mulato* chile, stem and seeds removed	2	cloves garlic
1	*ancho* chile, stem and seeds removed	½	teaspoon salt
		2	teaspoons Mexican oregano
1	*pasilla* chile, stem and seeds removed	2	tablespoons white wine vinegar
	Hot water as needed	2	tablespoons olive oil

Bring a small pot of water to a boil. Rinse the shrimp in cold water, then add the shrimp to the boiling water. Boil for 3 minutes or until the shrimp turn pink. Drain the shrimp and peel them when they are cool enough to handle; set aside.

Toast the chiles in a skillet, over low heat, for 1 minute, tossing them and taking care that they don't burn. Remove the pan from the heat, cover the chiles with hot water, soak them for 10 minutes.

Place the chiles and the soaking water in a blender and add the onion, garlic, salt, oregano, and white wine vinegar. Purée until smooth.

Heat the oil in a small skillet and pour in the puréed chile mixture and simmer for 5 minutes, adding more water if the mixture gets too thick. Add the shrimp, mix it with the chile sauce, and simmer for 30 seconds.

Pour the shrimp mixture into a lightly oiled, small casserole dish and bake for 5 minutes in an oven preheated to 350 degrees F. Serve the shrimp hot from the oven.

Serves: 4

Heat Scale: Medium

Camarones Adobados Estilo Veracruz
(Adobo Shrimp Veracruz Style)

The Veracruz style of this dish requires that the shrimp be sautéed rather than boiled, as in the Baja style. The chiles and the cider vinegar add spark to this recipe. Serve with warm tortillas and a shredded lettuce, tomato, and *jícama* salad with an oil and vinegar dressing.

4	tablespoons corn or canola oil	1	teaspoon ground black pepper
1	pound fresh shrimp, peeled	⅓	cup apple cider vinegar
1	onion, cut into eighths	½	teaspoon whole cumin seeds, crushed
2	cloves garlic		
5	*pasilla* chiles, seeds and stems removed, roasted		

Heat 2 tablespoons of the oil in a medium-sized skillet, add the shrimp, and sauté for 2 minutes. Using a slotted spoon, place the shrimp in a small bowl and set aside.

Add another tablespoon of the oil to the shrimp skillet and sauté the onion and garlic for 1 minute. Remove the skillet from the heat and stir in the chiles, black pepper, vinegar, and cumin. Allow the mixture to cool for a few minutes and then put the mixture into a blender and purée until smooth.

Heat the remaining tablespoon of oil in the skillet, add the puréed chile mixture, and simmer for 15 minutes, stirring frequently; add enough water to keep the mixture thick and heavy and to avoid burning.

Add the reserved shrimp to the sauce and simmer for 2 minutes, only long enough to heat the mixture and to allow the chile flavor to infuse the shrimp. Serve hot.

Serves: 2 to 3

Heat Scale: Medium

Barbacoa de Langostinos

(Barbecued Langostinos)

This is a beautifully spiced way of serving *langostinos!* Because the meat is so rich, serve the dish with simple but elegant side dishes, such as a tomato salad with balsamic vinegar dressing and maybe some good pasta. A citrus dessert would be the perfect finish. To give this recipe an authentic touch, serve the *langostinos* and chile sauce as they do in Veracruz—on banana leaves.

4	*ancho* chiles, seeds and stems removed	1	cup chopped onion
3	*pasilla* chiles, seeds and stems removed	¾	teaspoon ground black pepper
	Boiling water as needed	2	whole cloves, ground
6	tablespoons corn or canola oil	¼	teaspoon cinnamon
3	cups peeled, coarsely chopped tomatoes	½	teaspoon cumin
		2	tablespoons white wine vinegar
½	teaspoon salt	2	pounds cleaned *langostinos*, split lengthwise; or substitute lobster tails
10	cloves garlic, minced		

Tear the chiles into strips and cover with 1 cup boiling water. Soak the chiles for 10 minutes; put the chiles and soaking water into a blender, purée, and set aside.

  Heat 3 tablespoons of the oil in a medium-sized skillet and sauté the tomatoes, salt, half of the minced garlic, onion, ½ teaspoon of the ground black pepper, half of the ground cloves, cinnamon, cumin, and puréed chile mixture; simmer, covered, for 15 minutes. Remove from the heat and reserve.

  In a small bowl, mix the remaining garlic, ground cloves, and black pepper, and the vinegar. Set aside.

  Cook the *langostinos* in a pot of boiling water for 8 minutes. Drain them and plunge into cold water to cool them quickly. Cube the *langostinos*. Toss the meat in the bowl with the reserved garlic–vinegar mixture.

Heat the remaining 3 tablespoons of oil in a saucepan, add the *langostino* mixture, and sauté for 30 seconds. Next, add the reserved chile mixture, bring the mixture to a boil, then quickly reduce the heat to a simmer, cover, and simmer for 5 minutes, or until it is hot. Serve immediately.

Serves: 3 to 4

Heat Scale: Mild

Cuisine Arthropoda

Mexican cuisine has all the colors of the rainbow and even the food has exotic names: *escamoles* (ant's eggs), *acociles* (tiny river shrimp), *chapulines* (grasshoppers), *gusanos de maguey* (agave worm), *jumiles* (green pyramidal insects). Scorpions are eaten in the states of Durango—famous for its large, blond ones—and Sonora. They are fried and dipped in sauce and eaten. We take off the poison sac and stinger before frying.

—Beatriz Cuevas Cancino

Chiles Rellenos de Mariscos
(Seafood-Stuffed Poblano Chiles)

The state of Quintana Roo has become popular, along with the rest of the Yucatán peninsula, for both its Mayan ruins and delicious seafood. The use of *habanero* chiles in this recipe is also very typical of this area.

3 tablespoons corn oil	1 whole egg and 1 egg white, beaten
1 pound mixed seafood, cleaned and chopped	¾ cup flour
2 cloves garlic, finely chopped	Oil for frying
½ teaspoon salt	2 tablespoons oil
¼ teaspoon freshly ground black pepper	1 cup chopped onion
½ teaspoon dried Mexican oregano	1 *habanero* chile, seeds and stems removed, minced
3 tablespoons finely chopped cilantro	1 *xcatic* chile seeds and stems removed, minced; or substitute yellow wax hot
3 tablespoons white sauce	4 cups peeled, deseeded, chopped tomatoes
6 *poblano* chiles, roasted and peeled, seeds removed	

Heat the oil and sauté the seafood; add the garlic, salt, black pepper, oregano, and cilantro and simmer until the seafood is cooked. Remove the skillet from the heat and stir in the white sauce to bind the ingredients. Add more white sauce, if necessary.

Using a small spoon, stuff the seafood mixture into the chiles. Dredge the chiles in the flour, dip them into the beaten egg mixture, and fry in the hot oil for 2 minutes on each side. Drain them on paper towels and place them on a heated platter.

Heat the 2 tablespoons of oil in a medium skillet and sauté the onion, *habanero,* and *xcatic* chiles for 1 minute. Add the tomatoes and cook the sauce for 2 minutes over a low heat.

Spoon the sauce over the rellenos and serve.

Serves: 3

Heat Scale: Hot

Ensaladas y Arroz y Frijoles

Salads and Accompaniments

Vegetables and side dishes—what we all bring to potluck parties. But take a look at their history, and it may inspire you to create even tastier accompaniments. Think of spicy Mexican, with its herbs, spices, and chiles, and you too can create something so dynamic that it will outshine the standard potluck entrée!

The New World vegetables that were cultivated in Mexico sustained both rich and poor alike. Corn, beans, squash, and chiles were nutritious and valuable as commodities. Wild corn and squash are reputed to have been the first cultivated crops in the ancient Valley of Mexico, circa 4000 B.C.

Squash is available to everyone, but fresh squash blossoms, piled high in Mexican markets, are some of the most fragrant and delectable parts used in special recipes, such as Lula Bertrán's elegant *Ensalada de Flor de Calabaza con Vinagre Enchilado* (Squash Blossom Salad with Chile Vinegar, page 206).

The chayote squash is well seasoned in the Hidalgan recipe *Chayotes Exquisitos* (Exquisite Chayotes, page 205), with its simple but tasty composition of corn, chiles, and cheese. Equally as delicious and easy to prepare is *Calabacitas en Adobillo* (Squash in Adobo Sauce, page 208), a side dish from Sinaloa, with its infusion of garlic, herbs, and *ancho* chiles.

Another side dish equally spiced with chiles is the Sonoran *Ensalada de Garbanzos* (Chickpea Salad, page 209). A healthy mix of garbanzo beans laced with chile, citrus juice, and cilantro will give a new meaning to salad!

The next recipes are called enchiladas, but they are side dishes as well and are often served with spicy grilled meat. The recipe for *Echiladas Estilo Sonora* (Sonoran Enchiladas, page 210) was given to us by a native of Sonora. *Chiltepines* make the sauce fiery but delicious, as these enchiladas are served over homemade puffy tortillas sprinkled with cheese. Another very different style of enchilada is included from Yucatán. *Papadzul* (Enchiladas Stuffed with Hard-Cooked Eggs, page 214) are distinguished by the use of a green oil that is squeezed from toasted pumpkin seeds.

Other ingredients particularly used in the Yucatán (cilantro, *habanero* chiles, and epazote) spice up *Huevos Uxmal* (Uxmal-Style Eggs, page 212). The eggs are served with either a green or red sauce. Another egg recipe from Yucatán—*Huevos Motuleños* (Motuleño Eggs, page 215)—comes from the city of Motul. Fried eggs are smothered with beans and a fiery Yucatán-style tomato sauce, laced with the local *habanero* chiles.

Even mushrooms do not escape the fire of chiles in Mexico. A great variety of wild mushrooms can be found in the markets, particularly during the rainy season. From Morelos comes the recipe for *Hongos con Chile Pasilla*

(Mushrooms with Pasilla Chiles, page 216), which is an excellent dish to serve with grilled beef or pork. Served hot or cold, *Setas à la Vinagreta* (Mushrooms Vinaigrette, page 217) from Veracruz are marinated and cooked with vinegar, herbs, and vegetables.

Two rich and delicious side dishes are presented next. *Rajas con Crema* (Sliced Chile with Cream, page 218) from Jalisco includes fried *poblano* chiles enriched with cream and served over rice. Corn is given an elegant treatment in the rich recipe, *Elote con Crema y Chiles Serranos* (Spicy Creamed Corn and Serrano Chiles, page 219), from Morelos. The combination of fresh sweet corn, serranos, and cream make a lively side dish. The importance of corn cannot be underestimated in Mexico.

Chiles can be stuffed with practically anything, as evidenced in the next recipes, and served as an attractive addition to any meal. *Chiles Rellenos de Aguacate* (Avocado Rellenos, page 220) from Zacatecas are served at room temperature or chilled. The last-minute addition of sour cream makes this dish rather like guacamole in a chile. Warm rellenos stuffed with squash blossoms and corn are featured in *Chiles Rellenos de Verdura* (Vegetable Rellenos, page 221), a specialty of Morelos. Dried *pasilla* chiles are also stuffed in the recipe *Chiles Pasillas Tlaxcaltecas* (Pasilla Chiles in Sweet Sauce, page 222). In this recipe from Tlaxcala, the stuffed chiles are braised in a *piloncillo* (brown sugar) sauce and are delicious served with chicken or duck.

Beans are served all day, every day in Mexico—breakfast, lunch, dinner—the omnipresent bean is there. And everyone eats beans, from the society matron to the peasant; in fact, it was the combination of beans and corn that was the food foundation of the Indian civilization in this hemisphere. The Coahuilan *Frijoles Charros Numero Uno* (Cowboy Beans #1, page 224) is loaded with a variety of meats, chiles, and good taste. This recipe will convert even a nonbean eater! A Sonoran recipe of the same name, *Frijoles Charros Numero Dos* (Cowboy Beans #2, page 228), differs from the previous one in that homemade salsa is added at the end of cooking, along with *chicharrón* or crisp fried pork rind. *Frijoles Zacatecanos* (Zacatecas-Style Beans, page 226) is a combination of two kinds of dried beans, pork ribs, chiles, and cream. The beans are drained and mashed and served on a platter.

Rice, like beans, is featured predominantly in Mexican cuisine. Rice was introduced into Mexico in the 1600s and has been a popular foodstuff ever since. *Arroz con Chiles Poblanos Rojos* (Rice with Red Poblano Chiles, page 229) from Nuevo León is a full-bodied dish with the addition of *jalapeños*, beef stock, red *poblanos*, and a topping of hard-boiled eggs. From Veracruz comes

Arroz Con Rajas y Elotes (Rice with Sliced Chiles and Corn, page 230), a delicious dish accented with *poblano* chiles, cream, and Gruyére cheese. Since it is so rich, serve it with simple, grilled meat.

Ironically, Mexican cuisine focuses heavily on rice, while potatoes, native to the New World, have largely been ignored. (Rice recipes probably outnumber potato recipes five to one—we will attempt to remedy that!) The first potato recipe, *Papitas con Chile* (Potatoes with Chile, page 231), uses one of Sonora's hottest chiles, the *chiltepín*, to spice up the potatoes. From Tlaxcala comes *Barbacoa de Papa* (Barbecued Potatoes, page 232) with its multitude of ingredients—herbs, spices, chiles, fresh mint—all blending together to spark up the blandness of the potatoes.

An unusual taste treat that needs little enhancing is the Guerreran side dish *Chile de Mango* (Mango Chile, page 233). The delicious mango (a fruit that you should eat while you are naked in the shower) is turned into a chunky, cooked sauce spiked with *guajillo* chiles and garlic. Serve it alongside roast pork, and you'll never serve applesauce again!

Chayotes Exquisitos

(Exquisite Chayotes)

Squash is one of the staples of the New World foods, and in this recipe from Hidalgo it is chayote squash that plays the starring role. Chayote has a delicate taste and takes well to any type of seasoning. Serve this side dish with a spicy pork recipe from Chapter 5.

4	*poblano* chiles, roasted, peeled, seeds and stems removed	Water as needed
1	tablespoon vegetable oil	½ cup milk
2	tablespoons butter	½ teaspoon salt
1	cup chopped onion	¼ teaspoon freshly grated black pepper
5	chayotes, washed and cut into eighths	1 cup grated Monterey Jack cheese
1½	cups whole corn kernels, preferably fresh off the cob	

Cut the roasted chiles into 1-inch square pieces and set aside.

Heat the oil and the butter in a skillet, add the onion, and sauté for 1 minute. Next, add the chayote squash and the corn and sauté over low heat for 2 minutes. If the mixture starts to dry out, add a few tablespoons of water.

Stir in the cubed chiles, milk, salt, and pepper and simmer until the chayote has softened.

Remove the sautéed mixture to a small glass baking dish, cover with the cheese, and bake at 350 degrees F for 10 minutes, or until the cheese has melted.

Serves: 6

Heat Scale: Mild

Ensalada de Flor de Calabaza con Vinagre Enchilado

(Squash Blossom Salad with Chile Vinegar)

According to Lula Bertrán, "We use squash blossoms very often in our recipes. We think they are very Mexican. What I wanted to do in this recipe was use my vinegar because everyone loves it so much. The vinegar will work in any kind of salad." Note that the vinegar must sit for at least 2 days.

Chile Vinegar

1	cup apple cider vinegar	4	*chiltepines,* or substitute chile *piquins*
2	cloves garlic		
6	black peppercorns	1	*serrano* chile, seeds and stem removed, halved
6	white peppercorns		
6	green peppercorns	1	sprig fresh basil
1	*chile de árbol,* or substitute ½ New Mexican chile	2	sprigs fresh rosemary
		1	bay leaf

Combine all ingredients for the vinegar in a bottle. Cover and let sit in a cool place for at least 2 days, but preferably 1 month.

Squash Blossom Salad

1½	cups julienned *jicama*	½	teaspoon roasted sesame seeds
	Watercress	½	cup Chile Vinegar
	Mixed lettuce leaves		Salt and freshly ground pepper to taste
8	large squash blossoms (or substitute other edible flowers), minced	½	cup grated goat cheese
½	cup sesame oil		

To assemble the salad, place the julienned *jícama* in a cross-hatched pattern on the center of each of four salad plates. Cover partially with the watercress and lettuce leaves. Sprinkle on the minced squash blossoms.

In a jar, mix together the sesame oil, sesame seeds, Chile Vinegar, and salt and pepper. Lightly pour the dressing over the salads and top with the goat cheese.

Yield: 1 cup vinegar; 4 servings of salad

Heat Scale: Mild

Note: Requires advance preparation.

Mexican Chile Defined

It is a product of acrid flavor, piquant and heat-generating, which from the earliest times the Indian made a part of his diet, approaching it with a kind of mystical and religious unction. Over the years it has come to set the tone, both in its general and special application, of the original Mexican cuisine.

—Amando Farga

Calabacitas en Adobillo

(Squash in Adobo Sauce)

When you eat chayote squash, you are eating a part of history, starting with the Aztecs and the Mayas. Chayote was one of the mainstays of their diet. The squash has a delicate taste and takes well to high seasoning. This side dish from Sinaloa goes well with any recipe from Chapters 5, 6, and 7.

2	*ancho* chiles, seeds and stems removed	2	teaspoons butter or vegetable oil
1	cup hot water	¼	chopped onion
3	cloves garlic	3	tablespoons dried bread crumbs
1	teaspoon dried thyme	2	tablespoons cider vinegar
¼	teaspoon ground cumin	1	pound chayote squash, peeled and sliced into ¼-inch slices
½	teaspoon salt	½	cup water to steam squash

Tear the *ancho* chiles into strips, put them into a small dish, add 1 cup of hot water, and let the chiles rehydrate for 20 minutes.

Pour the chiles and water into a blender and add the garlic, thyme, cumin, and salt and purée until smooth. Set aside.

Heat the butter in a skillet and sauté the onion for 1 minute. Add the chile purée to the onion, along with the bread crumbs and cider vinegar, cover, and simmer for 10 minutes. Stir the mixture and add more water or stock if the mixture gets too thick.

While the sauce is simmering, steam the chayote squash in ½ cup water for 8 minutes. Drain and then add to the simmering sauce. Serve immediately.

Serves: 5 to 6

Heat Scale: Mild

Ensalada de Garbanzos

(Chickpea Salad)

Serve this delicious Sonoran-style dish over shredded mixed greens to accompany one of the fish dishes from Chapter 7. We recommend using freshly cooked chickpeas, but the canned variety will also work if the peas are thoroughly rinsed.

	Juice of 1 lemon	6	ounces cream cheese, softened
	Juice of 2 limes	2	*poblano* chiles, roasted and peeled, seeds and stems removed, chopped fine
¼	cup minced cilantro		
¼	cup olive oil		Mixed greens
¾	cup minced onion		
2½	cups cooked chickpeas		

Mix the citrus juices, cilantro, olive oil, and onion in a medium-sized glass bowl. Allow to stand at room temperature for 3 hours.

In a small bowl, combine the cooked chickpeas, softened cream cheese, and the chiles and mix thoroughly. Add this mixture to the marinated citrus mixture and mix thoroughly.

Serve the mixture over shredded mixed greens.

Serves: 4

Heat Scale: Mild

Note: Advance preparation required.

Enchiladas Estilo Sonora

(Sonoran Enchiladas)

These enchiladas are not the same as those served north of the border. The main differences are the use of freshly made, thick corn tortillas and the fact that the enchiladas are not baked. Cindy Castillo, who is well versed in Sonoran cookery, prepared these for us. Serve the enchiladas with some grilled chicken and drizzle some of the red chile sauce over the chicken before serving.

The Sauce

15	to 20 *chiltepínes,* crushed	3	cloves garlic
15	dried red New Mexican chiles, seeds and stems removed	1	teaspoon vegetable oil
1	teaspoon salt	1	teaspoon flour
	Water to boil chiles		

In a saucepan, combine the chiles, salt, and enough water to cover. Boil for 10 or 15 minutes or until the chiles are quite soft.

Allow the chiles to cool and then purée them in a blender along with the garlic. Strain the mixture, mash the pulp through the strainer, and discard the skins.

Heat the oil in a saucepan and add the flour. Brown the flour, taking care that it does not burn. Add the chile purée and boil for 5 or 10 minutes until the sauce has thickened slightly. Set aside and keep warm.

The Tortillas

2	cups masa *harina*	1	teaspoon salt
1	egg		Water
1	teaspoon baking powder		Vegetable oil for deep frying

Mix the first four ingredients together thoroughly, adding enough water to make a dough. Using a tortilla press, make the tortillas. Deep fry each tortilla in vegetable oil until it puffs up and turns slightly brown. Remove, drain on paper towels, and keep warm.

To Assemble and Serve

2   cups grated *queso blanco* or
    Monterey Jack cheese
    Shredded lettuce

3   to 4 scallions, minced (white
    part only)

Place a tortilla on each plate and spoon a generous amount of sauce over it. Top with the cheese, lettuce, and scallions.

Serves: 4 to 6

Heat Scale: Hot

A Lust for Chiles

Chile peppers were such a novelty to the Spanish explorers in Mexico that rumors were rampant about their medical properties. The Jesuit priest, poet, and historian, José de Acosta, wrote in 1590, "Taken moderately, chile helps and comforts the stomach for digestion." The priest undoubtedly had heard rumors about the reputed aphrodisiac qualities of chiles because he continued his description of chile with the following warning: "But if they take too much, it has bad effects, for of itself it is very hot, fuming, and pierces greatly, so the use thereof is prejudicial to the health of young folks, chiefly to the soul, for it provokes to lust." Despite the good father's suspicions, the only thing lustful about chiles was the desire everyone, including the Spanish, had to devour them.

Huevos Uxmal

(Uxmal-Style Eggs)

All the flavors of Yucatán—including cilantro, *habanero* chiles, and epazote—
are found in this dish. The diner has a choice of green or red sauce over the
poached eggs. Cook the sauces first, so that they are ready when the eggs are
done.

Green Sauce

1	teaspoon vegetable oil	½	teaspoon salt
4	epazote leaves, chopped	1	green bell pepper, roasted,
10	tomatillos, coarsely chopped		peeled, seeds and stem
¾	to 1 cup water		removed, quartered
1	*habanero* chile, seeds and stems removed, halved	2	teaspoons coarsely chopped epazote
4	tablespoons coarsely chopped cilantro		

Heat the oil in a small skillet and sauté the epazote and the tomatillos for
1 minute, or until the tomatillos are softened. Allow the mixture to cool for
a few minutes, and then place it in a blender with the water, *habanero* chile,
cilantro, salt, green bell pepper, and the epazote and purée the mixture.
Return this mixture to the skillet and keep it warm.

Red Sauce

1	teaspoon vegetable oil	½	teaspoon salt
8	tomatoes, roasted, peeled, and quartered	1	*habanero* chile, seeds and stem removed, cut in half
½	cup coarsely chopped onion	2	tablespoons chopped cilantro
¼	cup coarsely chopped cilantro		

Heat the oil in a small skillet and add the tomatoes, onion, cilantro, salt, and chile and sauté for 1 minute. Allow the mixture to cool slightly and then pour it into a blender and purée. Return this mixture to a small saucepan, add the 2 tablespoons chopped cilantro, and keep the sauce warm.

The Eggs

12   fresh eggs, poached in molds, or in a large skillet with 2 table-spoons vinegar added to the water

Place two poached eggs on a warm dinner plate and serve with the red and/or green sauce.

Serves: 6

Heat Scale: Medium

Papadzul
(Enchiladas stuffed with Hard-Cooked Eggs)

We want to thank Nancy and Jeff Gerlach for this recipe, which is unique to Yucatán. They note: "These enchiladas are traditionally served garnished with a green oil that is squeezed from toasted pumpkin seeds. This is a very old recipe and it was reputed to have been served by the Maya to the Spaniards when they arrived in the New World, which is possible since the name means 'food of the lords.'"

2   large tomatoes, peeled and chopped

1   *habanero* chile, stem and seeds removed; or substitute 2 *jalapeño* or 3 *serrano* chiles

2   leaves fresh epazote; or substitute 1 tablespoon dried

2   cups chicken broth

1   small onion, chopped

2   tablespoons vegetable oil

1   cup toasted pumpkin seeds, finely ground

8   corn tortillas

6   hard-cooked eggs, peeled and chopped

Combine the tomatoes, chiles, epazote, and broth in a pan. Bring to a boil and cook for 5 minutes. Remove and strain, saving both the tomatoes and the broth.

Sauté the onion in half of the oil until softened. Place the onion in a blender or food processor, and add the tomato mixture. Purée until smooth. Sauté this sauce in the remaining oil for 5 minutes.

Heat the strained tomato broth and slowly stir in the pumpkin seeds. Simmer until the mixture thickens and has the consistency of thick cream, stirring constantly. Be careful the sauce does not boil or it may curdle.

Dip the tortillas in the warm pumpkin seed sauce to coat and soften. Place some of the chopped eggs in the center, roll up, and place on a platter. Pour the remaining pumpkin seed sauce over the top, then the tomato sauce, and serve.

Serves: 4

Heat Scale: Medium

Huevos Motuleños

(Motuleño Eggs)

The city of Motul near Mérida is where this recipe originated. This is Yucatán's version of *huevos rancheros*. The *chiltomate* is a very traditional Yucatecan tomato sauce; some cooks say that the tomatoes should just be grilled and never fried, and still others maintain that frying brings out additional flavor. Serve this as an accompaniment with some spicy grilled fish from Chapter 7 for a big, luscious Yucatán-style dinner.

2	tablespoons corn oil
1	cup chopped onion
1	clove garlic, minced
3	tomatoes, grilled, peeled, and chopped
1	*habanero* chile, seeds and stem removed, minced
½	teaspoon salt
¼	teaspoon freshly ground black pepper
¼	cup chicken stock or water

10	corn tortillas, cut into eighths, fried, drained, and coarsely crushed by hand; or substitute 3 cups coarsely crushed packaged corn tortilla chips
3	cups refried black beans, thinned with 3 tablespoons water
10	fried eggs
1	cup chopped boiled ham
1½	cups cooked peas
1½	cups crumbled *queso blanco*; or substitute goat cheese or feta

Optional garnish: sliced bananas

Heat the oil in a medium-sized skillet and sauté the onion for 1 minute, and then add the garlic, tomatoes, *habanero* chile, salt, and pepper and simmer for 5 minutes, adding chicken stock if the mixture gets too thick.

While this mixture is simmering, arrange the tortilla chips on a warm platter and cover them with the hot refried beans.

Top the beans with the fried eggs, ham, and peas, and cover with the simmering tomato sauce. Sprinkle the cheese over the top and serve.

Serves: 5

Heat Scale: Medium

Hongos con Chile Pasilla

(Mushrooms with Pasilla Chiles)

Mushrooms are very plentiful in Morelos and throughout most of central Mexico. The following recipe is very easy to prepare and is a great favorite with cooks throughout the region. If wild mushrooms are not available, we suggest a mixture of button, oyster, shiitake, and maybe even a small portabello for interest. Serve this with a meat dish from Chapter 5.

3	*pasilla* chiles, toasted, seeds and stems removed	1	to 2 tablespoons oil
	Hot water as needed	¾	cup thinly sliced onion
8	cloves garlic, 4 whole and 4 minced	1	pound wild mushrooms, left whole if small, thickly sliced if large
3	tablespoons butter	¼	cup chopped epazote

Soak the toasted chiles in hot water for 15 minutes. Drain and reserve the water. Place the chiles in a blender with the 4 whole garlic cloves and purée, adding a few tablespoons of the reserved water to make a thick sauce.

Heat the butter and oil in a large saucepan and sauté the onion and minced garlic over low heat for 1 minute, stirring constantly, so the garlic doesn't burn.

Add the mushrooms and toss with the onion mixture over low heat for 2 minutes. Next, add the chile purée and epazote and simmer for 5 minutes. Serve hot.

Serves: 6

Heat Scale: Mild

Setas à la Vinagreta
(Mushrooms Vinaigrette)

Since a wide variety of mushrooms is found in Mexico, it is no wonder that they are used extensively in many different kinds of dishes. This spicy side dish is from Veracruz, and we suggest serving it with one of the fish dishes from Chapter 7, or one of the meat entrées from Chapter 5.

3 tablespoons olive oil	1 tablespoon Mexican oregano
1½ cups thinly sliced carrots	1 tablespoon dried thyme
2 cups thinly sliced onion	¼ teaspoon cumin
3 *jalapeño* chiles, seeds and stems removed, sliced into rings	1 tablespoon whole black peppercorns, coarsely ground in a food processor
5 cups cleaned, sliced mushrooms	
2 whole bay leaves	5 cloves garlic, minced
½ teaspoon salt	¼ cup cider vinegar

Heat the oil in a saucepan and add the carrots, onion, chiles, and mushrooms and sauté the mixture for 1 minute, tossing and stirring. Add the bay leaves, salt, oregano, thyme, cumin, ground peppercorns, garlic, and vinegar. Cover and simmer for 15 minutes.

Remove the bay leaves. Serve the mushrooms hot, or chill the mixture for several hours and serve cold.

Serves: 5

Heat Scale: Medium

Rajas con Crema
(Sliced Chiles with Cream)

This accompaniment is from Jalisco, an area rich in food and traditions, and boasting the famous city of Guadalajara. Mary Jane ate in a large restaurant there that specialized in *cabrito* (goat), and the waiters wore roller skates! Serve this classy dish over hot, cooked rice, and, for the entrée, serve a simple, spicy grilled fish recipe from Chapter 7.

8	*poblano* chiles, roasted, peeled, seeds and stems removed	2	to 2½ cups chicken broth
3	tablespoons butter	¾	cup cream
3	tablespoons oil	¼	pound grated *asadero* cheese; or substitute *queso blanco* or Monterey Jack cheese
3	cups thinly sliced onion		
½	teaspoon salt		
¼	teaspoon freshly ground black or white pepper		

Slice the *poblano* chiles into strips and set aside.

Heat the butter and oil in a medium-sized saucepan and add the onions; sprinkle with the salt and pepper and sauté the onions for 3 minutes, or until they just begin to brown.

Stir in the reserved chile strips and toss the mixture over low heat for 1 minute.

Add 2 cups of the chicken broth and the cream to the onion–chile sauté; bring the mixture to a light boil and reduce the heat immediately to a simmer. Stir the mixture frequently until it starts to thicken slightly, about 1 minute. If it thickens too much, too fast, add a few tablespoons of the chicken stock.

Sprinkle the cheese over the mixture and gently mix into the simmering mixture. Serve immediately over hot, cooked rice.

Serves: 4 to 5

Heat Scale: Mild

Elote con Crema y Chiles Serranos
(Spicy Creamed Corn and Serrano Chiles)

The state of Morelos is beautiful and diverse. Mary Jane lived in Cuernavaca for 3 months while going to summer school language classes and ate herself silly the entire time! This rich side dish is very typical of the area, and we suggest serving it with a simple, spicy grilled meat from Chapter 5.

5	ears fresh corn, steamed for 3 minutes
2	tablespoons butter or vegetable oil
¼	cup minced onion
4	*serrano* chiles, seeds and stems removed, minced
¼	cup chopped epazote
2	tablespoons water
¼	cup milk
½	teaspoon salt
¼	teaspoon freshly grated black pepper
¾	cup cream, warmed
½	cup grated white cheese, such as Mexican *queso blanco*

When the corn has cooled enough to handle, cut the kernels from the ears and set aside.

Heat the butter in a small saucepan and add the onion, chiles, and epazote and sauté for 30 seconds. Next, add the water, milk, salt, black pepper, and the reserved corn and bring the mixture to a light boil. Reduce the heat to a simmer and add the cream and the cheese; simmer only until heated through, and the cheese is melted, and do not let the mixture boil.

Serves: 4

Heat Scale: Medium

Chiles Rellenos de Aguacate

(Avocado Rellenos)

Mary Jane first saw Zacatecas from a train in 1970, and she bought some beautiful wool ponchos, negotiating the whole deal from the train window. She also ate some great food from the vendors; the train system had forgotten to attach the dining car! These tasty rellenos can be served at room temperature or slightly chilled. Try serving them at a buffet; the entrée could be a spicy meat or chicken entrée from Chapter 5 or 6.

3	large, ripe avocados, peeled and pitted	¾	cup grated *queso blanco* cheese, or substitute Monterey Jack
2	teaspoons fresh lemon juice	3	tablespoons olive oil
1	teaspoon fresh lime juice	6	*poblano* chiles, roasted, peeled, seeds and stems removed, left whole
½	teaspoon salt		
¼	teaspoon freshly ground black pepper	6	tablespoons sour cream
¼	cup minced onion		

In a ceramic or Pyrex bowl, coarsely chop the avocados; next, add the citrus juices, salt, pepper, onion, cheese, and olive oil and mix well with the avocados.

Stuff the avocado mixture into the chiles; arrange the stuffed chiles on a platter, and cover each chile with the sour cream. Serve at room temperature.

Serves: 6

Heat Scale: Mild

Chiles Rellenos de Verdura
(Vegetable Rellenos)

Squash blossoms are a common ingredient in many Mexican recipes. Check with a Latin American market in your area; if it doesn't carry them, you can probably special order them. The taste of the blossoms is exquisite. The heat of this recipe is mild, so serve it with one of the spicier fish or meat entrées.

2	tablespoons butter	½	teaspoon salt
2	tablespoons vegetable oil	¼	teaspoon freshly ground black pepper
1	cup coarsely chopped carrots		
1	cup chopped onion	1	cup milk
3	cups chopped chayote squash, or substitute zucchini	½	cup grated *queso blanco* cheese, or substitute Monterey Jack
½	cup fresh corn kernels	10	*poblano* chiles, roasted, peeled, seeds and stems removed
1	cup chopped squash blossoms	⅔	cup cream

Heat the butter and oil in a saucepan and add the carrots, onion, squash, and corn and sauté for 2 minutes. Add the squash blossoms, salt, and black pepper and sauté until the pan is almost dry.

Add the milk, bring the mixture to a boil, reduce the heat to a simmer, and simmer until the mixture has thickened, about 4 to 5 minutes. Stir in the cheese and remove the pan from the heat.

Using a teaspoon, stuff the chiles with the cooked squash mixture. Arrange the stuffed chiles on a warmed serving platter and drizzle 1 tablespoon of cream over each chile. Serve warm.

Serves: 5

Heat Scale: Mild

Chiles Pasillas Tlaxcaltecas

(Pasilla Chiles in Sweet Sauce)

Here's a dish from Tlaxcala that *norteamericanos* will find very unusual! *Piloncillo* is unrefined brown sugar, and dark brown sugar makes a good substitute. It is delicious, especially if you serve it with a spicy seafood dish from Chapter 7; the sweet taste will complement the hot and spicy flavoring of the seafood.

5   tablespoons olive oil

1   tablespoon butter

3   cups thinly sliced onion

5   cloves garlic, minced

2   cups water

2   cups *piloncillo*, or substitute dark brown sugar

12   *pasilla* chiles, seeds and stems removed

½   pound *manchego* cheese, cut into 12 thick strips; or substitute Parmesan

Heat the oil and the butter in a large saucepan and sauté the onions for 1 minute. Add the garlic and sauté for 2 minutes more.

Add the water and the *piloncillo*, bring the mixture to a boil, reduce the heat, and simmer the mixture until it thickens to the consistency of honey.

Stuff each chile with a piece of the cheese, taking care not to break the chile. Place the stuffed chiles in the simmering skillet and sauté over low heat until the cheese starts to soften.

Place two chiles on a plate and drizzle some sauce over them.

Serves: 6

Heat Scale: Mild

Stalking the Flaming Canary

The chile *canario,* which is found in limited quantities in the Oaxaca and Michoacán areas of Mexico, is the only member of the species *Capsicum pubescens* found in North America. At first glance, the pods look much like Habanero chiles. They are found green, but more often they are bright yellow or orange, hence the name: canary peppers. There is no mistaking the *canario* for the Habanero once you've cut one open, however; the seeds of the *canario,* like all members of the *pubescens* species, are always black. The plant itself is also impossible to mistake. *Capsicum pubescens* features purple flowers and dark purplish stalks which are covered with hairy fuzz. The chile *canario* is usually roasted, cut into strips and combined with lengthwise slices of raw onion and moistened with lime juice. This salsa is traditionally served with *totopos,* the Oaxaqueño version of tortilla chips. The chile *canario* is very thick-walled and has a rich, fruity flavor when roasted. Whether eaten raw or roasted, *canarios* are hot, but nowhere near as hot as habaneros. The mystery of the *canario* pepper is how this lone member of the South American rocoto family came to grow in North America. Does it represent the beginning of a northward spread of the species *Capsicum pubescens?* If so, why are the recipes for its use so well-known among the Zapotec Indians of Oaxaca? Could the chile *canario* be the last vestige of an "endangered species," an old strain of *Capsicum* that is dying out in North America?

—Robb Walsh

Frijoles Charros Numero Uno

(Cowboy Beans #1)

Beans, or *frijoles*, are an integral part of Mexican cuisine—from border to border and from coast to coast. There are many kinds of dried beans available, and they are cooked in every possible method and manner, sometimes adding a bit of this and that. A rich bean pot in Mexico is akin to a multi-ingredient omelet or a casserole in the states! Our first version of Cowboy or Ranch-Style Beans is from Coahuila.

2	pounds *flor de mayo* beans, or substitute pink or pinto beans
	Water to cover
5	*serrano* chiles, seeds and stems removed, cut into slices
1	cup coarsely chopped onion
1	cup chopped tomato
½	cup chopped cilantro
4	cloves garlic, chopped

¼	teaspoon freshly ground black pepper
¼	pound chopped bacon or salt pork
¼	pound pork sausage
½	pound pork meat, cut into ¼-inch cubes
¼	pound chorizo
¼	pound chopped ham

Wash and pick over the beans. Place the beans in a very large, heavy casserole pot, cover with cold water, bring to a boil for 2 minutes, and then turn off the heat. Allow the beans to sit, covered, for 1 hour. Drain the beans, return them to the pot, cover with hot water, and bring them to a boil; add the chiles, onion, tomato, cilantro, garlic, and black pepper. Reduce the heat to a simmer and cover.

Sauté all of the meats together in a large skillet for 3 minutes. Drain off all of the fat and blot the meat with paper towels. Add the meats to the simmering beans, cover, and simmer for 3½ hours. Stir the beans several times during the cooking and, if more water is needed, add hot water only. The bean mixture should have a slightly soupy consistency.

Serve hot with any type of entrée or with warmed tortillas.

Serves: 10 to 12

Heat Scale: Medium to Hot

Note: Advance preparation required.

Frijoles Zacatecanos
(Zacatecas-Style Beans)

This side dish is very substantial and should be served with a light entrée, such as one of the chicken recipes in Chapter 6 or fish recipes in Chapter 7. The layering of the different colors of the mashed beans gives this dish an artistic look that will most certainly please both the eye and the mouth.

½ pound canary beans, washed and picked over; or substitute pinto beans

½ pound black beans, washed and picked over

Water to cover

½ pound pork ribs, excess fat removed

6 tablespoons vegetable oil

1½ cups chopped onion

4 *poblano* chiles, roasted, peeled, seeds and stems removed, and cut into strips

2 cups roasted, peeled, chopped tomatoes

¾ cup cream

½ cup grated aged *cotija* cheese; or substitute mild Cheddar

4 corn tortillas, quartered and fried; or substitute store-bought tortilla chips

Place the two different types of beans into separate large saucepans, cover with cold water, bring to a boil, cover, and boil for 1 minute. Turn off the heat and allow the beans to soak for 1 hour. Drain the beans and return them to their separate pans. Cover them with hot water, bring to a boil, cover, and simmer for 1 to 1½ hours, or until tender.

While the beans are cooking, wash the pork ribs. Place them in a small saucepan, cover with cold water, bring the water to a boil, reduce the heat to a simmer, and cook for 20 minutes. Remove the ribs from the water and drain, reserving the cooking broth. Remove the bones and coarsely shred the pork, discarding any fat that remains. Set aside.

When the beans are done, drain them and keep the two types separate. Heat 2 tablespoons of the oil in each of two separate small skillets and add the beans. Mash them with a potato masher, add ½ cup of the onion to each skillet, and simmer for a minute or two. If the beans start to get too thick, add a few tablespoons of the reserved pork cooking broth to thin slightly.

Heat the remaining 2 tablespoons of oil in another skillet and sauté the remaining ½ cup onion and the shredded pork. Add the chiles and the tomatoes and simmer for 1 minute. Next, stir in the cream and remove the skillet from the heat and let it sit for 3 minutes.

On a small, decorative heated platter, spread a thin layer of the canary beans, top with some of the pork mixture, then spread a thin layer of black beans, and repeat the layers until all of the beans and pork are used up. Sprinkle the top with the grated cheese and arrange the tortillas (or corn chips) around the platter.

Serves: 5

Heat Scale: Mild

Note: Advance preparation required.

Mexican Cuisine, circa 1890

During this epoch, Mexico attained a high degree of grandeur in its cuisine, which had been endowed with a sense of universality. This was the result of the crops of the Indian; the innumerable contributions from Spain; the spices, fruits, and rice which poured in with every arrival at Acapulco of the historic *Nao de la China,* the Manila galleon, which arrived from the distant Philippine archipelago. This splendor also derived from the use of slaves; the visits by pirates who made frequent incursions along the Mexican coasts; the French invaders; immigrants from all parts of the world, bringing about a veritable gastronomic revolution of major proportions, unequalled by most countries of the world.

—Amando Farga

Frijoles Charros Numero Dos

(Cowboy Beans #2)

Here is our second version of Cowboy Beans, this one from Sonora. The *chicharrón* in this recipe is fried pork cracklings, and can be seasoned with different sauces and seasonings, depending on the region. In the United States, *chicharrón* can be purchased in many grocery stores, since former President George Bush made them famous—as his favorite snack!

1	pound pinto beans, cleaned	¼	cup ground *ancho* chiles
	Water to cover	2	cups *Salsa Chile de Árbol*
2	cups beer, not dark		(page 21)
3	tablespoons vegetable oil	¾	cup *chicharrónes*
1	pound cooked pork, shredded		

Place the beans in a large, heavy casserole pot, cover with cold water, bring to a boil, and boil for 2 minutes. Turn off the heat and allow the beans to sit for 1 hour. Drain the beans and return them to the cleaned casserole. Add the beer, and enough hot water to cover (to about 2 inches above the beans). Bring the mixture to a boil, reduce the heat to a simmer, and partially cover.

Heat the oil in a skillet and sauté the shredded pork, *ancho* chiles, and salsa and simmer for 1 minute. Stir this sautéed mixture into the cooking beans, cover, and simmer for 3 to 3½ hours, stirring occasionally, and adding more water if the beans get too dry. You want a semisoupy consistency.

Just before serving, stir the *chicharrón* into the beans.

Serves: 6

Heat Scale: Medium

Note: Advance preparation required.

Arroz con Chiles Poblanos Rojos
(Rice with Red Poblano Chiles)

This rice recipe from Nuevo León is unusual because of the addition of tomatillos and sliced hard-boiled eggs. The roasted red *poblano* chiles add color and a dash of heat. Serve the rice with a chicken dish from Chapter 6.

3	tablespoons olive oil	½	teaspoon salt
2	cups rice	¼	teaspoon freshly ground black pepper
1	cup minced onion		
2	cloves garlic, minced	4	cups chicken or beef stock
2	*jalapeño* chiles, seeds and stems removed, cut into thin rings	2	red *poblano* chiles, roasted, peeled, and chopped
1	cup chopped tomatillos	2	hard-boiled eggs, sliced
½	teaspoon ground cumin		

Heat the oil in a medium-sized saucepan and sauté the rice, onion, garlic, *jalapeño* chiles, tomatillos, cumin, salt, and black pepper for 2 minutes, or until the rice turns golden. Stir in the broth, bring the mixture to a boil, cover, and reduce the heat. Cook the rice for 20 minutes.

Stir in the red *poblano* chiles and the eggs and serve.

Serves: 4 to 6

Heat Scale: Medium

Arroz con Rajas y Elotes
(Rice with Sliced Chiles and Corn)

Rice, chiles, and corn are all combined in this delicious side dish from Veracruz. Serve it with a fish recipe from Chapter 7, befitting Veracruz's seaside location.

4	tablespoons vegetable oil	¾	cup whole-kernel corn, canned or frozen
1	cup rice	¼	cup cream
1	cup chopped onion	¾	cup grated Gruyère cheese
2	cloves garlic, minced	4	*poblano* chiles, roasted, peeled, seeds and stems removed, and chopped
2	cups water		
½	teaspoon salt		

Heat 3 tablespoons of the oil in a small saucepan and sauté the rice over low heat until it turns golden, about 1 minute, stirring constantly. Add half of the chopped onion and all of the garlic and sauté for 1 minute more. Next, add the water and salt, and bring the mixture to a boil. Reduce the heat to a simmer, cover, and cook for 20 minutes.

While the rice is cooking, heat the remaining 1 tablespoon of oil in a small skillet and sauté the remaining ½ cup of chopped onion for 1 minute. Then add the chopped chiles and sauté for 30 seconds. Add the corn and the cream and heat the mixture at low heat; do not boil.

Spoon the cooked rice into a small, oven-proof glass baking dish (such as Pyrex) and mix in the chile–corn–cream sauté. Cover the mixture with the grated cheese and bake for 10 to 15 minutes at 350 degrees F, or until the cheese has melted and the mixture is heated through.

Serves: 4

Heat Scale: Mild

Papitas con Chile
(Potatoes with Chile)

This recipe is extremely hot and very typical of Sonora, where people make *Salsa Casera* (page 20) with 2 to 3 cups of *chiltepines!* To reduce the heat, add fewer *chiltepines.* Serve this with a mild fish entrée from Chapter 7.

3	tablespoons butter	5	cloves garlic
3	tablespoons olive oil	¼	cup *chiltepín* chiles
2	pounds potatoes, peeled and diced into ½-inch cubes	1	cup water
		½	teaspoon salt
3	tablespoons water		

Heat the butter and olive oil in a large skillet and add the diced potatoes. Toss and turn the potatoes with a spatula for 1 minute. Reduce the heat to a simmer, add 3 tablespoons of water, and cook the potatoes at low heat while you make the chile sauce.

Place the garlic, chiles, 1 cup water, and salt in a blender and purée thoroughly. Pour this mixture over the potatoes and simmer for 10 to 15 minutes, or until the potatoes are tender.

Serves: 4

Heat Scale: Extremely Hot

Barbacoa de Papa

(Barbecued Potatoes)

Potatoes, one of the New World crops, stars in this recipe from Tlaxcala. It's a new twist to warm potato salad, redolent with chile, herbs, and spices; serve it at your next hot and spicy Mexican barbecue.

4	*guajillo* chiles, seeds and stems removed; or substitute New Mexican dried red chiles	½	teaspoon ground cumin
		1	teaspoon dried thyme
	Hot water to rehydrate	1	teaspoon Mexican oregano
3	tablespoons vegetable oil	½	teaspoon salt
1	cup chopped onions	2	whole bay leaves
3	cloves garlic, minced	½	cup chopped mint
¼	teaspoon cinnamon	4	cups potatoes, cut in ½-inch cubes
2	whole cloves, ground in processor		

Tear the chiles into strips, place them in a small saucepan, cover with boiling water, and rehydrate for 20 minutes. Pour the mixture into a blender and purée until smooth. Set aside.

Heat the oil in a medium-sized skillet and sauté the onion and garlic for 1 minute. Pour in the chile purée and add the cinnamon, ground cloves, cumin, thyme, oregano, salt, bay leaves, and mint and simmer for 2 minutes. If the mixture starts to thicken too much, add a few tablespoons of water.

Add the cubed potatoes and coat with the chile mixture. Cover and simmer the potatoes for 15 to 20 minutes, or until the potatoes are tender. Remove the whole bay leaves and serve.

Serves: 4 to 5

Heat Scale: Medium

Chile de Mango

(Mango Chile)

This recipe from Guerrero is unusual—a fruity and slightly spicy dish. Mango and chile have a natural affinity for each other, as their flavors blend and meld to create a most delicious taste. Serve this dish with a chicken or fish entrée from Chapter 6 or 7.

7	*guajillo* chiles, toasted, seeds and stems removed	½	teaspoon salt
	Hot water to rehydrate	3	tablespoons butter
3	cloves garlic	6	ripe mangos, peeled and cut into small cubes

Place the toasted chiles in a small bowl, cover with hot water, and soak them for 15 minutes. Drain the chiles and reserve the soaking water; place the chiles in a blender with the garlic and the salt and purée, adding a few tablespoons of the reserved soaking water if the chile mixture becomes too thick. Heat the butter in a small saucepan, add the puréed chile mixture, and simmer for 10 minutes. Remove the purée from the heat and allow it to cool.

When the mixture has cooled to room temperature, stir in the cubed mangos and serve.

Serves: 4

Heat Scale: Medium

Bebidas y Postres
Drinks and Desserts

What a wealth of drinks and desserts has Mexico! As with sauces, entire
books have been written on the subject, so our approach is simple: We
have selected our favorite accompaniments and finishes to the other recipes in
this book.

The drinks of Mexico range from simple punches to more complicated
mixed drinks. In some cases, chile still plays a role. In Oaxaca, according to
Patricia Quintana, "In the better bars of the capital, cocktail glasses are often
rimmed with *sal de gusano*—a mixture of salt, crushed chile, and dried maguey
worms—and filled with *mezcal*." The recipe for *Tequila Enchilado* (Chilied
Tequila, page 238) eliminates the insects, but still has chiles and chile powder—
along with other spices—to fire it up.

Of course, one of the most famous Mexican drinks is the margarita, and
dozens of stories tell of its supposed invention. One of our favorite tales holds
that the drink was invented by Francisco "Pancho" Morales in 1942. We have
no idea if that story is true, but Francisco "Pancho" Morales' Perfect, Original
Margarita (page 239) is by far our favorite version of the drink. For more margarita tales, and for the complete story of tequila drinks, we highly recommend
the book *¡Tequila!* by Lucinda Hutson (Ten Speed Press, 1995). A fine chaser
for tequila is *Sangrita de Chapala* (Chapala's Little Bloody Drink, page 240),
which is sweet and spicy at the same time.

No Mexican cookbook would be complete without a hot chocolate drink,
and we offer a slightly modified recipe from Tabasco, *Chocolate con Canela*
(Hot Chocolate with Cinnamon, page 241). Chocolate was often combined
with chile powder as a royal drink at the court of Moctezuma.

Fruit drinks are very popular in the country, and *Ponche de Piña* (Pineapple Punch, page 242) from Colima uses strawberries—a favorite fruit. *Bebida
de Piña y Mango con Mezcal* (Pineapple–Mango Drink with Mescal, page 243)
combines mango and mescal with pineapple. Other favorite fruits—oranges and
bananas—meet in *Bebida de Naranja y Plátano* (Orange–Banana Drink, page
244). Our final two drinks are fruitlike, but one is based on a flower and the
other on a bean: *Ponche de Jamaica* (Hibiscus Punch, page 245) is based on *flor
de Jamaica*, a flavorful hibiscus, while the tangy tamarind bean stars in *Agua
Fresca de Tamarindo* (Tamarind Refresher, page 246).

Our desserts begin with puddings. *Flan Estilo Rancho Aurora*, or
Coconut Ginger Flan from Rancho Aurora (page 247), is a creative version of
the classic Mexican pudding, *flan. Capirotada Mexicana Estilo Zacatecas*
(Mexican Bread Pudding Zacatecas Style, (page 248) is our favorite bread pudding, while our favorite Mexican rice pudding is *Arroz con Leche* (page 249).

Postre de Jícama y Coco (page 250) is an interesting dessert featuring coconut and *jícama,* a vegetable not often associated with desserts. Also flavored with coconut is *Mermelada de Piña, Manzana, Naranja y Coco* (Mixed Fruit Marmalade with Coconut, page 251).

Cakes, pies, breads, and their like complete our selection of Mexican desserts. *Buñuelos Estilo Querétaro,* or Dessert Fritters Querétaro Style (page 252), are unusual because they are made with corn instead of wheat flour and are not leavened. A delicious festival cake, *Pastel de Festejo* (page 254), from Yucatán is served at weddings and other celebrations. Delicate ladyfingers, almonds, raisins, and cinnamon make *Ante de Almendra* (Almond Dessert, page 253) a delicious offering. *Pan de Muertos* (page 256), the "Bread of the Dead," is served on All Souls Day as a tribute to ancestors. The famous Mexican cookies called *Bizcochitos de Naranja* (page 257) complete our sampling of Mexican desserts.

The Ten-Year Crop

There is no vintage tequila. One reason is that agave is harvested continuously—there is no single harvest to which a vintage could be attributed. Another reason is the agave's slow growth cycle. Season variations in the big weather picture don't affect it as they do grapes. Theoretically, a single load of *piñas* would manifest the composite effect of a decade's worth of weather. Not even the most slavish wine nerd could hope to make much of that.

—Rod Smith

Tequila Enchilado
(Chilied Tequila)

Lula Bertrán says that she invented this recipe about 20 years ago, after hearing about spiced vodkas. She said to herself, "Why not put some Mexican spices with a Mexican liquor?" It makes eminent sense to us, Lula.

1	liter white tequila	2	long lime peels
10	coriander seeds	2	tablespoons salt
10	*chiltepínes* or *piquín chiles*	1	teaspoon *chile piquín* powder
10	black peppercorns	½	lime
2	sprigs cilantro		

Open the bottle of tequila and add the coriander seeds, *chiltepínes*, peppercorns, cilantro, and lime peels. Close the bottle and refrigerate for at least 4 hours, preferably overnight.

Combine the salt and *chile piquín* powder in a shallow bowl and mix.

To serve, pass the lime over the rims of shot glasses, dip the glasses in the salt mixture, and pour in the chilled and chilied tequila.

Yield: 1 liter

Heat Scale: Medium

Note: Requires advance preparation.

Francisco "Pancho" Morales's Perfect, Original Margarita

This recipe was collected by Elaine Corn, writing in *Chile Pepper*. According to her research, a bartender by the name of Francisco "Pancho" Morales claimed the invention of the margarita in Ciudad Juárez in 1942. "The two parts doesn't mean jigger and it doesn't mean bottles," warns Pancho. "I've seen this all mixed up."

Juice of ½ lime		2	parts white tequila
Salt		1	part Cointreau

Squeeze about an ounce of lime juice from a Mexican *limón* (not a Persian lime) into a shaker glass filled with chunks (not cubes) of ice (never shaved). Take the squeezed *limón* and run it around the rim of a cocktail glass. Put the glass on a towel, sprinkle it lightly with salt, and then shake off *all* the excess salt. Now, allowing for the juice already in the glass, and any ice that may have melted to contribute to the 4-ounce final tally of liquid, the remainder of the formula requires enough tequila (please, a great tequila like Herradura) and Cointreau (never Triple Sec), two parts to one, to equal exactly 4 ounces of drink to be shaken, strained, and poured off into a 4-ounce cocktail glass. This takes some skill, but it's not brain surgery.

Serves: 1

Sign in a 17th Century *Pulquería*

Vayan entrando, vayan bibiendo;
Vayan pagando, vayan saliendo.

(Keep coming in, keep drinking,
Keep paying up, keep leaving.)

Sangrita de Chapala
(Chapala's Little Bloody Drink)

This particular version of *sangrita*, or "little bloody drink," comes from Chapala, where the bartenders have not succumbed to the temptation of adding tomato juice to this concoction, as the *norteamericanos* do. The bloody color comes from the grenadine, so this is truly a sweet heat drink that is also salty. Some people take a sip of tequila after each swallow of *sangrita*, while others mix one part tequila to four parts *sangrita* to make a cocktail.

2 cups orange juice	1 tablespoon salt
¾ cup grenadine syrup	
2 teaspoons Mexican hot sauce of choice (or substitute any *habanero* hot sauce)	

Combine all ingredients in a jar, shake well, and chill.

Yield: About 3 cups

Heat Scale: Medium

It Should Have Been Titled
Under the Tequila

The boy brought them camarones, red shrimps in a saucer, and had to be told again to get the tequila. At last it arrived . . .

"Do you really like it?" M. Laurelle asked him, and the Consul, sucking a lemon, felt the fire of the tequila run down his spine like lightning striking a tree which thereupon, miraculously, blossoms.

—Malcolm Lowry, *Under the Volcano*, 1947

Chocolate con Canela
(Hot Chocolate with Cinnamon)

Traditionally, Mexican hot chocolate is beaten at the table with a *molinillo*, a carved wooden stirrer made specifically for preparing hot chocolate—it is rubbed between the palms. *Molinillos* are available in Mexican specialty shops. The hot chocolate should be served in heavy earthenware mugs—preferably emblazoned with chile peppers. This drink is our version of a recipe from Tabasco.

⅓	cup cocoa	2	cups half-and-half
1	tablespoon flour	1	cup milk
⅓	cup sugar	1½	teaspoons vanilla
¾	teaspoon ground cinnamon	1	cup whipped cream
¼	teaspoon ground cloves		Freshly grated nutmeg
1	cup water	6	whole cinnamon sticks

Combine the cocoa, flour, sugar, cinnamon, and cloves with the water in a large saucepan. Stir or whisk until well blended. Heat until bubbling and just barely beginning to simmer.

   Gradually add the half-and-half, then the milk, in a very fine stream, stirring all the time. Beat with your *molinillo* or a whisk. Heat until hot, but do not boil, and keep warm for at least 5 minutes.

   Whip the chocolate again with the *molinillo* until it is frothy, just before serving. Top with a dollop of whipped cream, a pinch of nutmeg, and then insert a cinnamon stick into the cream.

Serves: 6

Ponche de Piña

(Pineapple Punch)

From Colima comes this refreshing—and powerful—punch that utilizes one of Mexico's favorite fruit. This recipe makes enough punch for a medium-sized party.

3	ripe pineapples, peeled, cored, and chopped	2	cups red wine
4	quarts water	2	cups rum
2	cups sugar (or more to taste)		Sliced fresh strawberries for garnish
4	large lemons, juiced		

In batches in a blender, combine the pineapple and water and purée. Set aside.

Place the sugar in a saucepan and heat until the sugar melts. Add the pineapple, lemon juice, wine, and rum and stir well. Serve over ice in large glasses garnished with the strawberry slices.

Serves: 12 to 16

---

400 Bottles of *Pulque* on the Wall . . .

The Romans had only one god of drunkenness: Bacchus. The Aztecs had four hundred. Called the Four Hundred Rabbits, these deities presided over the four hundred different kinds of drinks that could be made with *pulque*— and the four hundred different ways you get crocked from drinking them.

—Patricia Sharpe

Bebida de Piña y Mango con Mezcal

(Pineapple–Mango Drink with Mescal)

Here is a tasty dessert drink from the state of Sinaloa. It is interesting because of the combination of fruits and mescal.

2	ripe mangoes, peeled, pitted, and chopped	1	cup orange juice
½	ripe pineapple, peeled and chopped	1	cup mescal
¼	cup sugar	½	cup sweet cream, whipped
			Fresh mint leaves for garnish

In batches in a blender, combine the mangoes, pineapple, sugar, and orange juice and purée. Remove from the blender and stir in the mescal. Refrigerate for about 3 hours. Serve in individual glasses, topped with whipped cream and garnished with mint leaves.

Serves: 6

Note: Advance preparation required.

The Legacy of Tequila

The Spanish conquerors in Mexico were quick to learn that the heart of the agave contained a sap that could be distilled. During the nineteenth century, the spirits produced in Tequila gained a considerable reputation, and in 1873 there were already sixteen distilleries in the little town in the province of Jalisco. Today, some 435 million agave plants are to be found in the landscape surrounding Tequila.

—Charles Schumann

Bebida de Naranja y Plátano

(Orange–Banana Drink)

Here is another dessert drink, this time from Nuevo León. This one is fruit based as well, but combines yogurt and rum to make a seemingly innocent drink.

1	banana, peeled	½	cup yogurt
1	cup orange juice	2	tablespoons sugar
1	tablespoon lemon juice	¼	cup rum

Cut the banana into quarters crosswise. Slice one of the quarters and reserve the slices. Combine the remaining banana with the orange juice, lemon juice, yogurt, and sugar and purée. Once blended, add the rum and mix well. Serve garnished with the banana slices.

Serves: 2

Mexican Alcoholic Drinks
Not Included in This Book

Curados: Pulque enriched with oats, celery, and almonds, from Mexico City

Teshuino: Corn fermented with brown sugar, from Jalisco

Tlanichicole: Macerated aromatic and medicinal herbs in alcohol, from Veracruz

Tuba: Fermented coconut palm sap, from Guerrero

Ponche de Jamaica

(Hibiscus Punch)

Known as *roselle* and Jamaican sorrel in the Caribbean, these hibiscus flowers are popular in Mexico as the basis of many drinks. This particular one from Colima is served garnished with ground peanuts. *Flor de Jamaica* is available from Latin markets and mail-order spice suppliers.

¼	pound dried *flor de Jamaica*	½	cup sugar
1½	quarts water	¼	cup finely ground peanuts
½	liter dark rum		

In a pan, combine the flowers and water and bring to a boil. Boil briskly for 10 minutes. Remove from the heat and allow to cool. In a blender, liquefy the flower mixture. Add the rum.

Heat the sugar in a saucepan until melted. Remove from the heat and slowly add the flower water, mixing well.

Serve warm in mugs and add peanuts to taste.

Serves: 6

Mezcal Ritual

It is interesting to note that in drinking *mezcal* or tequila, a special custom has been developed, which has become almost a ritual. First, a small amount of salt is placed between the thumb and index finger of the left hand. Then, the salt is picked up by the tongue as the liquor is lifted with the other hand. The drinker alternately sucks half a lime as he imbibes the drink and licks the salt.

—Amando Farga

Agua Fresca de Tamarindo

(Tamarind Refresher)

This recipe, a favorite all over Mexico, was collected by Robb Walsh. He wrote in *Chile Pepper*: "This is the perfect drink for a hot day. I like beer too, but you can only drink so many of them. *Agua Fresca* is thirst-quenching, has more nutritive value than tea or water, and you can drink lots without worrying about caffeine or alcohol. Kids love it and it goes great with spicy food, too!"

½   pound tamarind beans   1   gallon water
¾   cup of sugar or honey

Rinse the beans and drain them. Put the beans in a soup pot and add enough water to cover them. Cook at a low boil for 10 minutes or so. Mash the softened beans vigorously with a potato masher. Strain the coffee-colored liquid into a gallon container, throwing away the seeds and outer pods as you go. Add the sugar or honey while the liquid is hot. Add water to fill the container. Refrigerate and serve over ice.

Yield: 1 gallon

Variation: Adjust the sugar level to your taste. Use the specified equivalent amount of artificial sweetener for the diet version. Serve over more or less ice to make it as strong or weak as you like.

Flan Estilo Rancho Aurora

(Coconut Ginger Flan from Rancho Aurora)

From our correspondent in Oaxaca, Susana Trilling, comes this tasty variation on traditional flan. She noted in *Chile Pepper:* "This is one of the favorite desserts of my students at Rancho Aurora. It's much better to make it a day ahead and chill it icy cold."

¼	cup plus 3 tablespoons sugar	6	eggs
½	cup sliced almonds	5	egg yolks
2	12-ounce cans coconut milk (not sweetened coconut milk or coconut cream)	¼	teaspoon vanilla extract
		1	tablespoon crystallized ginger, minced
½	cup milk		

Preheat the oven to 350 degrees F. In a saucepan melt ¼ cup of the sugar over medium heat until brown and bubbly; do not stir. Remove and pour into a *flan* pan (a round, 9-inch pan) and rotate the pan so the sugar syrup completely covers the bottom. Top with the almonds and set the pan aside.

Combine the coconut milk, remaining 3 tablespoons of sugar, milk, eggs, egg yolks, and vanilla and whisk well. Add the ginger, stir well, and pour the mixture into the pan.

Place the pan in a water bath, cover with aluminum foil, and bake for 1 hour. Remove from the oven and chill.

To serve, flip the pan over on a platter, garnish with more ginger, and slice thinly.

Serves: 6

Capirotada Mexicana Estilo Zacatecas

(Mexican Bread Pudding Zacateca Style)

This is a version of bread pudding as prepared in Zacatecas. This dessert is served during Lent. Feel free to substitute French bread for the *bolillos*. Serve it with ice cream or whipped cream.

3 cups water	⅓ cup peanuts, peeled and coarsely chopped
2 cups *piloncillo,* or substitute brown sugar	⅓ cup raisins, coarsely chopped
1 cinnamon stick	Melted butter as needed for the mold
2 cloves	2 eggs, separated
4 cups dried *bolillos* or other rolls, broken up into small cubes	3 teaspoons sugar
¼ cup vegetable oil for frying	⅔ cup shredded coconut
1 cup grated *añejo* cheese; or substitute mild Cheddar	

Combine the water, *piloncillo,* cinnamon, and cloves in a saucepan and bring to a boil. Boil until it becomes a syrup about as thick as honey. Remove the cinnamon stick and cloves.

In a pan, fry the bread in the oil, stirring constantly, until it is slightly browned. Remove and drain on paper towels.

In a bowl, combine the cheese, peanuts, and raisins and mix well.

Grease a baking dish with enough butter so that the sugar won't stick. Coat the dish generously with the syrup, then alternate adding the bread and cheese mixtures in layers. Pour the remaining syrup over all.

Beat the egg whites until stiff; carefully spoon the beaten egg whites over the top layer in the pan, covering it. Mix the coconut and sugar and sprinkle on top of the meringue. Bake at 350 degrees F until the meringue starts to brown, about 20 minutes.

Serves: 6 to 8

Arroz con Leche

(Rice Pudding)

Here's a version of rice pudding that's popular all over the country. Legend holds that, like *mole poblano*, this recipe was invented by nuns in Puebla.

2	cups water		1	cup milk
½	cup uncooked rice		1	cup sugar
1	cinnamon stick		¼	cup raisins
2	eggs			

Combine the water, rice, and cinnamon stick in a large saucepan and mix well. Let stand overnight.

Over low heat, cook the mixture, stirring frequently, until the water is absorbed. Cool the mixture to room temperature.

Beat the eggs with the milk and stir in the sugar until well mixed. Add the egg mixture and the raisins to the rice mixture. Simmer, stirring constantly, until thickened (about 10 minutes). Remove the cinnamon stick; serve the pudding warm or cold.

Serves: 4

Note: Requires advance preparation.

Postre de Jícama y Coco

(Jícama–Coconut Dessert)

Jícama, the succulent tuber that is so tasty in salads, is transformed into a unique but simple dessert in this recipe from Nayarit. Serve this with one of our favorite dessert drinks, *Bebida de Naranja y Plátano* (page 244).

½ pound *jícama*, peeled and grated	1½ cups sugar
½ cup shredded coconut	Dash ground cinnamon or nutmeg (optional)
Juice of 1 orange	

In a saucepan, mix the *jícama* and coconut together, then add the orange juice and sugar. Cook gently over medium heat for about 10 minutes, stirring constantly.

Transfer the mixture to a bowl and refrigerate. When thoroughly chilled, transfer to individual bowls and dust with the cinnamon or nutmeg.

Serves: 4

Cacao Currency

Chocolate was so expensive that it could hardly have been the drink of poor peasants. It was used in Mexico as a currency instead of the coinage that the Aztecs had never originated. The pods of the cacao were made up into packs of 24,000 pods as a standard unit of currency.

—Carson Ritchie

Mermelada de Piña, Manzana, Naranja y Coco

(Mixed Fruit Marmalade with Coconut)

Although called a marmalade, this delicious dessert from Hidalgo can be served in a bowl, topped with whipped cream, or as a topping itself for ice cream or bread pudding.

2½ cups pineapple, finely chopped	1 teaspoon orange zest
2½ cups apples, finely chopped	2 cups sugar
Juice of 2 oranges	1½ cups shredded coconut

Combine the pineapple, apples, orange juice, and orange zest in a saucepan and cook over low heat for about 5 minutes, stirring constantly. Add the sugar and continue cooking until the sugar is dissolved. Add a little water if the mixture becomes too dry.

Remove the pan from the heat, stirring constantly, and add the coconut. Allow to cool and serve.

Serves: 6

Buñuelos Estilo Querétaro

(Dessert Fritters Querétaro Style)

Most *buñuelos* are made from wheat flour and are leavened with yeast or baking powder. These from Querétaro use corn masa and are not leavened. Traditionally they are served on Christmas Eve with a hot chocolate such as *Chocolate con Canela* (page 241).

10 tablespoons butter
3   cups corn masa (dough)
8   eggs
1   teaspoon anise
1   cup sugar mixed with 1
    teaspoon cinnamon

6   cups dark brown sugar
2   cups water
3   cinnamon sticks

Heat 3 tablespoons of butter in a skillet. Add the masa to the skillet and fry, stirring well, until the masa is dry and slightly toasted.

Remove the skillet from the heat and add the eggs, one by one, and the anise, stirring well until completely mixed.

Form the masa mixture into any desired shapes and fry the *buñuelos* in the remaining butter. When they are browned, remove them from the skillet and drain on paper towels. Dust them with the sugar and cinnamon.

To make the syrup, combine the brown sugar, water, and cinnamon sticks in a saucepan and cook over high heat until reduced to a thick syrup. Remove the cinnamon sticks and serve over the *buñuelos*.

Serves: 6 to 8

Ante de Almendra

(Almond Dessert)

In Oaxaca, *antes* are special desserts like this one. Serve this with hot chocolate or coffee with Kahlúa.

1½ cups ground almonds	2 cups sugar
3 cups milk	2 cups water
1 cup sugar	2 cinnamon sticks
Prepared ladyfingers or spongecake	2 cups dry sherry

Garnishes:

¼ cup slivered almonds
¼ cup raisins
   Ground cinnamon

In a saucepan cook the almonds, milk, and 1 cup sugar over very low heat until the flavors are blended (approximately 1 hour and 15 minutes).

Arrange a single layer of ladyfingers or spongecake on the bottom of an 8- by-8-inch baking dish and set aside.

To make the syrup, combine 2 cups sugar, water, cinnamon sticks, and sherry in a saucepan and boil until it reaches a thick consistency. Remove the cinnamon sticks.

Pour the syrup over the ladyfingers until they are covered. Then add half of the almond mixture. Cover the almond mixture with another layer of syrup (leaving a little in reserve) and another layer of ladyfingers. Allow to sit for about 10 minutes, then pour the remaining almond mixture over it. Garnish with the almonds, raisins, and cinnamon and serve.

Serves: 8

Pastel de Festejo

(Festival Cake)

This exquisite cake from Yucatán is served at weddings and other festivities. Some cooks shave bittersweet chocolate over the finished cake.

Cake

1	pound butter	1	tablespoon vanilla
2	cups sugar	2	tablespoons cognac
12	eggs	3	cups flour
1	cup milk	2	tablespoons baking powder

Filling

¾	cup water	¾	cup ground almonds
2	cups sugar	3	egg yolks, beaten

Meringue

2	cups sugar	1	tablespoon lemon juice
1	cup water		Lemon zest to taste
2	egg whites		

To make the cake, grease three round cake pans and cut out a piece of parchment paper to fit the bottom of each. Preheat the oven to 300 degrees F.

In a bowl, cream the butter and sugar together and add the eggs, one at a time, along with the milk, vanilla, and cognac, stirring well. In another bowl, mix together the flour and baking powder, then add the dry mixture to the liquid mixture and mix well.

Pour an equal amount of this batter into each of the cake pans and bake for 25 to 20 minutes, or until a toothpick comes out clean; let the cakes cool.

To make the filling, dissolve the water and sugar in a saucepan over high heat. Remove the saucepan from the heat, add the almonds, and beat well. Add the egg yolks and cook for a few minutes until it becomes thick.

To make the meringue, heat the sugar in a saucepan with the water until it becomes thick; you should be able to create threadlike strands. In a separate bowl, beat the egg whites until they become stiff. Beat in the lemon juice and lemon zest, then add the sugar.

To assemble: Once the cakes have cooled, place them on a cake plate, alternating cake and filling. Then frost with the meringue.

Serves: 12

A Dessert So Big They Couldn't Eat It

The high point of the evening was the monumental "Mapa Mundi" cake, which consisted of a large base, from which there rose several architectural columns supporting a large globe of the earth, complete with continents and waters, all done in pastry and whipped cream frosting, in a variety of resplendent colors. A magnificent impression was made among the guests by this masterpiece of the pastry cook's art. Nobody dared suggest that this work be sliced up, and it was finally decided to follow the suggestion of the ASTA American directors, that it be offered, as a gesture of courtesy and as a souvenir, to Miguel Alemán, then president of the Republic.

—Amando Fargas, writing about the banquet for
the American Society of Travel Agents,
Chapultepec Castle, October 1949

Pan de Muertos
(All Souls Day Bread)

It is a tradition to bake this bread for Mexico's Day of the Dead (All Souls Day), which is celebrated on November 2. The round loaves are decorated with small "bones" and are taken to the cemetery as an offering to those who have passed on, and that's why an alternate name for this bread is "bread of the dead."

2	packages active dry yeast	2	tablespoons finely grated orange peel
½	cup warm water		
4	cups flour	1	teaspoon ground anise
½	cup sugar	1	cup butter or margarine at room temperature
½	teaspoon salt		
2	whole eggs	1	beaten egg for glaze
6	egg yolks	¼	cup sugar for topping

Dissolve the yeast in the warm water. Add enough flour (about ⅔ cup) to make a light dough. Knead on a lightly floured board until smooth and elastic. Shape into a ball and put in a warm place until doubled in size.

Sift the remaining flour together with the sugar and salt. Add the whole eggs, egg yolks, grated orange peel, anise, and butter. Knead until soft. Add the risen yeast dough. On a lightly floured board knead the dough until smooth. Place in a greased bowl and let rise in a warm place. When the dough has doubled, knead lightly and shape into two round loaves, setting aside a small amount of dough to shape as "bones."

Roll the dough into small ropes resembling bones. Brush the loaves with the beaten egg. Attach the "bones" in the shape of a cross. Bake in the oven at 350 degrees F for about 30 minutes, or until the bread is golden brown. Remove from the oven and dust with sugar.

Yield: 2 loaves

Bizcochitos de Naranja
(Orange Cookies)

Bizcochitos are a favorite Mexican snack or dessert that is commonly served with coffee or hot chocolate. They are commonly flavored with anise, although this version has orange rind as well. This particular recipe comes from Mexico City.

2	cups flour	½	cup lard or shortening
½	cup sugar	1	egg, slightly beaten
4	teaspoons baking powder	1	cup milk
½	teaspoon salt	2	tablespoons grated orange rind
½	teaspoon cream of tartar	½	teaspoon powdered anise

Preheat the oven to 450 degrees F. Grease a baking sheet or cookie sheet.

In a large bowl, sift together the flour, sugar, baking powder, salt, and the cream of tartar. With a pastry blender, cut the shortening into the flour until the mixture resembles coarse crumbs.

Mix together the egg and milk and add this mixture to the dry ingredients. Stir until the dough is just mixed and place on a lightly floured surface. Add the orange rind and anise to the dough and knead very gently for 30 seconds. Drop the dough a teaspoonful at a time onto the greased baking sheet. Bake for 12 to 15 minutes.

Yield: 24 cookies

One Version of the Invention of the Margarita

It was American Independence Day, 1942. The heat was sweltering, and the scene was Ciudad Juárez, Mexico. Not that you couldn't celebrate the independence of America in Mexico. During those days, just over the bridge in Juárez's busiest commercial district, you could celebrate anything you wanted.

Pancho Morales was tending bar at Tommy's Place, a favorite hangout for GIs from Fort Bliss. A lady walked in, sat at the bar, and ordered a magnolia. The only thing Pancho knew about a magnolia was that it had lemon or lime in it and some kind of liquor. So he did what any good bartender would do—he winged it and used the most popular liquor served in Juárez: tequila.

With a single taste, the woman, who knew a magnolia was made of gin, cream, lemon juice, and grenadine, realized that the drink was an impostor, but liked it anyway because Pancho had loaded it up with enough tequila to make anyone smile. When she asked what the new drink was called, Pancho's brain was thinking flowers and m's, and had leaped from magnolia to *margarita*—Spanish for daisy. And so mixology history was made, and Pancho later immortalized the drink when he taught at the bartender's school in Juárez before immigrating to El Paso in 1974.

—Elaine Corn

Glossary of Mexican Chiles

Mexican chiles are available by mail order and can be found in natural foods markets, Latin markets, and some supermarkets in the West and Southwest. Unless otherwise specified, the chiles defined here are of the species *Capsicum annuum*. Researchers and cooks alike should be forewarned that the chile nomenclature of Mexico is often confusing. Some of the varieties have multiple names, and some names are used to describe multiple varieties. We have attempted to sort it out here.

Achocolatado: "Chocolaty"; another name for *pasilla*, probably a reference to its dark brown color.

Acorchado: "Corky"; A cultivated variety of *jalapeño*. The name is a reference to the "corking," or brown streaks, on the pod.

Ahumado: "Smoke-cured"; referring to *chipotle* chiles.

Altamira: A cultivated variety of *serrano*.

Amarillo: Any yellow chile, but specifically *chilcoxtle*.

Amash: A *piquín* chile that grows wild in Tabasco, Chiapas, and Yucatán. Very hot and consumed in the green form.

Amomo: A variety of *piquín* chile. *Amomo* is a botanical name referring to the pepper's resemblance to grains of paradise; also called *malegueta* pepper.

Anaheim: *See* New Mexican.

Ancho: "Wide" or "broad"; a dried *poblano* chile. It is a large, broad, mild chile with a raisiny aroma and flavor. Confusingly, *ancho* is called *pasilla* in Morelia and Michoacán, and *chile joto* in Aguascalientes. It is also called *pasilla* in some northern states and in California.

Apaseo: A cultivated variety of *pasilla*.

Balín: "Bullet"; a cultivated variety of *serrano* chile.

Bandeño: In the state of Guerrero, a name for the green *costeño*. The name refers to the bank of a river.

Bola: "Ball" or "marble"; *see Cascabel*. Also, in Jalisco, a word for a round *piquín*.

Bolita: "Little ball"; *see Cascabel*.

Boludo: "Bumpy"; *see Cascabel*.

Bravo: "Brave, wild, savage"; a local name for *chile de árbol*.

Caballo: "Horse"; another name for *rocoto*.

Cambray: A long, narrow chile grown in San Luis Potosí and marketed in Monterrey.

Canario: "Canary"; a yellow variety of the *rocoto*, or *chile manzano*.

Candelaria: A cultivated variety of *jalapeño*.

Capon: An emasculated chile; one with the seeds removed.

Caribe: A variety of *güero* grown in Aguascalientes; usually found fresh, it has a conical shape, is about 1½ inches long, and is colored yellow.

Carrocillo: A name in central Mexico for the *güero*.

Cascabel: "Jingle bell" or "rattle"; an allusion to the seeds rattling in the pods of this oval chile, which is about 1½ inches in diameter and dark red in the dried form. When fresh it is called *bola*, *bolita*, and *boludo*. Dried, *cascabeles* are also known as *coras* and *guajones*. Grown in Jalisco and Guerrero.

Casero: "Homemade"; in the state of Guerrero, a name for the green *costeño*.

Catarina: A dried chile from the state of Aguascalientes; it is 1 to 2 inches long, ½ inch wide, and the seeds rattle in the pods. Possibly a variety of *de árbol*.

Chiapas: A name for the *chiltepín* in Chiapas.

Chilaca: Fresh form of the *pasilla* chile. This term is also used to refer to New Mexican types of pepper grown in Mexico.

Chilacate: A chile eaten both fresh and dry in Jalisco; it resembles a small New Mexican type. Also called *tierra*.

Chilaile: *See Mora.*

Chilcoxtle: A dried yellow chile used in the *mole amarillo* of Oaxaca. Also spelled *chilcostle* and *chilcoxle*.

Chile colorado: Generally, any red chile; usually *guajillo*.

Chile seco: Any dried chile; in various states of Mexico the term refers to different chiles. For example, in the state of Colima, the term most often refers to *guajillos*. In other parts of Mexico it refers to *chipotles*.

Chilhuacle: A Oaxacan chile primarily used in *moles*. Some sources say that it is a regional variety of *guajillo*, but to our eyes it more closely resembles a small *poblano*. There are three forms: *amarillo*, *rojo*, and *negro*. Also spelled *chilguacle*.

Chililo: "Little chile"; a variety of *piquín* in Yucatán.

Chilpaya: A variety of *chiltepín* in Veracruz.

Chiltepín: A spherical wild chile varying from ¼ to ½ inch in diameter. Extremely hot. Also spelled *tepín*, *chiltepe*, and *chiltipín*. Also called *chilpaya*. They are pickled when fresh or added to soups and stews. Dried, they are a year-round spice.

Chino: Another term for a dried *poblano* chile, especially in central Mexico and San Luis Potosí.

Chipotle: Any smoked chile, but most often used to refer to a *jalapeño* that is smoked until it is very dark and stiff. Also spelled *chilpotle* and *chipocle*. A typical *chipotle* sold in North American markets is a *jalapeño* that is smoked while green, rather than red, and thus has a whitish, tan color. They are often so dehydrated that they need to be reconstituted by soaking in hot water.

Cola de rata: "Rat's tail"; a term for a long, thin variety of *chile de árbol* in Nayarit.

Colorado: Another term for a dried red New Mexican chile.

Comapeño: A small, orange chile consumed both fresh and dry in Veracruz. Also called *ozulyamero*.

Cora: A cultivated variety of *cascabel* grown in Nayarit, where it is also called *acaponeta* and *cuerudo*. It is eaten both fresh and in dried form. *Cora* is also the name of an Indian tribe.

Corazón: A spicy, heart-shaped *poblano* grown in Durango.

Corriente: In the state of Guerrero, a name for the green *costeño*.

Costeño: A small, dried red chile about an inch long that is a variety of *chile de árbol*. Commonly found in the states of Veracruz, Oaxaca, and Guerrero. Also spelled *costeña*. Other regional terms for this chile are *bandeño*, *casero*, *criollo*, and *corriente*.

Cotaxtla: A cultivated variety of *serrano*.

Cuaresmeño: *See Jalapeño*. The name refers to Lent, probably an allusion to the agriculture of the chile at that time of year.

Cuauhchilli: In Jalisco, Nayarit, and Aguascalientes, a variety of *de árbol*.

Cuicatleco: A variety of chile consumed by the indigenous people of the district of Cuicatlán, Oaxaca.

de Agua: "Water chile"; a fairly long (to 4 inches), conical chile that grows erect on plants in Oaxaca. It is used both in its green and dried red forms in sauces and stews. Some sources say it is a variety of *poblano*, but that is doubtful.

de Árbol: "Tree chile"; so named because the bush resembles a small tree. The hot pods are red and about ¼ inch wide by 1½ inches long. Also called *puya*, *cuauhchilli*, *alfilerillo*, *pico de pájaro*, and *cola de rata*. Grown primarily in Jalisco and Nayarit.

de Chorro: "Irrigated chile"; a variety of *poblano* so named because each plant is irrigated separately. Grown only in Guanajuato and Durango. The pods are used only in the green form.

de Color: "Of color." There are two types: *chile pasera*, a dried *poblano* that is left on the plant until the pods turn red and then are removed and dried in the sun, and *chiles secadora*, which is a green *poblano* that is removed from the bush and dried in a dehydrator.

de la Tierra: Another term for a dried red New Mexican chile.

de Monte: "Hill chile"; a general term for wild chiles, the *chiltepines*.

de Onza: "By the ounce"; a small dried, brick-red Oaxacan chile about 3 inches long and ½ inch wide. It is used in *moles*.

Diente de tlacuache: "Opossum tooth"; The name for *chiltepín* in Tamaulipas.

Dulce: "Sweet"; a term for bell peppers and *pimiento* (defined below).

Esmeralda: "Emerald"; a cultivated variety of *poblano*.

Espinateco: "Spiny"; a cultivated variety of *jalapeño*.

Flor de pabellón: "Flower of the pavilion"; a cultivated variety of *poblano*.

Gachupín: Name for *piquín* in Veracruz.

Guajillo: A common chile in northern and central Mexico, it resembles a small, dried, red New Mexican chile. It is used primarily in sauces. Grown primarily in Zacatecas, Durango, and Aguascalientes.

Güero: "Blonde"; a generic term for yellow chiles. *See Xcatic.* Other terms are *carricillo*, *cristal*, and *cristalino*.

Habanero: "From Havana"; the hottest chile in the world, this pod is of the species *Capsicum chinense.* The fresh pods, usually orange, are about an inch wide and 1½ inches long, with a distinct aroma reminiscent of apricots. Grown in the Yucatán peninsula.

Huauchinango: Another term for a large *jalapeño*; also a term for *chipotle* in Oaxaca.

INIA: A cultivated variety of *habanero*.

Jalapeño: The familiar small green chile about ¾ inch wide and 1½ to 2 inches long. Of medium heat, it is often called *chipotle* in its dried, smoked form. Also spelled *xalapeño*. Also called *cuaresmeño*.

Japón: "Japan"; a small, pointed chile grown in Veracruz and San Luis Potosí.

Joto: The term for *chile ancho* in Aguascalientes.

La blanca: "The white one"; a cultivated variety of *mirasol*.

Largo: "Long or large"; a cultivated variety of *serrano*.

Loco: "Crazy"; a term for mutants and hybrids, especially those chiles hotter than normal.

Loreto 74: A cultivated variety of *mirasol*.

Macho: "Manly"; another name for *piquín*.

Manzano or **Manzana:** "Apple"; of the species *Capsicum pubescens.* Grown in the states of Michoacán, Chiapas, Guerrero, and Mexico, these chiles resemble small apples and are usually used in the red form. One variety is yellow and is termed *canario.* They have thick flesh and black seeds. The variety is also called *cirhuelo* in Querétaro. The *manzano* is also called *cera*, *malinalco*, and *rocoto*.

Max: Another name for *piquín* in Yucatán.

Meco: A blackish-red smoked *jalapeño*.

Miahuateco: Grown only in the states of Puebla and Oaxaca, this large variety of *poblano* is used only in its green form.

Mirasol: "Looking at the sun"; the erect (sometimes pendant) pods are 2 to 4 inches long, are quite hot, and are used both fresh and dry. It is grown primarily in Zacatecas. Also called *miracielo*, "Looking at the sky."

Mora: "Mulberry" or "blackberry"; a smoked red *serrano* or *jalapeño* that is pliable. Also called *morita* in many parts of Mexico and *chilaile* in Quintana Roo.

Morelia: A variety of *poblano* that is grown only in Queréndaro, Michoacán. The pods dry to a black color, so it is also known as *chile negro.* Named for the capital of Michoacán.

Morita: A cultivated variety of *jalapeño*.

Morrón: Generally, a bell pepper but also another name for *pimiento*.

Mosquito: "Mosquito chile"; another name for the *piquín*.

Mulato: A variety of dried *poblano* chile that has very dark brown—almost black—pods. Grown primarily in Jalisco, Guanajuato, and Puebla.

Negro: "Black"; *see Morelia*. Also sometimes refers to a dark *pasilla* chile.

New Mexican: Formerly called Anaheim, this pod type is grown in Chihuahua and other northern states and then imported into the United States. It is a long (up to 8 inches), fairly mild pod that is used both in green and red forms.

Pabellón 1: A cultivated variety of *pasilla*.

Pánuco: A cultivated variety of *serrano*. Named for a river in northern Veracruz.

Papaloápan: A cultivated variety of *jalapeño*.

Parado: A name for *piquín* in Oaxaca.

Pasado: In Mexico, another name for *chilaca*; in New Mexico, roasted and peeled New Mexican chiles that are sun-dried.

Pasilla: "Little raisin"; a long, thin, mild, dark Mexican chile that is used in *mole* sauces. It has overtones of chocolate and raisin in its flavor. Fresh, it is called *chilaca*. It is grown primarily in Guanajuato, Aguascalientes, Zacatecas, and Jalisco.

Pasilla Oaxaqueño: A smoked *pasilla* in Oaxaca.

Pátzcuaro: A dark variety of *pasilla* grown in Michoacán. Named for the famous lake.

Peludo: "Hairy"; a cultivated variety of *jalapeño*.

Pequín: *See Piquín*.

Perón: "Pear-shaped"; a regional name for the *rocoto* or *manzano* chile.

Pichichi: A name for *piquín* in Puebla.

Pico de Pájaro: "Bird's beak"; another name for *chile de árbol*; also, *pico de paloma*, "dove's beak."

Pimiento: The familiar, sweet, mild, olive-stuffing pepper.

Piquín: Small, erect pods 1 inch or less in length; quite hot. Usually used in dry form. Also spelled *pequín*.

Poblano: "From Puebla"; one of the most common Mexican chiles, it is heart-shaped and dark green, about 3 inches wide and 4 inches long. Called *miahuateco* in southern Mexico and the Yucatán peninsula. The dried form is *ancho*.

Pochilli: Náhuatl name for smoked chiles.

Pubescens: The species of *Capsicum* that includes the Mexican *rocoto*.

Pulga: "Flea chile"; another name for the *piquín* chile.

Pulla: *See Puya*.

Puya: *See de Árbol*. Also, a form of *mirasol* or *guajillo*.

Ramos: A cultivated variety of *poblano* in Coahuila.

Real mirasol: A cultivated variety of *mirasol*.

Rocoto: The Peruvian name for *Capsicum pubescens* grown in mountainous regions of Mexico, where they are called *manzano* and *canario* (when yellow). The pods are thick-walled, quite hot, and have black seeds. Also spelled *rocote*.

Roque: "Rook"; a cultivated variety of *mulato*.

Serrano: "From the highlands"; a common, small, bullet-shaped chile, about 1½ inches long and ½ to ¾ inch wide, used in salsas. Also called *balín* and *serranito*. It is the chile most commonly canned in Mexico. Grown all over Mexico, but primarily in Nayarit, San Luis Potosí, Sinaloa, and Tamaulipas.

Siete caldos: "Seven broths"; a chile from Chiapas that is supposedly so hot that one is enough to spice up seven pots of soup.

Tabiche: A Oaxacan chile similar to a *jalapeño*, consumed both fresh and in dried form.

Tampiqueño-74: A cultivated variety of *serrano*.

Típico: A cultivated variety of *jalapeño*.

Travieso: "Naughty"; another term for *guajillo*.

Trompo: "Child's top"; another term for a *cascabel*.

Tuxtla: A *piquín* from southern Mexico.

Uxmal: A cultivated variety of *habanero*.

Veracruz S-69: A cultivated variety of *serrano*.

Verde: "Green or unripe"; any green chile, but typically *serrano*.

Verdeño: A pale green, cultivated variety of *poblano*.

Xcatic: A fairly mild chile grown in the Yucatán peninsula that is related to yellow wax and banana chiles. Sometimes called *güero* ("blonde"), it usually is yellow in color.

Glossary of Mexican Cheeses

Cheese is *queso* in Spanish. Some of these cheeses can be found in natural foods stores, Latin markets, and some supermarkets, especially in the West and Southwest.

Adobera: Shaped like an adobe brick; looks and tastes like Monterey Jack cheese, but holds its shape when heated.

Añejo: Meaning "aged," this is a dry, salty cheese that is also called *queso cotija.* Substitute Parmesan, Italian Romano, or even feta.

Asadero: "Broiler" or "roaster" cheese from Coahuila; a mild, soft, often braided cheese. Sold in tortilla-size slices or wound into balls. Substitute mozzarella or Monterey Jack.

Chihuahua: Mild, spongy, creamy, and pale yellow. It gets stringy when heated. Substitute a mild Cheddar such as Longhorn. Also called *queso menonita.*

Cotija: A dry, salty, aged cheese. Subsitute Parmesan.

Cuajada: Finely ground curds are football-shaped. Mild flavor.

Enchilado: Firm, dry cheese; surface colored with annatto. Used sliced or grated.

Fresco: A fresh, salty, crumbly white cheese served with salads and salsas; substitute goat cheese or feta. Also called *queso blanco, ranchero, quesito,* and *estilo casero.*

Manchego: A sharp, hard Mexican cheese; substitute pecorino Romano or Parmesan.

Panela: A soft, salty cheese from central Mexico; the curds are scooped into baskets and drained. Substitute mozzarella.

Queso Oaxaqueño: Similar to *asadero.* Substitute Monterey Jack.

Glossary of Mexican Food Terms

Many of the ingredients in the following list are available in Latin, Caribbean, and Asian markets and from our mail-order sources.

Achiote: The orange-colored seeds of the annatto tree; used as a coloring agent and seasoning. Also called annatto.

Aceite: Cooking oil, usually corn oil.

Aceituna: Olive.

Adobado: Marinated meat.

Adobo: Spicy seasonings rubbed on meat before cooking; also, a thick cooking sauce with vinegar and tomatoes.

Agave: The century plant; its succulent leaves are the source of tequila.

Agua: Water.

Aguacate: Avocado.

Aguardiente: Brandy.

Aguas frescas: Fresh fruit drinks.

Ají: The South American term for chile; often used by early Spanish explorers or conquerors in Mexico.

Ajo: Garlic.

Ajonjolli: Sesame.

Albóndigas: Meatballs.

Alcaparra: Caper.

Al carbón: Charcoal grilled.

Al horno: Oven baked.

Almendra: Almond.

Almuerzo: Brunch, lunch.

Al pastór: Cooked on a spit over a fire.

Anchoa: Anchovy.

Añejo: Aged.

Anjonjolí: Sesame seed.

Annuum: The species of chile that includes the *jalapeño* and most familiar Mexican and American varieties.

Antojito: Literally, "little whim"; an appetizer. Any popular street food.

Apio: Celery.

Arroz: Rice.

Asada or **asado:** Grilled, roasted, or broiled.

Atole: A gruel made with cornmeal.

Azafran: Saffron.

Azúcar: Sugar.

Bacalao: Salt cod.

Barbacoa: Pit barbecue, especially a cow's head.

Bebida: Drink.

Biftec or **bistec:** Beef steak.

Bitter orange: *Naranja agria,* the Seville orange. Substitute ½ cup orange juice mixed with ¼ cup Key lime juice.

Bolillo: Hard roll.

Borracho: Literally, "drunken"; foods containing beer or liquor.

Budín: Pudding.

Buñuelo: Fritter.

Cabrito: Young goat or kid.

Cacahuate: Peanut.

Café: Coffee.

Calabacita: Squash, usually zucchini types.

Calabaza: Pumpkin, gourd.

Calamari: Squid.

Caldo: A broth, stock, or clear soup.

Camarón: Shrimp.

Camote: Sweet potato.

Canela: Cinnamon.

Cangrejo: Crab.

Carne: Meat.

Carne seca: Jerky.

Carnitas: Fried pieces of pork.

Cazuela: A pottery cooking dish or the stew cooked in one; a Chilean stew.

Cebolla: Onion.

Cena: Dinner, supper.

Cerdo: Pork.

Cerveza: Beer.

Ceviche: Raw seafood combined with citrus juice, which "cooks" the fish by combining with its protein and turning it opaque.

Chalupa: "Boat"; a boat-shaped tortilla filled with toppings.

Chayote: A pear-shaped squash.

Chicharrones: Fried pork skins; also, spare ribs.

Chico: Roasted and steamed dried corn.

Chilaquiles: Stale tortillas that are fried and cooked in a chile–tomato sauce.

Chilatole: A dish consisting of corn on the cob that is cooked with pork and hot chile powder.

Chilchote: A very hot chile salsa or paste.

Chile: Referring to the plants or pods of the *Capsicum* genus.

Chilorio: Cooked and shredded pork with chiles.

Chimole: A general term for stews flavored with chile.

Chinense: The species of chiles that includes the *habanero.*

Chirmole: A seasoning paste of blackened chiles.

Chorizo: A spicy sausage made with pork, garlic, and red chile powder.

Cilantro: An annual herb (*Coriandrum sativum*) with seeds that are known as coriander. Substitute: Italian parsley, or *culantro* (*Eryngium foetidum*). Commonly used in salsas and soups.

Clavo: Clove.

Cochinita: A small pig.

Cocina: Kitchen; cuisine.

Coco: Coconut.

Col: Cabbage.

Comida: Meal, dinner.

Comino: Cumin, an annual herb (*Cuminum cyminum*) whose seeds have a distinctive, musty odor.

Cuitlacoche: Corn fungus, used like mushrooms in cooking.

Desayuno: Breakfast.

Durazno: Peach.

Elote: Corn.

Empanada: A pastry turnover, often filled with ground meat.

Empanadita: A small pastry turnover.

Enchiladas: Rolled or stacked corn tortillas filled with meat or cheese and covered with chile sauce.

Ensalada: Salad.

Epazote: Known as "ambrosia" in English, this perennial herb (*Chenopodium ambrosioides*) is strong and bitter and is used primarily to flavor beans.

Escabeche: Foods marinated or pickled in vinegar.

Estilo: In the style of.

Flan: A baked caramel custard dessert.

Flauta: "Flute"; rolled, stuffed tortillas that are deep-fried.

Flor de Jamaica: Sorrel, the flowers of a Jamaican hibiscus, used in drinks.

Fresa: Strawberry.

Frijoles: Beans.

Frito: Fried.

Fruta: Fruit.

Frutescens: The species of chile that includes the *tabasco*.

Gallina: Hen.

Gallo: Rooster.

Garbanzo: Chickpea.

Ginebra: Gin.

Gorditas: "Little fat ones"; an appetizer.

Guacamole: An avocado, tomato, and chile salad.

Guajolote: Turkey.

Helado: Ice cream.

Hongo: Mushroom.

Huachinango: Red snapper.

Huevo: Egg.

Jaiba: Crab.

Jamón: Ham.

Jengibre: Ginger.

Jerez: Sherry.

Jícama: A white tuber (*Pachyrhizus erosus*) used in salads; tastes like a cross between an apple and a potato.

Jitomate: Tomato.

Jugo: Juice.

Langosta: Lobster.

Leche: Milk.

Lengua: Tongue.

Lima: Lime.

Limón: In Mexico, *limón* means the small Key lime.

Lomo: Loin.

Longaniza: Pork sausage.

Machaca: Meat, usually beef, stewed with chiles until it falls apart.

Maíz: Corn.

Manteca: Lard.

Mantequilla: Butter.

Manzana: Apple.

Marisco: Shellfish.

Masa: Corn dough.

Masa harina: Corn flour.

Metate: A stone used to grind corn and spices.

Mezcal: Mescal (distilled agave juice).

Miel: Honey; syrup.

Molcajete: A stone mortar used to grind chiles and other vegetables into salsas.

Moles: Thick chile sauces with many ingredients; popular in Mexico and northern Central America.

Molinillo: A wooden beater used to whip Mexican chocolate into a froth.

Naranja: Orange.

Natillas: A custard dessert.

Nopales or **nopalitos:** Prickly pear cactus pads, spines removed.

Nueces: Nuts; walnuts.

Olla: A round, earthenware pot.

Oregano: A Mexican herb, *Lippia graveolens;* distinctly different from European or Greek oregano, *Origanum vulgare.*

Ostione: Oyster.

Paloma: Dove.

Pan: Bread. *Pan dulce* is sweet bread.

Panuchos: Tortillas stuffed with black beans and topped with shredded turkey.

Papas: Potatoes.

Parrilla: Grill or broiler.

Pasa: Raisin.

Pastel: A pastry turnover; pie.

Pato: Duck.

Pavo: Turkey.

Pepino: Cucumber.

Pepitas: Toasted squash or pumpkin seeds.

Perón: Pear.

Pescado: Fish.

Pibíl: "Pit-baked"; usually a stewed pork dish seasoned with a *recado.*

Picadillo: Shredded beef, spices, and other ingredients usually used as a stuffing.

Picante: Hot and spicy.

Piloncillo: Unrefined, dark brown sugar that is sold in cones.

Pimenta: Black pepper.

Pimento: Allspice.

Pimentón: Ironically, this can mean either paprika or cayenne.

Piña: Pineapple; also, the harvested portion of the agave plant, which resembles a huge pineapple.

Pinole: Toasted corn meal.

Piñon: Pine nut.

Plátano: Banana.

Plátano macho: Plantain.

Pollo: Chicken.

Porro: Leek.

Postre: Dessert.

Puerco: Pork.

Pulpo: Octopus.

Pulque: The fermented juice of the agave plant.

Queso: Cheese. *Queso blanco* is white cheese.

Rábano: Radish.

Rajas: Strips; usually refers to strips of chiles.

Recado: A Yucatán seasoning sauce made with achiote.

Refrito: Fried; refried.

Relleno: Stuffed.

Repollo: Cabbage.

Res: Beef.

Ristra: A string of red chile pods.

Romero: Rosemary.

Ron: Rum.

Salbutes: In Yucatán, fried tortillas topped with shredded turkey, pickled onions, and other toppings.

Salchicha: Sausage.

Salsa: Literally, "sauce," but usually used to describe uncooked sauces (*salsa cruda*).

Sandía: Watermelon.

Seta: Mushroom.

Sopa: Soup.

Tamal (plural, **tamales**): Any filling enclosed in masa, wrapped in a corn shuck or banana leaf, and steamed.

Tamarindo: Tamarind.

Té: Tea.

Tequila: The fermented, distilled juice of the agave plant.

Tocino: Bacon.

Tomate: Tomato in northern Mexico.

Tomatillo: Green tomato; a member of the potato family, which includes both the tomato and the gooseberry. Sometimes called *tomate verde*.

Tomillo: Thyme.

Torta: Tart, cake, and sometimes pie.

Tortillas: Thin cakes made with corn masa.

Tostada: Thinly fried corn chip.

Trucha: Trout.

Tuna: Fruit of the prickly pear cactus.

Venado: Venison.

Verdura: Vegetable.

Vinagre: Vinegar.

Yerba buena: Spearmint.

Zanahoria: Carrot.

Bibliography

Banco Nacional de Crédito Rural. *Comida Familiar en la Ciudad de México.* México, D.F.: Impresora La Palma, 1987.

Banco Nacional de Crédito Rural. *Comida Familiar en el Estado de Aguascalientes.* México, D.F.: Impresora La Palma, 1988.

Banco Nacional de Crédito Rural. *Comida Familiar en el Estado de Baja California.* México, D.F.: Impresora La Palma, 1988.

Banco Nacional de Crédito Rural. *Comida Familiar en el Estado de Baja California Sur.* México, D.F.: Impresora La Palma, 1988.

Banco Nacional de Crédito Rural. *Comida Familiar en el Estado de Campeche.* México, D.F.: Impresora La Palma, 1988.

Banco Nacional de Crédito Rural. *Comida Familiar en el Estado de Chiapas.* México, D.F.: Impresora La Palma, 1988.

Banco Nacional de Crédito Rural. *Comida Familiar en el Estado de Chihuahua.* México, D.F.: Impresora La Palma, 1988.

Banco Nacional de Crédito Rural. *Comida Familiar en el Estado de Coahuila.* México, D.F.: Impresora La Palma, 1988.

Banco Nacional de Crédito Rural. *Comida Familiar en el Estado de Colima.* México, D.F.: Impresora La Palma, 1988.

Banco Nacional de Crédito Rural. *Comida Familiar en el Estado de Durango.* México, D.F.: Impresora La Palma, 1987.

Banco Nacional de Crédito Rural. *Comida Familiar en el Estado de Guanajuato.* México, D.F.: Impresora La Palma, 1988.

Banco Nacional de Crédito Rural. *Comida Familiar en el Estado de Guerrero.* México, D.F.: Impresora La Palma, 1988.

Banco Nacional de Crédito Rural. *Comida Familiar en el Estado de Hidalgo.* México, D.F.: Impresora La Palma, 1988.

Banco Nacional de Crédito Rural. *Comida Familiar en el Estado de Jalisco.* México, D.F.: Impresora La Palma, 1988.

Banco Nacional de Crédito Rural. *Comida Familiar en el Estado de México.* México, D.F.: Impresora La Palma, 1988.

Banco Nacional de Crédito Rural. *Comida Familiar en el Estado de Michoacán.* México, D.F.: Impresora La Palma, 1988.

Banco Nacional de Crédito Rural. *Comida Familiar en el Estado de Morelos.* México, D.F.: Impresora La Palma, 1988.

Banco Nacional de Crédito Rural. *Comida Familiar en el Estado de Nayarit.* México, D.F.: Impresora La Palma, 1988.

Banco Nacional de Crédito Rural. *Comida Familiar en el Estado de Nuevo León.* México, D.F.: Impresora La Palma, 1988.

Banco Nacional de Crédito Rural. *Comida Familiar en el Estado de Puebla.* México, D.F.: Impresora La Palma, 1988.

Banco Nacional de Crédito Rural. *Comida Familiar en el Estado de Querétaro.* México, D.F.: Impresora La Palma, 1988.

Banco Nacional de Crédito Rural. *Comida Familiar en el Estado de Quintana Roo.* México, D.F.: Impresora La Palma, 1988.

Banco Nacional de Crédito Rural. *Comida Familiar en el Estado de San Luis Potosí.* México, D.F.: Impresora La Palma, 1988.

Banco Nacional de Crédito Rural. *Comida Familiar en el Estado de Sinaloa.* México, D.F.: Impresora La Palma, 1988.

Banco Nacional de Crédito Rural. *Comida Familiar en el Estado de Sonora.* México, D.F.: Impresora La Palma, 1988.

Banco Nacional de Crédito Rural. *Comida Familiar en el Estado de Tabasco.* México, D.F.: Impresora La Palma, 1987.

Banco Nacional de Crédito Rural. *Comida Familiar en el Estado de Tamaulipas.* México, D.F.: Impresora La Palma, 1988.

Banco Nacional de Crédito Rural. *Comida Familiar en el Estado de Tlaxcala.* México, D.F.: Impresora La Palma, 1987.

Banco Nacional de Crédito Rural. *Comida Familiar en el Estado de Veracruz.* México, D.F.: Impresora La Palma, 1987.

Banco Nacional de Crédito Rural. *Comida Familiar en el Estado de Yucatán.* México, D.F.: Impresora La Palma, 1988.

Banco Nacional de Crédito Rural. *Comida Familiar en el Estado de Zacatecas.* México, D.F.: Impresora La Palma, 1988.

Booth, George C. *The Food and Drink of Mexico.* Menlo Park, CA: The Ward Richie Press, 1964.

Cancino, Beatriz Cuevas. "A Glimpse into Mexico and Mexican Cuisine." México, D.F.: Unpublished ms., c. 1989.

Chapa, Martha. *La Cocina Mexicana y Su Arte*. México, D.F.: Editorial Everest Mexicana, 1983.

Chapa, Martha, and Martha Ortiz. *Sabor Regia*. Nuevo Léon: Gobierno del Estado de Nuevo Léon, 1986.

Chapa, Martha, and Martha Ortiz. *Sabor a Sinaloa*. Sinaloa: Gobierno del Estado de Sinaloa, 1989.

Chapa, Martha, and Martha Ortiz. *Cocina de Querétaro*. Querétaro: Gobierno del Estado de Querétaro, 1990.

Chapa, Martha, and Martha Ortiz. *Sabor a Eternidad*. Tlaxcala: Gobierno del Estado de Tlaxcala, 1992.

Coe, Sophie D. *America's First Cuisines*. Austin, TX: University of Texas Press, 1994.

Comida Oaxaqueña. México, D.F.: *México Desconocido, Guías Gastronómica*. No. 3 (April, 1994). Ed. Beatriz Quintanar Hinojosa.

Comida Yucateca. México, D.F.: *México Desconocido, Guías Gastronómica*. No. 2 (February, 1994). Ed. Beatriz Quintanar Hinojosa.

Condon, Richard. *Olé Mole*. Dallas, TX: Taylor Publishing, 1988.

Corn, Elaine, "Margarita Man," *Chile Pepper*, September–October 1992, 38.

de Benítez, Ana M. *Pre-Hispanic Cooking*. México, D.F.: Ediciones Euro-americanas Klaus Thiele, 1974.

DeWitt, Dave, and Chuck Evans. *The Hot Sauce Bible*. Freedom, CA: The Crossing Press, 1996.

DeWitt, Dave, and Nancy Gerlach. *The Whole Chile Pepper Book*. Boston, MA: Little, Brown & Co., 1990.

Farga, Amando. *Eating in Mexico*. México, D.F.: Mexican Restaurant Association, 1963.

Figel, Marta, "Laid Back Is Alive and Well in Isla Mujeres," *Chile Pepper*, September–October 1992, 23.

Flores y Escalante, Jesús. *Brevisima Historia de la Comida Mexicana*. México, D.F.: Asociación Mexicana des Estudios Fonografia, A.C., 1994.

Franz, Carl. *The People's Guide to Mexico*. Santa Fe, NM: John Muir Publications, 1992.

Galeano, Eduardo. *Memory of Fire: Century of the Wind*. New York: Pantheon Books, 1988.

Galicia, Yolanda Ramos. *Así Se Come en Tlaxcala*. Tlaxcala: Instituto Nacional de Antropología e Historia, 1993.

Gallantine, Kathy, "The Search for the Perfect Ceviche," *Chile Pepper*, September–October 1992, 18.

Gerlach, Nancy. "Mexico: A View from Two Coasts." *Chile Pepper*, September– October, 1992, 31.

Gerlach, Nancy, and Jeff Gerlach. *Foods of the Maya*. Freedom, CA: The Crossing Press, 1994.

Gerlach, Nancy, and Jeff Gerlach. "A Taste of Yucatán," *Chile Pepper*, January– February 1994, 18.

Guzmán de Vásquez Colmenares, Ana María. *Tradiciones Gastronomicas Oaxaqueñas*. Oaxaca, 1982.

Guzmán de Vásquez Colmenares, Ana María. *La Cocina de Colima*. México, D.F.: DIF Nacional, 1987.

Hernandez, Dolores Ávila, et al. *Atlas Cultural de México: Gastronomía*. México, D.F.: Secretaria de Educación Pública, 1988.

Hutson, Lucinda. *¡Tequila!* Berkeley, CA: Ten Speed Press, 1995.

Kennedy, Diana. *The Cuisines of Mexico*. New York: Harper & Row, 1972.

Kennedy, Diana. *Mexican Regional Cooking*. New York: Harper Perennial, 1990.

Kimble, Socorro Muñoz, and Irma Serrano Noriega. *Mexican Desserts*. Phoenix, AZ: Golden West Publishers, 1987.

Laborde, J.A., and E. Rendon-Poblete, "Tomatoes and Peppers in Mexico: Commercial Production and Research Challenges," in *Tomato and Pepper Production in the Tropics*, ed. T.D. Grillgs and B.T. McLean. Taipei, Taiwan: Asian Vegetable Research and Development Center, 1989.

Lomelí, Arturo. *El Chile y Otros Picantes*. México, D.F.: Editorial Premeteo Libre, 1986.

Long-Solís, Janet. *Capsicum y Cultura: La Historia del Chilli*. México, D.F.: Fondo de Cultura Económica, 1986.

Lucero, Al. *María's Real Margarita Book*. Berkeley, CA: Ten Speed Press, 1994.

Mackay, Ian. *Food for Thought*. Freedom, CA: The Crossing Press, 1995.

McMahan, Jacqueline Higuera. *Chipotle Chile Cook Book*. Lake Hughes, CA: Olive Press, 1994.

Mijares, Ivonne. *Mestizaje Alimentario*. México, D.F.: Facultad de Filosofía y Letras, Universidad Nacional Autónoma de México, 1993.

"Mild and White, Here Come Mexico's Rancho-Style Cheeses," *Sunset*, June 1985, 114.

Miller, Mark. *The Great Chile Book*. Berkeley, CA: Ten Speed Press, 1991.

Minor, Elliot, "Corn Smut: Nuisance to Farmers, Delicacy to Diners," *Albuquerque Journal*, August 8, 1991, B8.

Miranda, Catalina, "Los Chiles Rellenos, Tradicíon y Modernidad," in *María Orsini: El Arte del Buen Comer*, No. 35, April–May 1992.

National Pepper Conference. *Newsletter, San Miguel de Allende Conference*, January 1984.

O'Reilly, James, and Larry Habegger, eds, *Travelers' Tales of Mexico*. San Francisco, CA: O'Reilly and Habegger, 1994.

Orsini, María, "Lasagnas Mexicanas," *María Orsini: El Arte del Buen Comer*, No. 42, September–October, 1993, 33.

Ortiz, Elisabeth Lambert. *The Complete Book of Mexican Cooking*. New York: Bantam Books, 1968.

Ortiz, Elisabeth Lambert, "The Cuisine of Mexico. Part II: Fresh Green Peppers," *Gourmet*, March 1985, 56.

Palazuelos, Susanna and Marilyn Tausend. *México: The Beautiful Cookbook*. San Francisco, CA: Collins Publishers, 1991.

Peyton, James W. *El Norte: The Cuisine of Northern Mexico*. Santa Fe, NM: Red Crane Books, 1990.

Peyton, James W. "Puebla: An Encounter with Mexico's Culinary History," *Chile Pepper*, January–February 1994, 24.

Portillo de Carballido, María Concepcíon. *Oaxaca y Su Cocina*. México, D.F.: Litoarte, 1989.

Preston, Mark, "The Land with No Ketchup," *Chile Pepper*, September–October 1992, 35.

Quintana, Patricia. *The Taste of Mexico*. New York: Stewart, Tabori & Chang, 1986.

Quintana, Patricia. *Mexico's Feasts of Life*. Tulsa, OK: Council Oak Books, 1989.

Ritchie, Carson. *Food in Civilization*. Auckland, New Zealand: Methuen Australia, 1991.

Root, Waverly. *Eating in America*. Hopewell, NJ: The Ecco Press, 1976.

Rivera, Virginia Rodríguez. *La Comida en el México Antiguo y Moderno*. México, D.F.: Editorial Pormaca, 1965.

Schumann, Charles. *Tropical Bar Book*. New York: Stewart, Tabori & Chang, 1989.

Scott, David and Eve Bletcher. *Latin American Vegetarian Cookery*. London: Rider, 1994.

Sharpe, Patricia, "Viva Tequila!" *Texas Monthly*, August, 1995, 74.

Smith, Rod, "High Noon in Tequila," *Wine and Spirits*, October, 1991, 28.

Stockton, William, "Hunt for Perfect Mole Leads to Rich Delights," *The Albuquerque Tribune*, December 12, 1985, B6.

Stoopen, María and Ana Laura Delgado. *La Cocina Veracruzana*. Veracruz: Gobierno del Estado de Veracruz, 1992.

Taibo, Paco Ignacio. *Brevario del Mole Poblano*. México, D.F.: Terra Nova, 1981.

Trilling, Susana, "My Search for the Seventh *Mole*," *Chile Pepper*, January–February 1995, 22.

van Rhijn, Patricia. *La Cocina del Chile*. México, D.F.: Offset Multicolor, 1993.

Walsh, Robb, "*Ole Mole!* The Cuisine of Oaxaca," *Chile Pepper*, September–October 1992, 28.

Zavala, Bertha. *Gastronomía Mexicana*. Guadalajara, Jalisco: Ediciones Berticel, 1991.

Mail-Order Sources
and Retail Shops

Mail-Order Catalogs

These are the main mail-order suppliers of chile-related products and Mexican imports.

Blazing Chile Bros.
(800) 473-9040

Chile Pepper Magazine
P.O. Box 80780
Albuquerque, NM 87198
(800) 359-1483

Chile Today-Hot Tamale
919 Highway 33, Suite 47
Freehold, NJ 07728
(908) 308-1151

Colorado Spice Company
5030 Nome St., Unit A
Denver, CO 80239
(303) 373-0141

Coyote Cocina
1364 Rufina Circle, #1
Santa Fe, NM 87501
(800) 866-HOWL

Dean and DeLuca
Mail-Order Department
560 Broadway
New York, NY 10012
(212) 431-1691

Don Alfonso Foods
P.O. Box 201988
Austin, TX 78720
(800) 456-6100

Enchanted Seeds
P.O. Box 6087
Las Cruces, NM 88006
(505) 233-3033

Flamingo Flats
P.O. Box 441
St. Michael's, MD 21663
(800) 468-8841

Frieda's, Inc.
P.O. Box 584888
Los Angeles, CA 90058
(800) 421-9477

GMB Specialty Foods, Inc.
P.O. Box 962
San Juan Capistrano, CA 92693-0962
(714) 240-3053

Hot Sauce Club of America
P.O. Box 687
Indian Rocks Beach, FL 34635-0687
(800) SAUCE-2-U

Hot Sauce Harry's
The Dallas Farmer's Market
3422 Flair Dr.
Dallas, TX 75229
(214) 902-8552

Le Saucier
Faneuil Hall Marketplace
Boston, MA 02109
(617) 227-9649

Melissa's World Variety Produce
P.O. Box 21127
Los Angeles, CA 90021
(800) 468-7111

Mo Hotta, Mo Betta
P.O. Box 4136
San Luis Obispo, CA 93403
(800) 462-3220

Nancy's Specialty Market
P.O. Box 327
Wye Mills, MD 21679
(800) 462-6291

Old Southwest Trading Co.
P.O. Box 7545
Albuquerque, NM 87194
(505) 836-0168

Pendery's
304 E. Belknap
Fort Worth, TX 76102
(800) 533-1879

Pepper Gal
P.O. Box 23006
Ft. Lauderdale, FL 33307
(305) 537-5540

Pepper Joe's, Inc.
7 Tyburn Court
Timonium, MD 21093
(410) 561-8158

Santa Fe School of Cooking
116 W. San Francisco Street
Santa Fe, NM 87501
(505) 983-4511

Shepherd Garden Seeds
6116 Highway 9
Felton, CA 95018
(408) 335-6910

South Side Pepper Co.
320 N. Walnut St.
Mechanicsburg, PA 17055

Retail Shops

Here are the retail shops or markets that specialize in hot and spicy products. Some of them have mail-order catalogs. It has been difficult to keep up with the explosion in hot shop retailers, so we apologize in advance if we have missed any. For shops listed with post office boxes, call first for directions to their location.

Calido Chile Traders
5360 Merriam Dr.
Merriam, KS 66203
(800) 568-8468

Caribbean Spice Company
2 S. Church St.
Fairhope, AL 36532
(800) 990-6088

Central Market
4001 N. Lamar
Austin, TX 78756
(512) 206-1000

Chile Hill Emporium
P.O. Box 9100
Bernalillo, NM 87004
(505) 867-3294

Chile Pepper Mania
1709-F Airline Highway, P.O. Box 232
Hollister, CA 95023
(408) 636-8259

The Chile Shop
109 E. Water St.
Santa Fe, NM 87501
(505) 983-6080

Chili Patch U.S.A.
204 San Felipe N.W.
Albuquerque, NM 87104
(505) 242-4454; (800) 458-0646

Chili Pepper Emporium
328 San Felipe N.W.
Albuquerque, NM 87104
(505) 242-7538

Chutneys
143 Delaware St.
Lexington, OH 44904
(419) 884-2853

Colorado Spice Company
5030 Nome St., Unit A
Denver, CO 80239
(800) 67-SPICE

Coyote Cafe General Store
132 W. Water St.
Santa Fe, NM 87501
(505) 982-2454; (800) 866-HOWL

Dat'l Do-It Hot Shop
P.O. Box 4019
St. Augustine, FL 32085
(904) 824-5303; (800) HOT-DATL

Dat'l Do-It Hot Shop
Dadeland Mall
7535 N. Kendall Dr.
Miami, FL 37211
(305) 253-0248

Down Island Ventures
P.O. Box 37
Cruz Bay, St. John, U.S. Virgin Islands
(809) 693-7000

Eagle Mountain Gifts
634 S. China Lake Blvd.
Ridgecrest, CA 93555
(619) 375-3071

Fiery Foods
909 20th Avenue South
Nashville, TN 37212
(615) 320-5475

Free Spirit
420 S. Mill Avenue
Tempe, AZ 85281
(602) 966-4339

Garden Gate Gift Shop
Tucson Botanical Gardens
2150 North Alvernon Way
Tucson, AZ 85712
(602) 326-9686

GMB Specialty Foods, Inc.
P.O. Box 962
San Juan Capistrano, CA 92693-0962
(714) 240-3053

Gourmet Gallery
320 N. Highway 89A
Singua Plaza
Sedona, AZ 86336

Hatch Chile Express
P.O. Box 350
Hatch, NM 87937
(505) 267-3226

Hell's Kitchen
216 Lipincott Avenue
Riverside, NJ 08075
(609) 764-1487

Hell's Kitchen
Pennsasken Mart, Store #328
Route 130
Pennsasken, NJ 08019
(609) 764-1330

Hot Hot Hot
56 South Delacey Ave.
Pasadena, CA 91105
(818) 564-1090

Hot Kicks
4349 Raymir Place
Wauwatosa, WI 53222
(414) 536-7808

Hot Licks
P.O. Box 7854
Hollywood, FL 33081
(305) 987-7105

Hot Lovers Fiery Foods
1282 Wolseley Avenue
Winnipeg, Manitoba R3G IH4
(204) 772-6418

Hot Papa's Fiery Flavors
11121 Weeden Road
Randolph, NY 14772
(716) 358-4302

Hots for You-Chile Pepper Emporium
8843 Shady Meadow Drive
Sandy, UT 84093
(801) 255-7800

The Hot Spot
5777 South Lakeshore Dr.
Shreveport, LA 71119
(318) 635-3581

The Hot Spot
1 Riverfront Plaza, #300
Lawrence, KS 66044
(913) 841-7200

Hot Stuff
227 Sullivan Street
New York, NY 10012
(212) 254-6120; (800) 466-8206

Hot Stuff
288 Argonne Avenue
Long Beach, CA 90803
(310) 438-1118

Jones and Bones
621 Capitola Avenue
Capitola, CA 95010
(408) 462-0521

Le Saucier
Faneuil Hall Marketplace
Boston, MA 02109
(617) 227-9649

Lotta Hotta
3150 Mercier, Suite 516
Kansas City, MO 64111
1-800-LOTT-HOT

New Orleans School of Cooking
620 Decatur Street
New Orleans, LA 70130
(504) 482-3632

The Original Hot Sauce Company
Avenue of Shops
1421-C Larimer St.
Denver, CO 80202
(303) 615-5812

Pampered Pirate
4 Norre Gade
St. Thomas, U.S. Virgin Islands 00802
(809) 775-5450

Pepperhead Hot Shoppe
7036 Kristi Court
Garner, NC 27529
(919) 553-4576

Pepper Joe's, Inc.
7 Tyburn Court
Timonium, MD 21093
(410) 561-8158

Peppers
2009 Highway 1
Dewey Beach, DE 19971
(302) 227-1958; (800) 998-3473

Potpourri
303 Romero N.W.
Plaza Don Luis, Old Town
Albuquerque, NM 87104
(505) 243-4087

Pungent Pod
25 Haviland Road
Queensbury, NY 12804
(518) 793-3180

Rivera's Chile Shop
109 ½ Concho Street
San Antonio, TX 78207
(210) 226-9106

Salsas, Etc.!
3683 Tunis Avenue
San Jose, CA 95132
(408) 263-6392

Salsas, Etc.!
374 Eastridge Mall
San Jose, CA 95122
(408) 223-9020

Sambet's Cajun Store
8644 Spicewood Springs Road, Suite F
Austin, TX 78759
(800) 472-6238

Santa Fe Emporium
104 W. San Francisco Street
Santa Fe, NM 87501
(505) 984-1966

Santa Fe School of Cooking
116 West San Francisco Street
Santa Fe, NM 87501
(505) 983-4511

Santa Fe Trading Company
7 Main St.
Tarrytown, NY 10591
(914) 332-1730

Señor Chile's at Rawhide
23020 North Scottsdale Road
Scottsdale, AZ 85255
(602) 563-5600

Sherwood's Lotsa Hotsa
P.O. Box 2106
Lakeside, CA 92040
(619) 443-7982

Some Like It Hot
3208 Scott St.
San Francisco, CA 94123
(415) 441-7HOT

Some Like It Hot
301 S. Light Street
Harbor Place
Baltimore, MD 21202
(410) 547-2HOT

The Stonewall Chili Pepper Company
P.O. Box 241
Stonewall, TX 78671
(210) 644-2667; (800) 232-2995

Tabasco Country Store
Avery Island, Louisiana 70513
(318) 365-8173

Tabasco Country Store
Riverwalk Marketplace
1 Poydras Street
New Orleans, LA 70130
(504) 523-1711

Uncle Bill's House of Hot Sauce
311 N. Higgins Avenue
Missoula, MT 59801
(406) 543-5627

The Whole Earth Grainery
111 Ivinson Avenue
Laramie, WY 82070
(307) 745-4268

Index

Hot & Spicy Southeast Asian Dishes

Share Culinary adventures across the backroads of Thailand, Singapore, and Malaysia. This sumptuous array of fiery recipes and fascinating food history makes it a pleasure to prepare dishes like: Hot Beef Curry with Lemongrass and Citrus or Santaka Chicken in Lime and Coconut Milk Sauce.

Hot & Spicy Latin Dishes

You'll find delicious dishes that will tango with your taste buds and samba with your soul in Hot & Spicy Latin Dishes. These spicy dishes are sure to add a fiery dose of Latin romance to your kitchen: Peruvian Walnut Chicken, Guyana Pepperpot Soup, and Uruguayan Baked Beef.

Hot & Spicy Chili

Hot & Spicy Chili gathers 150 of the best and the hottest chili recipes from the chili capitols of America. Treat yourself and your family to delicious and authentic dishes like: Lone Star Red Chili, The Great Earth Veggie Chili, High-Octane Chili, Santa Fe Chile, and more!

Hot & Spicy & Meatless

Chile peppers are good for you, and when you include them in delicious meat-free recipes, they really warm the heart—while helping to keep it healthy. With these dishes you can eliminate the meat and increase the heat with recipes like: Two-Chile Quesadilla Ecstasy, Chile-Cheese Bisque, and Habanero Lasagna.

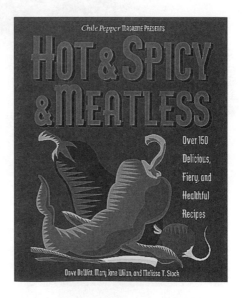

Hot & Spicy Caribbean

Along with mouthwatering food, you'll find amusing anecdotes revealing local color and history, a glossary of spicy terminology, and a listing of mail-order sources. You'll learn how to prepare such sensational dishes as: Jamaican Jerk Chicken Wings, Caribbean Crab Gumbo, and Beef Kebabs Tropicale.

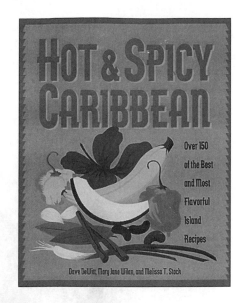

FILL IN AND MAIL TODAY

PRIMA PUBLISHING
P.O. Box 1260BK
Rocklin, CA 95677

USE YOUR VISA/MC AND ORDER BY PHONE
(916) 632-4400
Monday–Friday 9 A.M.–4 P.M. PST

I'd like to order copies of the following titles:

Quantity	Title		Amount
_____	*Hot & Spicy Southeast Asian Dishes*	$14.95	_____
_____	*Hot & Spicy Latin Dishes*	$14.95	_____
_____	*Hot & Spicy Chili*	$12.95	_____
_____	*Hot & Spicy & Meatless*	$12.95	_____
_____	*Hot & Spicy Caribbean*	$14.95	_____
_____	*Hot & Spicy Mexican*	$14.95	_____

Subtotal	_____
Postage & Handling ($5 for first book, $0.50 for additional books)	_____
7.25% Sales Tax (CA)	_____
5% Sales Tax (IN and MD)	_____
8.25% Sales Tax (TN)	_____
TOTAL (U.S. funds only)	_____

Check enclosed for $_____ (payable to Prima Publishing)

HAWAII, CANADA, FOREIGN, AND PRIORITY REQUEST ORDERS, PLEASE CALL (916) 632-4400.

Charge my   ❏ MasterCard   ❏ Visa

Account No. _____   Exp. Date _____

Print Your Name _____

Your Signature _____

Address _____

City/State/Zip _____

Daytime Telephone (___) _____